WORLD HERITAGE LIST NOMINATION FORM

Convention Concerning the Protection of the World Cultural and Natural Heritage

Under the terms of the Convention concerning the Protection of the World Cultural and Natural Heritage, adopted by the General Conference of UNESCO in 1972, the Intergovernmental Committee for the Protection of the World Cultural and Natural Heritage, called 'the World Heritage Committee', shall establish, under the title of 'World Heritage List', a list of properties forming part of the cultural and natural heritage which it considers as having Outstanding Universal Value in terms of such criteria as it shall have established.

The purpose of this form is to enable States Parties to submit to the World Heritage Committee nominations of properties situated in their territory and suitable for inclusion in the World Heritage List.

This Nomination Document has been prepared in accordance with the 'Format for the nomination of cultural and natural properties for inscription on the World Heritage list' issued by UNESCO.

The form has been completed in English and is sent in two copies to:-

The Secretariat
World Heritage Centre
UNESCO
7 Place de Fontenoy
75352 Paris 07 SP
France

UNITED NATIONS EDUCATIONAL SCIENTIFIC AND CULTURAL ORGANISATION

Published by Wrexham County Borough Council and the
Royal Commission on the Ancient and Historical Monuments of Wales in 2008,
with funding from Cadw, on behalf of the World Heritage Site Steering Group.

Further copies are available from
Royal Commission on the Ancient and Historical Monuments of Wales,
Crown Building, Plas Crug, Aberystwyth, Wales, SY23 1NJ,
United Kingdom.

Telephone 44 (0)1970 621200

e-mail nmr@rcahmw.gov.uk

www.rcahmw.gov.uk

ISBN 978-1-871184-31-0

Pontcysyllte Aqueduct and Canal World Heritage Steering Group
This bid is led by Wrexham County Borough Council, British Waterways and
the Royal Commission on the Ancient and Historical Monuments of Wales.

**Other organisations committed to the Pontcysyllte Aqueduct and Canal
nomination for World Heritage Status are:**

PONTCYSYLLTE
Aqueduct & Canal
NOMINATION AS A WORLD HERITAGE SITE

Nomination Document

2008

FOREWORD

by The Rt Hon James Purnell MP,
Secretary of State for Culture, Media and Sport

The World Heritage Convention has proved to be an effective and positive force in bringing together nations from all over the world to safeguard collectively sites of Outstanding Universal Value. Since the United Kingdom signed up to the Convention in 1984, we have fully supported UNESCO and the World Heritage Committee in its implementation. We continue to support UNESCO in its initiatives to achieve a thematic and geographical balance of properties on the World Heritage List and to identify potential World Heritage Sites in technological and other categories that are currently under-represented on the List.

I am therefore delighted that the United Kingdom Government is now able to nominate Pontcysyllte Aqueduct and Canal. Largely situated in Wales, the Site is a supreme example of a highly-engineered inland waterways transport route and an heroic monument which symbolises the technological innovation and technical achievement that played such a crucial role in, and contributed significantly to, the Industrial Revolution during the late eighteenth and early nineteenth centuries.

I am extremely grateful to the Welsh Assembly Government for their support for this nomination, the first from the United Kingdom for a site that extends across country borders. I would also like to express my thanks to the many people and organisations who have worked in a spirit of partnership to develop this nomination and its accompanying Management Plan. On behalf of the United Kingdom Government, I am delighted to give my full support to this nomination for World Heritage status.

James Purnell MP,
Secretary of State
for Culture, Media
and Sport

PREFACE

by The Right Honourable Rhodri Morgan AM
First Minister for Wales

Wales is a nation with a deep and diverse heritage. That is why we already have two unique and important World Heritage inscriptions, Blaenavon Industrial Landscape and the Castles and Town Walls of King Edward I in Gwynedd. This new nomination rightly places Pontcysyllte Aqueduct and Canal alongside these two and is the first since power over domestic affairs was devolved to Wales in 1999. If accepted, Pontcysyllte will join other sites of Outstanding Universal Value around the globe that are inscribed on the World Heritage List.

Pontcysyllte Aqueduct and its canal are loved and admired by the people of Wales and others from across the world. The aqueduct figured highly in a recent national poll to celebrate the wonders of Wales, and the consultation on this nomination has demonstrated overwhelming support from the general public: more than ninety-four per cent endorsed the proposal. The Site is appreciated internationally by those interested in the creative innovation of the Enlightenment or the history of early industrialisation and by those who have thrilled to the sheer mastery of the elements displayed by the 'sky-borne canal'. Since 1947 the canal has come to be known and enjoyed by hundreds of thousands of participants from all continents in the Llangollen International Eisteddfod that takes place on its banks every year, one of the largest international dance and music festivals in the world and the stage on which Luciano Pavarotti first performed.

I wish to thank especially the lead partners among many who have worked to make this such an excellent Nomination, particularly Wrexham County Borough Council, British Waterways, my officials in Cadw and the Royal Commission on the Ancient and Historical Monuments of Wales. I hope that in due course World Heritage Site status will allow Wales to share Pontcysyllte Aqueduct and Canal ever more effectively with the international community.

Rhodri Morgan

Rhodri Morgan AM
First Minister
for Wales

CONTENTS

Opposite:
Thomas Telford's curving
weir at Horseshoe Falls,
which extracts water
from the River Dee for
the whole canal.

Opposite: The central
spans of Pontcysyllte
Aqueduct from the
River Dee.

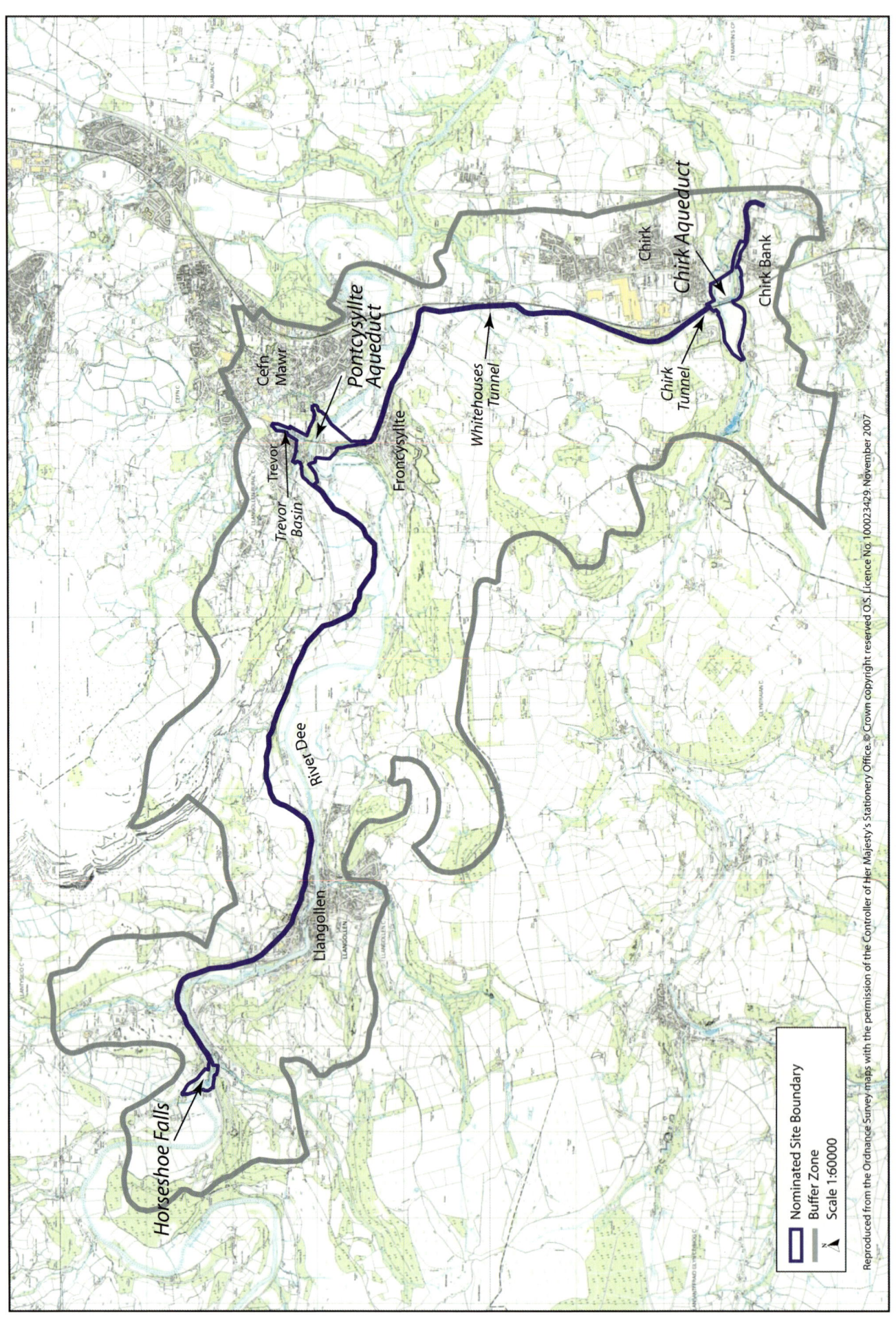

Chirk Aqueduct

Chirk Bank

Chirk

Chirk Tunnel

Whitehouses Tunnel

Pontcysyllte Aqueduct

Cefn Mawr

Froncysyllte

Trevor

Trevor Basin

River Dee

Llangollen

Horseshoe Falls

Nominated Site Boundary

Buffer Zone

Scale 1:60000

Reproduced from the Ordnance Survey maps with the permission of the Controller of Her Majesty's Stationery Office. © Crown copyright reserved OS, Licence No. 100023429. November 2007

EXECUTIVE SUMMARY

State Party

United Kingdom

State, Province or Region

Wales and England, with elements of the Site in Wrexham County Borough and the County of Denbighshire in Wales, and the Borough of Oswestry and County of Shropshire in England.

Name of Property/Site

Pontcysyllte Aqueduct and Canal

Geographical co-ordinates to nearest second

The centre of the nominated World Heritage Site, at Pontcysyllte Aqueduct, is at: Latitude: 52° 58' 13" N Longitude: 3° 5' 11" W.

Textual Description of the boundaries of the Nominated Property

The Nominated Site's boundaries have been drawn to include all those areas or attributes that are a direct and tangible expression of its Outstanding Universal Value: the canal and its engineering features together with remains associated with its construction and historical operation. It consists of 11 miles/18 kilometres of continuous waterway, from Horseshoe Falls near Llangollen to Gledrid Bridge near Rhoswiel. The boundary encompasses the full extent of the construction works of the canal and all its major engineering features together with areas of land relating to important views of and from the key structures.

The Buffer Zone takes in extensive land in the Dee Valley and the Ceiriog Valley. Landscape Planners from the respective Local Authorities have identified a boundary which follows the topographical ridgeline on both sides of the valley. In places where the ridgelines are less distinct, the Buffer Zone is drawn to incorporate all areas which contribute to the visual setting of the Site and features of related historic interest identified in an Industrial Archaeology study.

The area of the Nominated Site is 105 hectares. The area of the Site together with the Buffer Zone is 4,250 hectares.

Map of the Nominated Property

(see facing page)

Opposite: Map 1. A map showing the boundaries of the Nominated Site and Buffer Zone.

Proposed statement of Outstanding Universal Value

Pontcysyllte Aqueduct and Canal in North Wales, built between 1795 and 1808, is a masterpiece of historic transport development and the greatest work of two outstanding figures in the history of civil engineering: Thomas Telford and William Jessop. Pontcysyllte Aqueduct crossed the Dee Valley by nineteen spans at a height of 126 feet/38.4 metres. Its application of the new technology of cast iron to create the tallest and longest navigable aqueduct in the world was a daring and spectacular achievement. The associated 11 mile/18 kilometre section of navigable waterway is an outstanding example of advances in canal building in the Industrial Revolution, one of the fundamental turning points of human history. The Site exhibits important international interchanges of values in inland navigation, civil engineering and the application of iron to structural design.

The Nominated Site has a high degree of integrity and authenticity. The whole of the intensively-engineered section of the waterway is within the Site boundary and no major features have been lost or damaged. Changes made to the formation of the waterway and its engineering features during its continuing working life as a navigation have been largely superficial. Its central structure, Pontcysyllte Aqueduct, has been protected as a Scheduled Ancient Monument of National Importance since 1958 and was recently the subject of an exemplary conservation programme. The Nominated Site and its extensive Buffer Zone are protected and managed by multiple designations and planning controls. The canal is in state ownership through the medium of British Waterways. A robust World Heritage Site Management Plan has been prepared by the local authorities, British Waterways and national heritage bodies, who have come together in a strategic partnership for the purposes of its identification, protection, conservation, presentation and transmission to future generations.

Opposite: Aerial view of Trevor Basin and Pontcysyllte Aqueduct.

Criteria under which Inscription is proposed and justification

Criterion i)
The Nominated Site is the masterpiece of two of the exceptional figures in the heroic phase of civil engineering in the late eighteenth and early nineteenth centuries.

Criterion ii)
The Nominated Site exhibits important international interchanges of values in inland navigation, civil engineering and the application of iron to structural design.

Criterion iv)
The Nominated Site is an outstanding example of transport improvements in the Industrial Revolution, which initiated the process of industrialisation that spread to Europe, North America and the entire globe.

Name and contact information of official local institution/agency

ORGANISATION:
Wrexham County Borough Council

ADDRESS:
Economic Development Department
Lambpit Street
Wrexham
LL11 1AR
United Kingdom

Tel: 44 (0) 1978 292460
Fax: 44 (0) 1978 292445

E-mail: dawn.roberts@wrexham.gov.uk

Website: www.wrexham.gov.uk/aqueduct

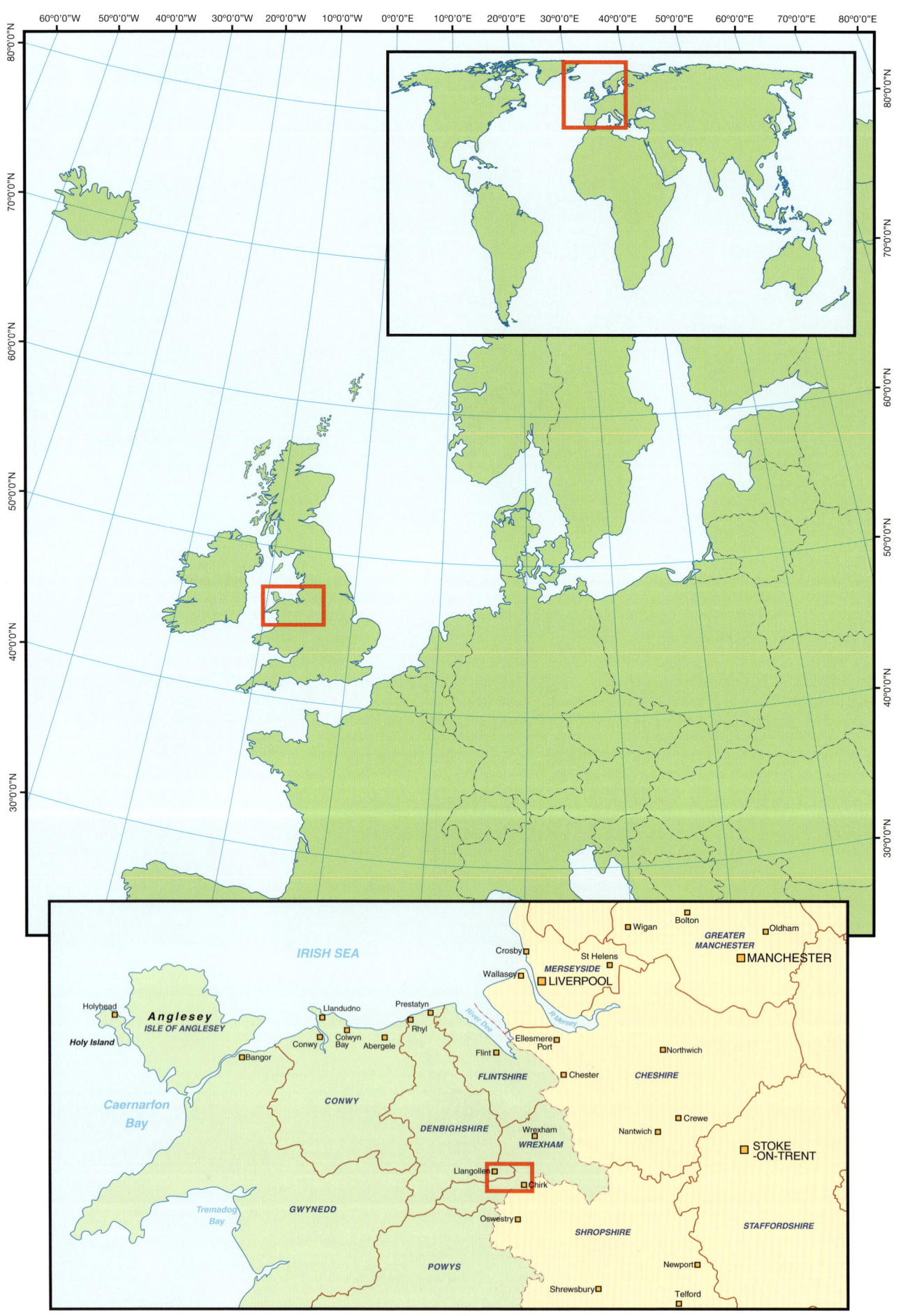

IDENTIFICATION OF THE PROPERTY

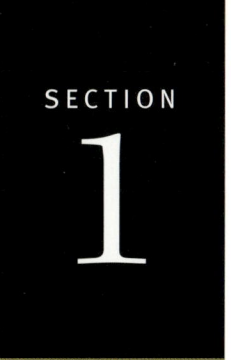

A very important improvement was made, in England, a few years since, in constructing aqueducts.

John White Webster, John Ware, Daniel Treadwell,
'Sketches of the Progress of Inventions, connected with Navigable Canals',
The Boston Journal of Philosophy and the Arts (1824)

1.a State Party and Country

The State Party is the UNITED KINGDOM

The nominated Site lies within two Countries:
10.5 miles/ 17 kilometres in Wales
0.5 miles/ 1 kilometre in England

1.b Region

Wales and England, with elements of the Site in Wrexham County Borough and the County of Denbighshire in Wales, and the Borough of Oswestry and County of Shropshire in England.

1.c Name of the Property

PONTCYSYLLTE AQUEDUCT
AND CANAL

1.d Geographical co-ordinates to the nearest second

Pontcysyllte Aqueduct is situated in Wrexham County Borough, in north-east Wales. The centre of the Nominated World Heritage Site, Pontcysyllte Aqueduct, is at:

Latitude: 52° 58' 13" N
Longitude: 3° 5' 11" W

(See Maps 2 and 3)

Opposite: Maps 2 and 3.
World and Regional
Maps showing the
location of Pontcysyllte
Aqueduct and Canal.

Pontcysyllte Aqueduct
contrasted with the
older Cysyllte Bridge
in a watercolour by
John Glover, c.1800.

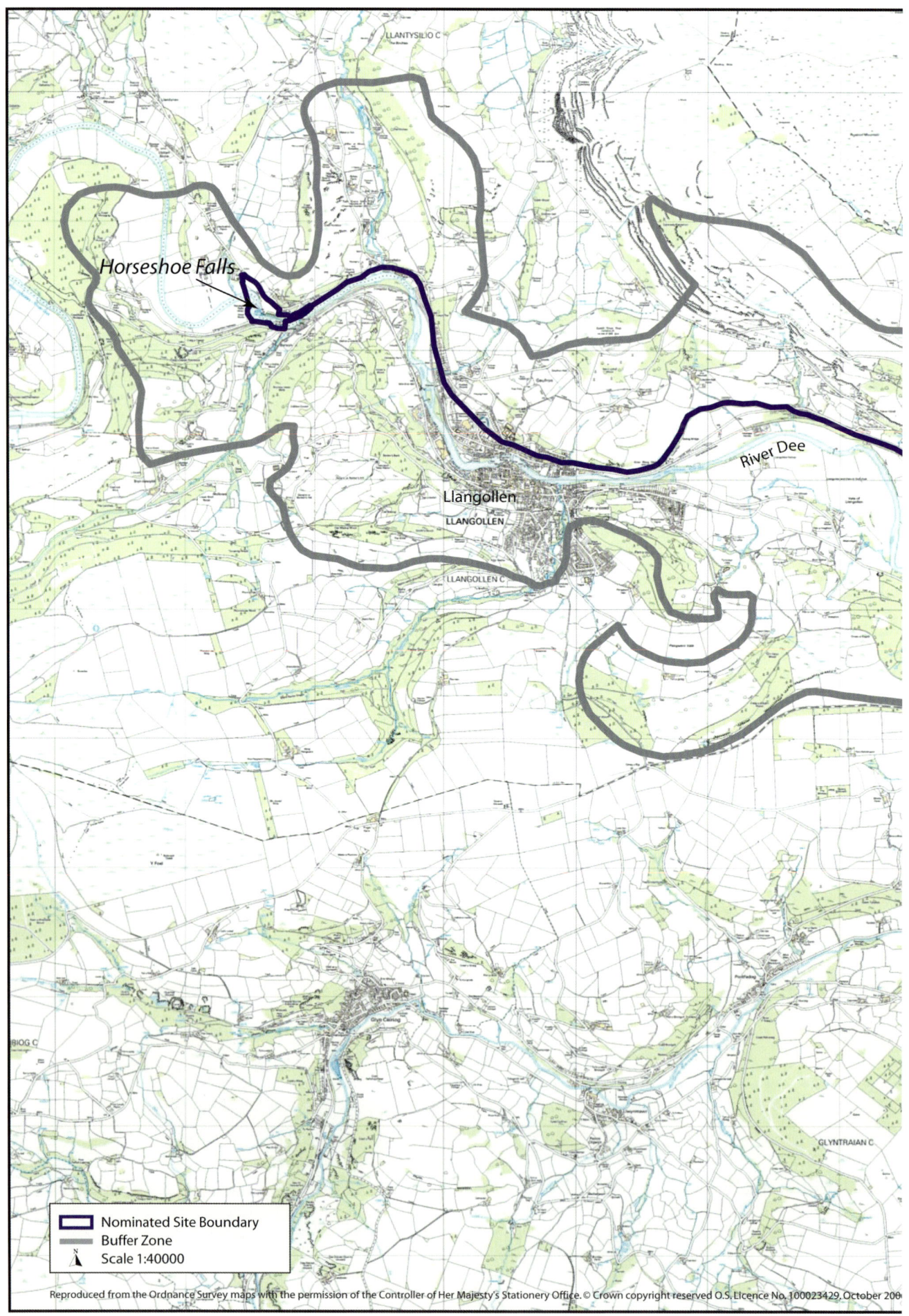

Map 4: A map showing the boundaries of the Nominated Site and Buffer Zone.

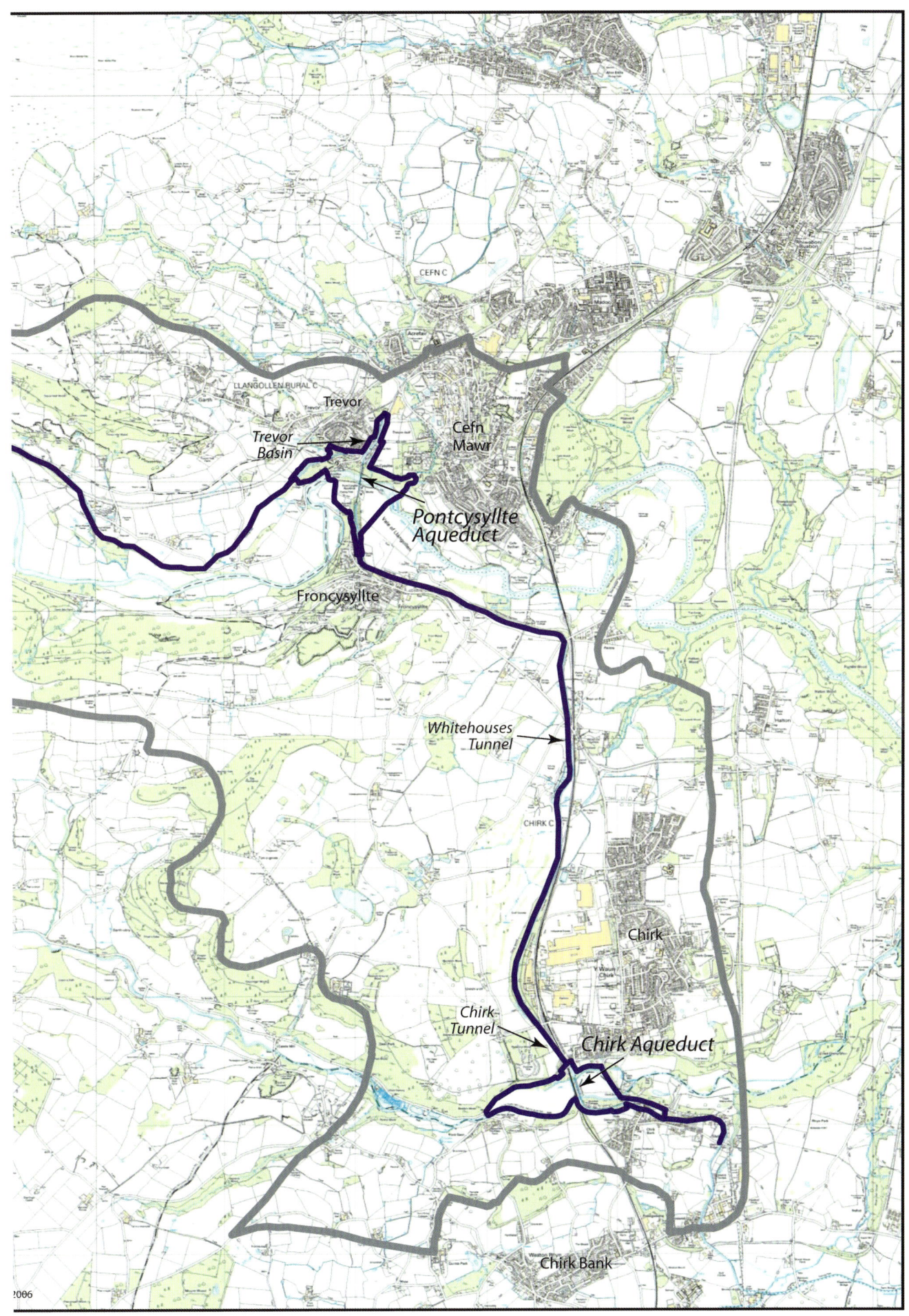

2006

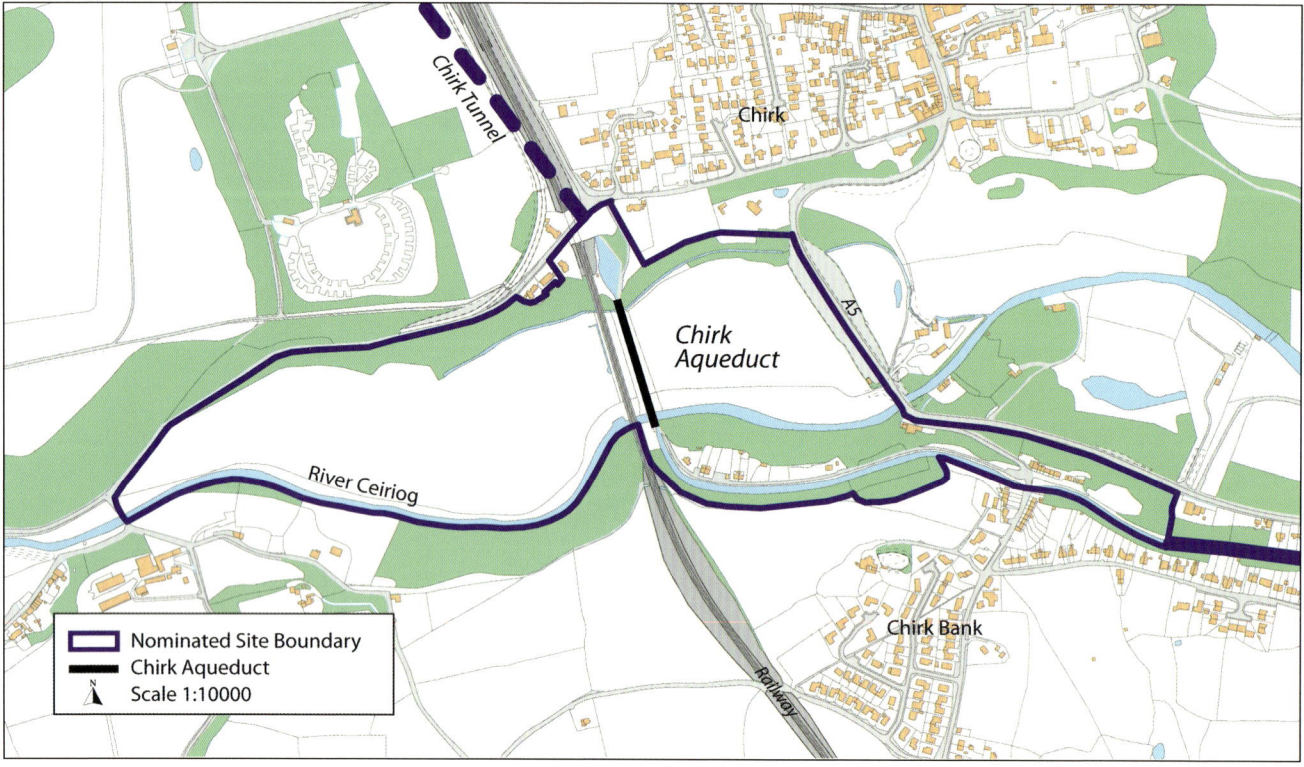

Map 5. A map detailing the Nominated Site boundary at Chirk Aqueduct.

1.e Maps and plans showing boundaries of the Property

i)   Map 4: Nominated Site and Buffer Zone – map at 1:35000 to show the 11 miles/18 kilometres Site and Buffer Zone;

ii) Map 5: Site boundary detail at Chirk Aqueduct;

iii) Map 6: Site boundary detail at Pontcysyllte Aqueduct; and

iv) Map 7: Site boundary detail at the Horseshoe Falls.

1.f Area of the Property

In accordance with World Heritage guidelines, the Nominated Site's boundaries have been drawn to include all those areas or attributes which are a direct and tangible expression of its Outstanding Universal Value – as a masterpiece of canal engineering and an outstanding representation of the improvement of transport during the Industrial Revolution. The Site includes the canal and its engineering features together with remains associated with its construction and historical operation such as engineer's houses, wharves and lengthman's cottages.

It contains 11 miles/18 kilometres of waterway from Horseshoe Falls to Gledrid Bridge near Rhoswiel; two major aqueducts at Pontcysyllte and Chirk plus two others; two tunnels at Chirk and Whitehouses; thirty-one bridges; fifteen embankments; sixteen cuttings; seven sluices; Horseshoe Falls and two floodweirs; eighteen culverts and associated buildings at Chirk Bank,

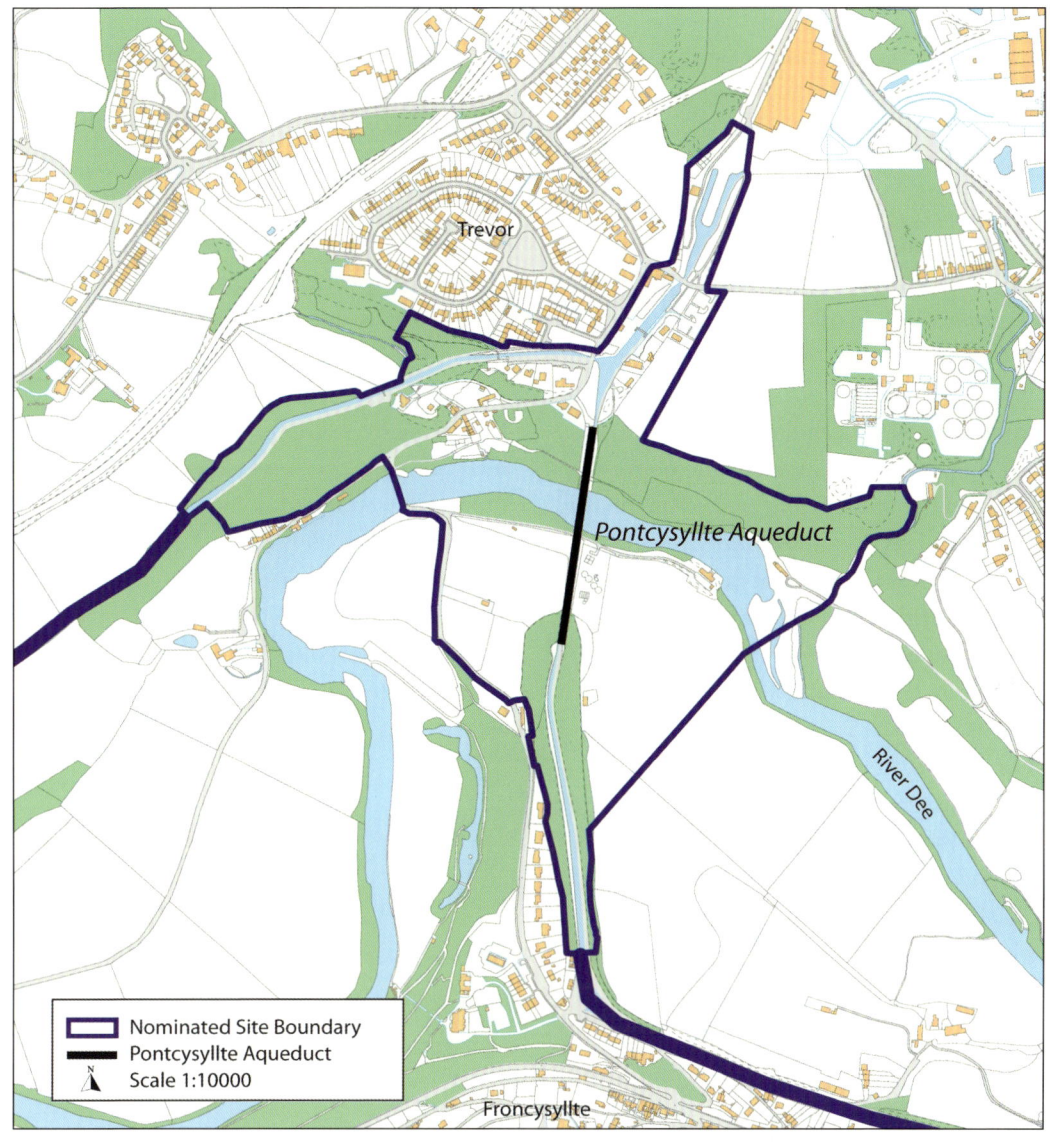

Map 6. A map detailing the Nominated Site boundary at Pontcysyllte Aqueduct.

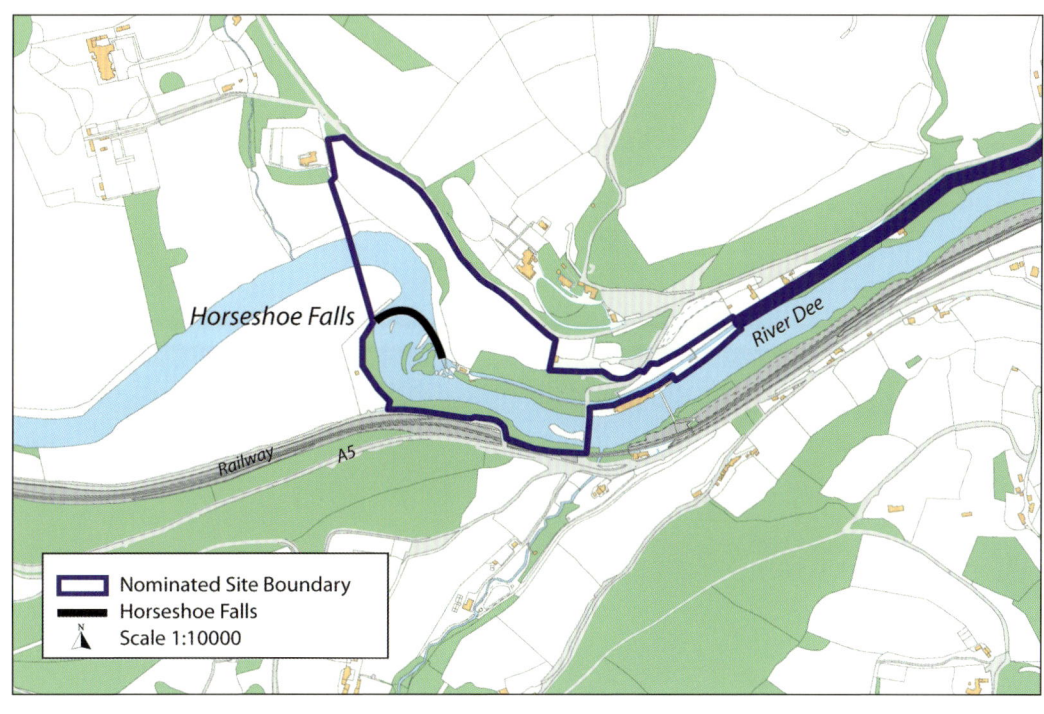

Map 7. A map detailing the Nominated Site boundary at Horseshoe Falls.

Froncysyllte, Trevor, Llangollen and Llantysilio. The Site boundary also includes limited areas of additional land relating to important views of the key structures, for instance upstream and downstream of Pontcysyllte Aqueduct itself.

The central feature of the proposed Site is Pontcysyllte Aqueduct. However, such is the sophistication of the engineering of the canal and the importance of Chirk Aqueduct (where Thomas Telford and William Jessop experimented with the use of cast iron) that the nomination includes the entire length of the feeder canal and of the heavily engineered section south of Pontcysyllte.

UNESCO requires that both the Site and its Setting are protected from any development which would be deemed harmful to the Site and its Outstanding Universal Value. In order to meet this requirement, many World Heritage Sites have a protective Buffer Zone drawn around them. A Buffer Zone has been designed for Pontcysyllte Aqueduct and Canal to encompass its visual setting and related industrial archaeological features

and safeguard it against inappropriate development.

The Buffer Zone (see Map 4, page 18) takes in land around Horseshoe Falls and most of the Dee Valley downstream before turning southwards to Chirk and the Ceiriog Valley. Landscape Planners from the respective local authorities have identified a boundary which follows the topographical ridgeline on both sides of the valley. In places where the ridgelines are less distinct, the Buffer Zone is drawn to incorporate all areas which contribute to the visual setting of the Site and features of related interest identified in an Industrial Archaeology study. The majority of the Site and Buffer Zone incorporates an area already designated as a Landscape of Special Historic Interest.

Area of Nominated Property and proposed Buffer Zone:

Nominated Site	105 hectares
Buffer Zone	4,145 hectares
Total	4,250 hectares

Opposite:
Thomas Telford with his masterpiece: an engraving after the painting by Samuel Lane of 1822, used as the frontispiece to the Atlas of Telford's works in 1838.

The grand Aqueduct, which had been, for some time past, constructing upon the Ellesmere Canal… has been lately completed. This very difficult and expensive work consists, of two large aqueducts, two tunnels, and a great extent of deep cutting; which… will bring the coal from the Ruabon collieries and Trevor lime-works, readily and fairly to proper markets; so that the county and the canal company will, by this mode of conveyance, reap the benefits resulting from a full competition; and, when the season of the year is favourable, it will not fail to display the beautiful scenery of the romantic vallies of Chirk and Llangollen. The canal, in its progress, works between the north bank of the river Dee and the south bank of the Ceiriog. It will have the effect, to create and establish a commercial intercourse and union between England and North Wales.

The Universal Magazine
(1806)

DESCRIPTION

Did the architecture of iron really rival the architecture of the cathedrals? It did. This was an heroic age. Thomas Telford felt that, spanning the landscape with iron. He was born a poor shepherd, then worked as a journeyman mason, and on his own initiative became an engineer of roads and canals, and a friend of poets. His greatest aqueduct that carries the Llangollen canal over the river Dee shows him to have been a master of cast iron on the grand scale. The monuments of the Industrial Revolution have a Roman grandeur, the grandeur of Republican men.

Jacob Bronowski, *The Ascent of Man* (1973)

Pontcysyllte Aqueduct and Canal consists of a continuous group of civil-engineering features from the heroic phase of transport improvement during the British Industrial Revolution. The canal brought water-borne transport from the English lowlands into the rugged terrain of the Welsh uplands, using innovative techniques to cross two major river valleys and the ridge between them. It was built between 1795 and 1808 by two outstanding figures in the development of civil engineering: Thomas Telford and William Jessop. Through their dynamic relationship the canal became a testing-ground for new ideas that were carried forward into subsequent engineering practice internationally.

At the centre of the Site is Pontcysyllte Aqueduct, which crosses the Dee Valley on nineteen cast-iron spans at a height of 126 feet/38.4 metres: a structure recognised internationally as a masterpiece of waterways engineering and a pioneering example of iron construction. The canal exemplifies the new approaches to engineering developed in Britain during

Thomas Telford in his early forties, a mezzotint after a portrait by Sir Henry Raeburn.

Pontcysyllte Aqueduct at the time of its completion, in a coloured aquatint after John Parry, 1806, commissioned by the influential landowner Sir Watkin Williams Wynn.

Pontcysyllte Aqueduct, 'the sky-borne canal', completed in 1805.

A portrait of William Jessop, by an unknown artist, c.1805.

the Industrial Revolution and taken up in subsequent waterway, railway and road construction throughout the world. The engineers intervened in the landscape with a new scale and intensity, challenged by the need to cut a waterway across the grain of the Welsh upland topography. At the time of its completion this length of canal was described as 'composed of works more difficult of execution than can perhaps be found anywhere within an equal distance of canal navigation'. It combined vigour of engineering with a particular sensitivity to its impact on a valued landscape.

All of the features that were to become characteristic of highly-engineered transport routes can be seen in the Nominated Site, including tunnels, cuttings, aqueducts and embankments, many of them technically innovative or of monumental scale, together with bridges, culverts, weirs and associated features. The whole Site has remained in use continuously for two hundred years - for some one hundred and thirty years by traffic in coal, iron, slate, limestone and general goods, and in more recent times to carry pleasure boats and convey drinking water. It is widely valued for its historical importance, beautiful environment and breathtaking structures, and attracts some 200,000 visitors a year.

Pontcysyllte Aqueduct and Canal are outstanding monuments of the Canal Age in the United Kingdom, which flourished from the 1760s until the establishment of a network of locomotive railways from the 1830s. Canal-building reached its zenith after 1790, during the so-called 'Canal Mania' that saw 1,180 miles / 1,900 kilometres of new waterway completed in just twenty years. The construction of a network of canals in Britain to provide transport for raw materials and goods represented a new phase in the history of inland navigation and was a fundamental factor in the Industrial Revolution, enabling and promoting rapid economic growth, regional specialisation and urbanisation. It contributed to wider developments in business organisation, capital mobilisation and engineering technology which were applied to construction projects all over the world.

2.a Description of the Property

The Canal Works between the north bank of the River Dee and the south bank of the Ceiriog, consisting of two large Aqueducts, two Tunnels and a great extent of deep cutting, will gratify those who enjoy the effects of works of art, when executed on a large scale.

Chester Courrier (26 November 1805)

The following Section of the nomination contains:

- a description of the canal route in its landscape setting, from east to west;

- descriptions of the principal components of the Nominated Site by functional type; and

- a descriptive gazetteer of the features of the Nominated Site, from east to west.

2.a.1 The canal route and its landscape setting

Telford, whether owing to his poetical temperament or not, appears to have had a peculiar tact in adapting his works to the scenes through which they passed, in this case some of the finest in Britain. The lover of the picturesque might tremble at the report that an engineer was about to carry a canal through the heart of North Wales, and to profane the most beautiful of valleys by locks and embankments, but Mr Telford executed the difficult task so as not only to avoid injuring the natural charms of the spots he touched upon, but absolutely to enhance their attractions in a high degree.

The Mechanics Magazine (1840)

The Nominated Site is located in the north-east corner of Wales, 40 miles / 65 kilometres south of the city of Liverpool, and crosses the border into England at its eastern extremity. It follows the route of the Ellesmere Canal, later known as the Welsh Arm of the Shropshire Union Canal or the Llangollen Canal. The Site is a continuous, linear property 11 miles / 18 kilometres

The rising ground of the Welsh borderland at Chirk. The canal follows the slope from bottom left, crosses the Ceiriog Valley on Chirk Aqueduct and enters a series of tunnels and cuttings below Chirk Castle park.

A depiction of the Vale of Llangollen centred upon the River Dee and the multiple piers of Pontcysyllte Aqueduct, seen from the south west, by an anonymous artist c.1825.

long which includes all those areas and attributes that are direct and tangible expressions of its Outstanding Universal Value as a masterpiece of canal engineering and a representation of the improvement of transport during the Industrial Revolution. It contains the engineering features of the canal, remains associated with its construction and historical operation, and the immediate visual surroundings of key monuments. The extensive Buffer Zone ensures that the Site can be protected and appreciated in its landscape setting.

The Site stands on the edge of the Welsh uplands. To its east is the level plain of northern Shropshire and southern Cheshire, lying at around 300 feet / 90 metres above sea level and incised by the River Dee as it flows northwards to the Irish Sea near Chester. From the Welsh border the land rises sharply through Carboniferous outcrops rich in coal and limestone to slate and granite uplands of 1,300 feet / 400 metres and higher. These mineral resources were exploited extensively after the canal was completed, creating new

industrial settlements in the nineteenth century around Trevor and northwards towards Wrexham, but the majority of the area remained largely rural: a landscape of lowland farms, densely wooded hillsides and upland grazing settled by dispersed farmsteads, scattered villages and small towns such as Chirk and Llangollen. The edge of the uplands is cut deeply by the valleys of the Ceiriog and Dee, the latter a classic glacial valley with a flat floor and steeply-sloping sides, offering an important route-way into the mountains of North Wales. To the south of the Dee is the ridge dividing it from the valley of the Ceiriog and the Berwyn Hills; and to its north the towering crags of Eglwyseg and Llantysilio mountains, at the southern tip of the Clwydian Range Area of Outstanding Natural Beauty.

The main line of the canal traverses the edge of the hills from the beginning of the Nominated Site at Gledrid Bridge, in increasingly difficult terrain, clinging to steep slopes, cutting through rising ground and crossing deep valleys as far

The Vale of Llangollen, looking east along the River Dee from Llangollen.

as Trevor, where it terminated. From here the Site extends westwards up the Llangollen Branch canal, which follows the Dee at a continuous level as the valley floor gradually climbs to meet it at Horseshoe Falls, the canal system's water supply. Such rugged topography challenged the skill and ingenuity of the canal's designers and promoters. The route was planned before relief maps were available, and success depended entirely on the engineers' own explorations, levelling surveys and distance measurements. The demands of powerful landowning interests also provided challenges. The area was rich in graceful country estates and was frequently visited by artists and members of the gentry undertaking the tour of Wales, especially during the period of the canal's construction when war with France (from 1793 to 1815) precluded the European 'Grand Tour'. Its mountain heights, rushing rivers, picturesque woods, ancient ruins and position as the gateway to the scenic beauty of North Wales brought appreciation of its physical attractions and Romantic

associations. Far from detracting from the landscape in the eyes of nineteenth-century visitors, the canal was seen to enhance its beauty. It continues to be one of the best-loved landscapes in the British Isles.

The 5 miles / 8 kilometres of the main line canal succeeded in maintaining a direct and level route without time-consuming diversions or water-hungry flights of locks, which crippled some canals of the period. It achieved this by an unprecedented sequence of major engineering features, culminating in Pontcysyllte Aqueduct itself.

At its eastern boundary, the Nominated Site begins at Gledrid Bridge with the canal terraced against a steep hillside, where coal mines and limestone quarries fed wharves. There is a substantial earthwork of Chirk Bank Embankment as the canal enters the valley of the River Ceiriog. Rather than follow the contour up the Ceiriog Valley or cross it by an obstructive embankment the canal utilises a ten-span aqueduct: a grand project that was considered a positive complement to the parkland of Chirk Castle. At its completion in 1801, Chirk

The Vale of Llangollen, looking east along the River Dee from Llangollen.

Top: Chirk Aqueduct, completed in 1801.

Above: The medieval fortress of Chirk Castle, managed by the National Trust.

A cross-section through the enormous approach embankment to Pontcysyllte Aqueduct.

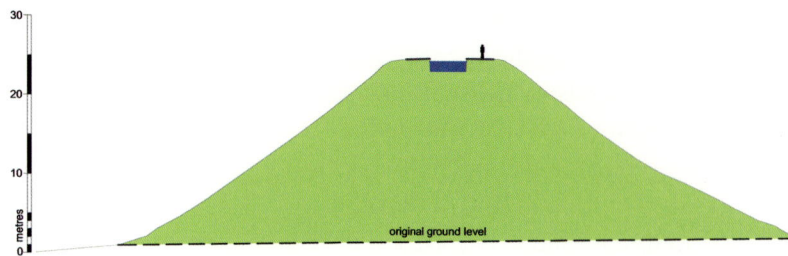

Aqueduct was the highest such structure to have been built, and it remained so until the completion of Pontcysyllte Aqueduct four years later. The Site includes the immediate visual setting of the water meadows of the Ceiriog in both directions. It is bounded at the east by an embankment on the Holyhead Road, built by Thomas Telford as part of his later scheme for a high-speed route linking London to Dublin. It includes the viaduct for the railway that later connected the coalfield to its markets, allowing an informative comparison of transport developments over half a century. A group of canal workers' houses from the later nineteenth century stands on the huge embankments approaching the aqueduct, where a construction yard was used to prepare stone from an adjacent quarry.

At the north end of Chirk Aqueduct a shelf cut into the hill provides space for a general trade wharf and a basin where boats could wait. The canal then enters the first of two tunnels and two long cuttings to the east of the medieval fortress of Chirk Castle. The Castle lies within the Buffer Zone and the house and grounds are managed and conserved by the National Trust. The cuttings and tunnels enabled the canal to take a direct route through higher ground rather than a long detour to the east while satisfying the desire of the landowners to preserve the approaches to their estate. Chirk Tunnel is followed by Irish Bridge Cutting and then Whitehouses Tunnel. These major civil engineering works required vast quantities of spoil to be excavated by hand and moved by construction railway or boat to provide material for embankments further north.

After Irish Bridge Cutting the canal is terraced against the slopes of the Dee Valley. It crosses Offa's Dyke, the early medieval boundary between the Welsh princedoms and the Saxon kingdom of Mercia. Now designated as one of the National Trails, the strategic routes taking walkers through the United Kingdom's finest countryside, Offa's Dyke is among the most popular long-distance walking routes in Europe. The Trail diverts onto the canal towing-path to Pontcysyllte Aqueduct. At Froncysyllte the canal continues in a terrace to a wharf and limekilns where limestone was brought to the canal. It is then carried out across the valley on a massive approach embankment towards the great aqueduct at Pontcysyllte.

The engineers had considered crossing the River Dee at a low level, on an aqueduct approached at either end by flights of locks. However, they made the daring choice to maintain the level – building an embankment that would be one of the world's most substantial earthen structures, and devising an aqueduct of such unprecedented scale that it necessitated a series of innovations in construction and design. The aqueduct was a waterway through the sky that amazed all who saw it. It still takes away the breath of visitors.

The Nominated Site encompasses the immediate setting of the embankment and aqueduct. To the west it includes Cysylltau Bridge, a three-arched crossing of the River Dee, which is a principal viewing point and appears in many contemporary depictions of the aqueduct, including Telford's official portrait in the Institution of Civil Engineers.

The main line of the canal terminates on the north side of Pontcysyllte Aqueduct at Trevor Basin, where wharves, dry docks, bridges, canal houses and traces of early railways are part of the Nominated Site. During the construction of the aqueduct, this was the preparation area for the stone and ironwork. Components were carried out across the valley on temporary bridges which were raised successively with the piers until the full height was achieved. Once the canal was completed, the basin became a hub of activity, servicing trade and transhipping goods to and from the boats. The new transport infrastructure stimulated the growth of collieries and ironworks. Several settlements grew up to house industrial workers. The largest is Cefn Mawr, within the Buffer Zone, where houses, shops, public houses and chapels have been designated as a Conservation Area and a Townscape Heritage Initiative has stimulated conservation projects.

The 6 mile / 10 kilometre Llangollen Branch extends to the west from Trevor Basin, along the north side of the Vale of Llangollen. Although proposed as early as 1791 it was begun under a separate Act of Parliament in 1804. Its purpose was to feed water to the Ellesmere Canal system, and also to serve the town of Llangollen and nearby slate and limestone quarries. It was narrower than the main canal, but was engineered skilfully to maintain a level route along the steep sides of the glacial valley.

The branch canal winds along slopes high above the river and offers panoramic views of the hills on either side and towards the eye-catching mountain-top ruins of Dinas Brân. This thirteenth-century Welsh castle, which was regarded during the Romantic period as a potent symbol of the ancient people of Wales, has been consolidated and interpreted for visitors by Denbighshire County Council. The canal takes a straighter line than the topography would suggest, crossing side valleys and bisecting spurs by embankments and cuttings. Telford wrote in 1805, 'This navigable feeder is about six miles; and on account of the difficult and rugged country through which it passes, the expense attending it will be great…'. Nearing Llangollen the hills are even steeper and the canal is constructed on a narrow terrace, often with rock walls to the north and earthen embankments to the south.

An aerial view of the Dee Valley looking towards the terminus of the main line of the canal at Trevor, with Pontcysyllte Aqueduct and its wooded approach embankment at the centre and Cefn Mawr to the right.

The Vale of Llangollen and the Romantic Movement: J.M.W. Turner's watercolour of the ruins of Valle Crucis abbey and Dinas Brân castle towering above, 1794-5.

The market town of Llangollen has been a centre for tourism since the late eighteenth century, stimulated initially by artists and writers who visited the area and recorded their impressions of it. The town lies in the Buffer Zone on the south bank of the River Dee and was served by a general goods wharf and warehouse on the canal. The multi-span bridge across the river is an impressive example of the achievements of bridge builders before the Industrial Revolution. On a hill above the town is Plas Newydd, the home between 1780 and 1829 of Lady Eleanor Butler and Miss Sara Ponsonby, 'the Ladies of Llangollen', whose fame drew numerous poets, writers, artists

and people of note to the Vale. The house is a museum, managed by Denbighshire County Council. Other historical landmarks in the beautiful countryside rising towards Llantysilio mountain have traditionally drawn visitors, including two monuments in the care of the government heritage body, Cadw: the Pillar of Eliseg and the Cistercian monastery of Valle Crucis, painted by J.M.W. Turner. The Buffer Zone includes these significant attractions together with slate and limestone quarries served by the canal in the hills around Llangollen.

The canal is at its narrowest in its last section from Llangollen to Horseshoe Falls, where it was relatively little-used by boats. However, substantial engineering work was still required, to cut a level shelf for the waterway and build a large masonry aqueduct over the River Eglwyseg and many culverts over streams flowing to the Dee. The last 0.2 miles / 0.3 kilometres is a rock-hewn watercourse from the elegantly-curved, cast-iron and masonry weir designed by Telford. The canal carries 11 million gallons / 50 million litres a day from this point to drinking-water reservoirs beyond the English border in Cheshire. The bowl of attractive parkland is included in the Nominated Site for its direct visual relationship with the weir. The river is a Special Area of Conservation, designated under the European Community Habitats Directive.

The picturesquely craggy and wooded aspect of this last section of the canal from Llangollen Wharf to Horseshoe Falls, running close to the rushing waters of the Dee, has made it popular among visitors for promenades and boat trips since the early nineteenth century. Among the groups who

Sections through the rock cutting at Chain Bridge, facing west.

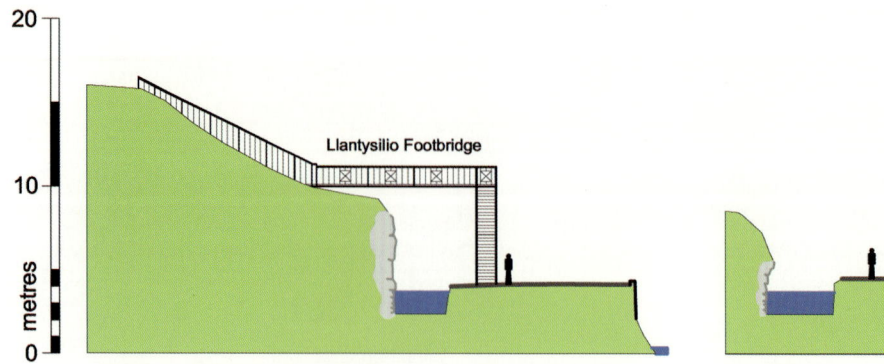

have used the canal regularly in the last sixty years have been hundreds of thousands of participants and visitors from around the world at the Llangollen International Musical Eisteddfod, established in 1947 and occupying a site near the bank of the canal. The stated aim of this music and dance festival has been to permit 'Welsh culture and a wider international movement in fostering the arts' to be 'happily reconciled for mutual enrichment.'

2.a.2 The canal formation

The bank of the canal forms a charming promenade of about six miles from its junction with the Dee to the Aqueduct, abounding with interesting and picturesque scenery.

W.T. Simpson, *Some Account of Llangollen and its Vicinity* (1827)

The scale and form of the canal in the Nominated Site is typical of those built in Britain during the early Industrial Revolution. Its earthwork formation incorporates the channel, a flat towing-path for the horses that drew the boats, hedges

to separate the towing-path from adjacent fields, and the wider land needed for embankments and cuttings. The majority of the formation is as it was built. It provides a tranquil, level route through spectacular scenery and has been well-used by boaters and walkers for two centuries. It also has biodiversity value as a habitat for birds, mammals and aquatic plants.

The channel was built flat at the bottom with banks that sloped up evenly to a vertical edge. It was designed to carry the typical English canal craft of the era, which had an elongated form 72 feet 6 inches / 22.1 metres by 6 feet 10 inches

Competitors from the Llangollen International Musical Eisteddfod taking a boat trip on the canal in about 1960.

The picturesque landscape of the head of the canal rising towards Llantysilio Mountain. The water source for the canal at Horseshoe Falls on the River Dee is near the centre of the picture and the feeder channel follows the valley to the right.

Above: A typical section of the canal formation, cut into the hill on one side and embanked on the other, with tall trees edging the towing-path, 1936.

wide/2.1 metres. Each 'narrow boat', as they came to be known, could carry up to 30 tons/30.5 tonnes. The largest of the pleasure boats using the canal today are of the same proportions. The main line is mostly 5 feet/1.5 metres deep and built to a standard width of about 30 feet/9.2 metres, sufficient to allow boats to pass one another unhindered. The channel is wider in some places, but is narrower on the tallest sections of embankment, and the aqueducts, tunnels and bridges are insufficient in width for boats to pass one another. Overall, the main line contrasts with the preceding generation of canals, many of which were far narrower and required designated passing places. The Llangollen Branch is smaller, typically about 26 feet/8 metres wide and with more frequent narrow sections, as it was expected to have less traffic and was terraced on steep slopes.

The channel was dug and waterproofed in clay by large gangs of labourers – the navvies – using picks and shovels and wheelbarrows on runs of planks. A rammed layer of 'puddled' clay was used for waterproofing, except in impermeable conditions such as

bands of naturally-occurring clay or the rock channels of the feeder watercourse. Some 55 per cent of the channel lining is unaltered, but from the 1960s onwards British Waterways re-lined sections at a high risk of breaching, mainly on high embankments or the steepest slopes. Past re-lining was usually carried out in asphalt or concrete, and banks in danger of erosion were protected with sheet piling, concrete or geotextile fabrics. Even in these locations, the canal width and depth, towing-path, earthworks and boundaries are all unchanged.

The towing-path is a broad, flat pathway. Where the canal is crossing slopes, cut into the hill on one side and embanked on the other, the towing-path is on the top of the down-hill embankment. As elsewhere on British canals, there are usually no boundaries on the far side but the towing-path is hedged to protect neighbouring crops and livestock. Hedges planted at the time of construction of the canal can still be seen and many oak trees, allowed to grow up to supply future timber, are now two hundred years old.

2.a.3 Pontcysyllte Aqueduct

*Tel est l'aqueduc de Pont-Cysylte, que, par
son légèreté, son élégance, est un modèle
dans son genre… un canal aérien, dont
l'enveloppe métallique est soutenue par
des piles hardies et légères. Des bateaux
à charge pesante, et les cheveaux que les
halent, franchissement, avec sécurité, cette
voie suspendue sur un abîme, et portent
vers Ellesmere, le charbon, la chaux et les
fers que fournissent les mines, les carrières
et les usines de la vallée de Llangollen'…
'Après une marche longue et pénible, je suis
entré dans cette vallée, par un beau soir
d'automne, presqu'au moment du coucher
de soleil. Jamais spectacle plus imposant
n'a frappé mes regards; au milieu d'une
végétation vigoureuse, et conservante encore
toute sa fraîcheur, des tourbillons de flamme
et de fumée, éruptions perpétuelles des
cratères de l'industrie; les hautsfourneaux,
les forges, les fours à chaux, et l'amas d'une
houille embrasée pour devenir, par l'ignition
même, un combustible parfait; des usines,
des maisons de plaisance, des villages, érigés
en amphithéâtre, sur les flancs de la vallée;
dans le fond un rapide torrent; audessus,
le pont-canal offrant son enveloppe de fer,
posée, comme par enchantement, sur les
hauts et minces piliers, d'une élégante et
simple architecture…*

[Such is Pontcysyllte Aqueduct, which
by its light appearance and its elegance is
a model of its kind… a sky-borne canal,
whose iron trough is held up by piers that
are both sturdy and delicate. Heavily laden
boats and the horses which haul them may
safely cross this passage over an abyss and
carry away towards Ellesmere the coal,
limestone and iron from the mines, quarries
and foundries of the Vale of Llangollen….
After a long and exhausting walk, I came
into the valley on a fine autumn evening,
just as the sun was setting. Never had I seen
such an imposing sight. In the midst of the
luxuriant woodlands, still flourishing with all
their natural freshness, arose whirlwinds of
flame and smoke, continual eruptions from
the craters of industry. There were blast
furnaces, forges, limekilns, piles of coal
being coked, workshops, fine mansions and
villages, built in an amphitheatre around
the flanks of the valley. At the bottom was
a foaming torrent, while above it the canal,
enclosed in its iron envelope, hung, like
something enchanted, on its high, slender
pillars, a supreme work of architecture,
elegant and unadorned…]

Charles Dupin, (1816)
[translation by Barrie Trinder]

Pontcysyllte Aqueduct
striding across the
Dee Valley towards
Froncysyllte.

Pontcysyllte Aqueduct is the monumental
centrepiece of the Nominated Site. It is
in excellent condition following an award-
winning conservation project before its
bicentenary in 2005. The aqueduct is
an acknowledged masterpiece of civil
engineering, the work of two of the creative
geniuses of the Industrial Revolution. The
historian Anthony Burton wrote in 1989, 'If
any one structure can be said to exemplify
the technical brilliance and innovation
that marked the work of the greatest canal
engineers, this is it.' J.P.M. Pannell, in his
Illustrated History of Civil Engineering
(1964) described it as 'perhaps the greatest
of all the works executed by British canal
engineers'.

The dimensions of the aqueduct are
staggering. It consists of eighteen tapering
stone piers, hollow in their upper sections
to reduce the load on the foundations. On
these a cast-iron trough is borne at a height
of 126 feet/38.4 metres on cast-iron arch
ribs. It was for two centuries the highest
navigable aqueduct in the world. The trough
stretches for 1,007 feet/307 metres. Such
a structure would not have been possible
using traditional techniques of navigable
aqueduct construction: masonry walls
retaining a thick waterproofing of puddled
clay, supported on massive piers and
imposing an unsustainable foundation load.

The trough is made up of plates one inch
/25 millimetres thick. It is constructed in
44 feet/13.4 metres spans, and is 11 feet
10 inches/3.61metres wide. The plates

Top: An elevation of Pontcysyllte Aqueduct from the Atlas of Telford's work published in 1838.

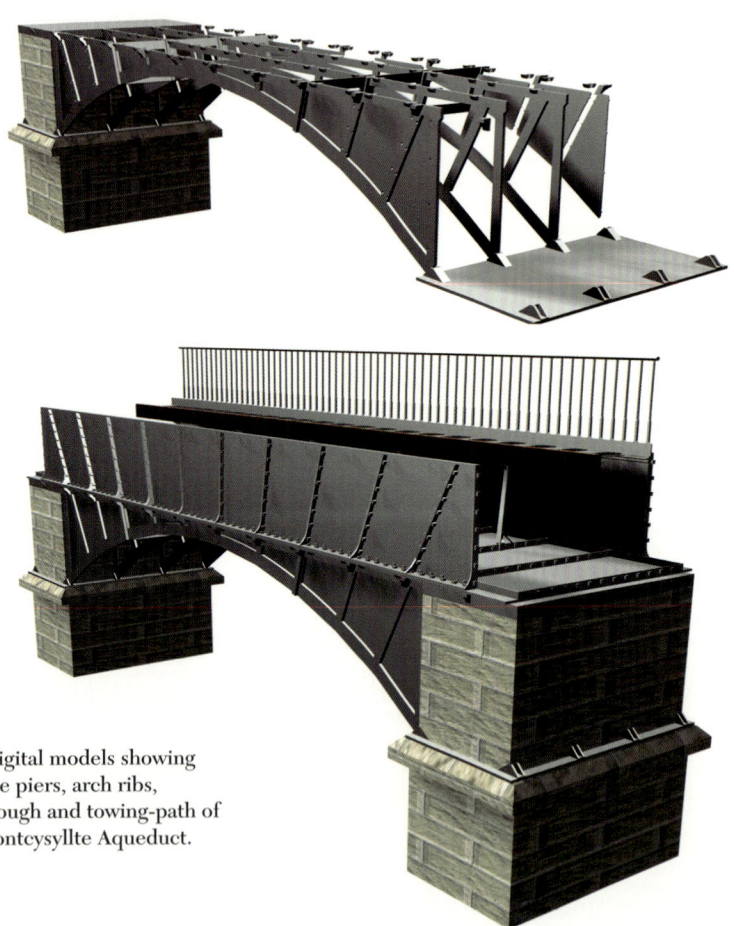

Digital models showing the piers, arch ribs, trough and towing-path of Pontcysyllte Aqueduct.

lock in a pattern similar to voussoirs in a flat stone arch and are bolted at the flanges, their joints made watertight with a mixture of flannel, white lead and iron borings. Supporting each span are four ribs, cast in three sections and bolted together with connecting plates. These sit on springing plates near the top of the piers. The outer-most ribs have infill plates giving the impression of a solid span. The trough is prevented from lateral movement by brackets and lugs on its under-side.

The towing-path is supported over the waterway on standards to allow circulation of water when a fully-laden narrowboat, which might draw several feet, moves through the trough. The uprights are secured to the flanged joints of the base plates with wedges and lugs. Cross-bearers support dished plates, over which is laid the top filling of the path. The towing-path is protected by a cast-iron handrail, but no railing was ever intended on the off-side of the canal - lug holes for uprights in the opposite trough plates simply reflect the fact that the same patterns were used to cast both sides.

The aqueduct's name, taken from the old Dee bridge below, translates from the Welsh as 'the bridge that joins': especially fitting for a structure that strides across a whole valley. The virtuosity and ambition displayed in Pontcysyllte are astounding, and all the more so as it came so soon after the first experiments with cast-iron troughs. The historian Tom Rolt wrote in 1950, 'Having compared Brindley's aqueducts with early Norman architecture then Telford's Pont Cysyllte can only be likened, in its airy lightness, to the full flower of the Gothic. The slender symmetry of Telford's aqueduct and of the great cathedral vault both display the exuberant craftsmanship of men who have won a new command over materials.'

An aerial view of
Pontcysyllte Aqueduct
from the east.

2.a.4 Chirk Aqueduct

6 June 1799… On my way stopped to take a view of the noble aqueduct forming across the valley under Chirk to convey the waters of the canal over a wide and deep valley. It consists of ten arches, half of which are nearly turned and some few finished. They are grand in their form and received an additional beauty in the picturesque light by the soft mellow yellow tint of the stone. On winding down the hill and just seeing this noble aqueduct (which for grandeur will vye with the Roman works of the same sort) the eye is sensibly struck with this new object; its present unfinished state renders it perhaps more picturesque to the painter's eye.

Sir Richard Colt Hoare (1799)

Below: Chirk Aqueduct with the railway viaduct of a generation later beyond.

Bottom: An elevation of Chirk Aqueduct from the Atlas of Telford's work published in 1838.

Chirk Aqueduct was completed before Pontcysyllte and was a transitional structure in its experimentation with masonry and iron construction. Problems of distortion had been identified with traditional masonry and puddled clay aqueducts, and the engineers recognised that a multi-span aqueduct of such height would require new techniques. The trough is supported by ten stone arches at 68 feet / 20.7 metres above the River Ceiriog – higher than any previous navigable aqueduct. The bottom of the trough was made up of cast-iron bed plates, but the sides originally were not. (Iron side plates were added in 1869 as a by-then conventional improvement to the ageing brickwork.) Although the engineers were not yet confident of using iron alone in such a major aqueduct, the iron bed plates and high-fired brick sides with hydraulic mortar removed the need for bulky puddled clay and therefore enabled a far smaller cross-section. The bed plates sit directly on the apex of each arch, minimising the depth of the masonry. In order to reduce the foundation load further, the masonry spans are hollow, with just cross-walls to strengthen them and support the trough. These are accessible for maintenance through openings in the undersides of the arches. A cast-iron balustrade runs along the towing-path side.

The stone for the aqueduct came from a quarry on the bank of the new canal just to the south, within the Nominated Site. Only that used for the quoins, stringcourses and subtly-emphasised keystones is ashlar, the majority being roughly-coursed rubble stone. The piers were constructed with finely-tapering engaged columns that rise

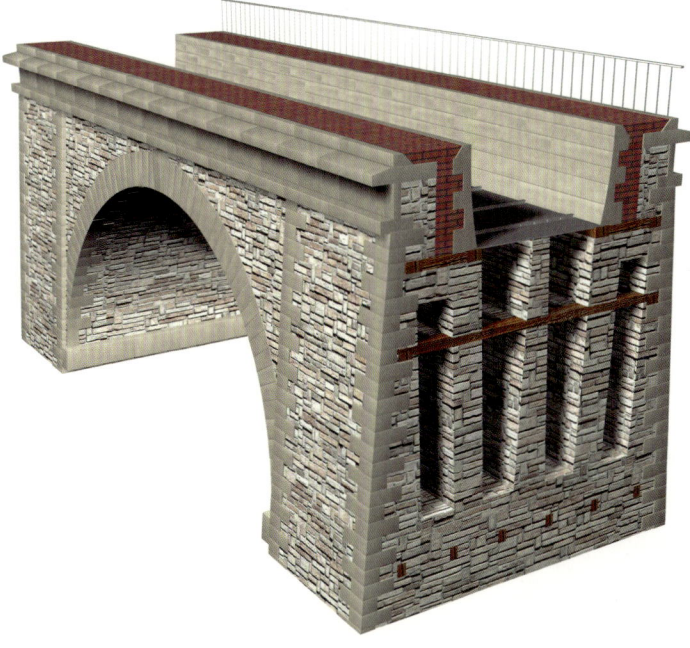

to a stringcourse at the deck level, echoing the Classical and Egyptian architecture in which Telford had an interest. However, the aqueduct achieves its elegance through a notably functional design, and can be contrasted strongly with the architecturally-embellished contemporary aqueducts of John Rennie on the Lancaster and Kennet and Avon canals.

The aqueduct is now paralleled by the railway viaduct of 1846-8, creating a remarkable pairing of great structures. The viaduct was designed by Henry Robertson and built by Telford's former assistant, Thomas Brassey. It is taller than the aqueduct, expressing the succession of one transport mode over another, and possesses architectural detailing such as dentillation and niches, in contrast to the functional integrity of the aqueduct. It provides impressive views of the canal for passengers on passing trains.

2.a.5 Conventional aqueducts and culverts

On the erection of Aqueducts… the least settling in brick or stone bridges, by letting through the water, may prove of the most fatal consequence. That the plan of an aqueduct-bridge should be curving inwards, that is, the ends should be wider than the middle, the walls should also not be upright, but buttering or diminishing upwards with-outside, to give greater strength and stability to the whole.

The Cyclopaedia; or Universal Dictionary of Arts, Sciences and Literature, (1802-20)

Two further aqueducts within the Nominated Site provide instructive comparisons with the innovative technology developed at Chirk and Pontcysyllte. Both are constructed conventionally using masonry walling for the exterior and trough and puddled-clay infill. The techniques chosen were sufficient to the demands of their locations, which required

Above left: the aqueduct and railway viaduct from Chirk basin.

Above right: A digital model of Chirk Aqueduct showing the original arrangement of iron plates on the bottom of the trough with brick and stone side walls. The bottom plates are supported by the centre of the arch and cross walls within the hollow spandrels.

only relatively low, small crossings. The substantial girth and great weight of both structures demonstrate the impossibility of using such techniques at the height and length needed to cross the valleys at Chirk and Pontcysyllte. Several conventional aqueducts of ambitious scale failed on other canals during the 1790s through their great weight and the instability of the clay interior, underlining the limitations of the traditional technology.

Cross Street Aqueduct at Froncysyllte was built for a track from a farm that was separated by the canal from its riverside meadows. It was later used by a railway to Froncysyllte limekilns. The single arch is set in curving rubble-stone wing walls with parapets, similar in appearance to the typical canal over-bridges. The canal continues at full width over the top, indicating the importance of limiting potential bottlenecks. The underside of the arch has been grouted to prevent leakage.

The aqueduct over the River Eglwyseg at Pentrefelin near Llangollen, is a visually impressive structure which demonstrates the high quality of Telford's masonry. The canal approaches it on a long causeway supported

Above and below left: The aqueduct over the River Eglwyseg at Pentrefelin.

Below right: A masonry culvert to carry a watercourse under the canal, at Trevor Mill.

by gently-curving retaining walls. The river arch is formed within a narrower middle section of the causeway and is emphasised architecturally by pilasters in a curved and battered facade. The downstream elevation, on the towing-path side, has a projecting stringcourse at the deck level and an elegant parapet unusually formed by setting large, tapering stone blocks on edge. The parapet follows the curves of the retaining wall for its full length of 115 feet/35 metres. A culvert to accommodate a watercourse from the pre-existing Pentrefelin corn-mill also passes through the causeway. The canal is wide enough throughout to allow boats to pass one another.

In places where a watercourse had to be carried under the canal but the terrain did not justify an aqueduct, a culvert was the most effective response. Culverts are simple but essential elements in the engineering of every transport line to prevent erosion of earthworks by streams or floodwaters. They are frequent where the canal crosses streams that could not be diverted into the waterway, because either they were used by landowners or they posed risks of silting and flooding.

Twenty-one culverts have been identified in the Nominated Site. At high embankments they usually follow a continuous gradient, but where embankments are shallow or the canal is embanked only on one side, a shaft may be incorporated to take the water to a lower level. All the original culverts are sturdily built of rubble masonry, sometimes with dressed stone portals set in retaining walls.

The longest passes diagonally for 330 feet/100 metres under the platform on which Trevor Basin is built, representing a substantial engineering work in its own right. A typical, small example, at Tŷ Uchaf near Llangollen, is 2 feet/0.6 metres wide. Another at Pen-y-bryn Embankment near Chirk, for a larger watercourse, is 3 feet 6 inches/1.1 metres wide. Some are linked to overflows and sluices for controlling the water level in the canal.

2.a.6 Embankments and Cuttings

…ein Teil des Kanals ruht auf einem aufgeschütteten Damm. Eine Meile davon ist der Kanal durch einen Berg und dann wieder über ein Tal auf massiven Bögem forteführt. Alles Werke des Herr Telford…

[…a section of the canal goes across an embankment of heaped-up earth. A mile or so further on the canal goes through a cutting through a hill, and then crosses another valley on a series of great arches. All of this is the work of Mr Telford…]

Karl Friedrich Schinkel (1826)
[translated by Barrie Trinder]

The scale and frequency of cuttings and embankments were among the characteristics that distinguished the canals of the heroic age of engineering in Britain from those that preceded them. As Robert Harris wrote in *Canals and their Architecture* (1969), 'The first canal lines were often notoriously winding, not because the navigators were paid by the mile but because they followed natural contours and avoided heavy earth-moving works wherever possible. Telford and his contemporaries had more sophisticated techniques and more confident promoters; their lines were cut through hills and carried over valleys.'

Cuttings and embankments were major construction works and are clear evidence of the vast commitment made to enable the engineers to command the landscape rather than respond to it. Jessop had long experience of excavating and depositing material successfully, and Telford ensured that embankments and cuttings were sloped to appropriate gradients and planted where necessary. Many are now densely covered with trees, but profile drawings reveal their true size. The earthworks are potent demonstrations of Telford's development of cut-and-fill calculations to enable material from one part of the project to be utilised in another, and of the use of construction railways to move spoil over considerable distances.

A high proportion of the canal in the Nominated Site is supported by artificially-constructed embankments. Fifteen have been identified. These include terraces with cuttings on one side and embankments on the other to support the canal on steep slopes and free-standing embankments that maintain a straight route by crossing

Rock cutting to create a terrace for the canal on the steep hillside at Wern-Isaf.

One of the deep cuttings on the main line of the canal near Chirk.

Below: A cross section through Wern Isaf Rock Walls, facing west, showing the steepness of the hillside occupied by the canal and the shelf made to accommodate it.

valleys and depressions. Virtually all the embankments remain intact as built, and protected from breaches by re-lining of the watercourse.

The largest of the free-standing embankments is Froncysyllte, the 90 feet/27.5 metres high earthwork leading to Pontcysyllte Aqueduct from the south. This was probably the largest civil earthwork of the eighteenth century, comparable with the greatest military earthworks of the period and ancient earthen structures such as construction ramps for Egyptian obelisks and Hindu temple towers. It is composed of enormous volumes of spoil from the cuttings and tunnels to the south. Telford wrote in a report of 1804 of 'The Earthen Embankment and Lining for the Canal, is carrying on by means of three Iron Railways; and it is proposed to have this Part finished at the same time as the Aqueduct.' This was one of the earliest engineering projects in which railways were used systematically to move materials.

The deep cuttings provide a direct route through higher ground. There are eight in the Nominated Site, six of which are on the section of canal that includes the two tunnels. Canal Wood Cutting is 0.75 miles /1.2 kilometres long, leading northwards from Chirk Tunnel. Irish Bridge Cutting is 1,247 feet/380 metres in length and is 33 feet/10 metres at its deepest. The sides of both cuttings are evenly sloped and planted. It is striking that the channel of the canal maintains its full width, with a generous towing-path throughout. A prodigious volume of material was excavated by navvies working with picks and shovels and innovative animal-powered barrow inclines. Two further cuttings on the Llangollen Branch cross hillside spurs at Bont Wood and Bryn Howel.

The greatest example of the terraces made from simultaneous cutting and embanking is at Chirk Bank. This extends for 0.7 miles /1.1 kilometres from the south end of Chirk Aqueduct. As it approaches the aqueduct it is 60 feet/18.3 metres high and 196 feet/60 metres across at the base. The spoil used was produced as a result of cutting the canal channel 25–40 feet/8–12 metres into the rock on its southern side. Terraced embankments cover much of the Llangollen Branch as it traverses the sides of the Dee Valley. The canal near Llangollen is notable for several lengths of solid rock-cutting, for example at Wern-Isaf Rock Walls and Chain Bridge. At Chain Bridge, spoil thrown to the south to embank the canal formation is protected by a stone retaining wall above the River Dee.

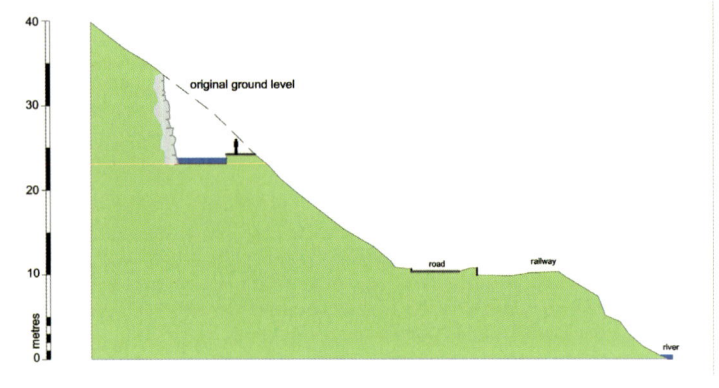

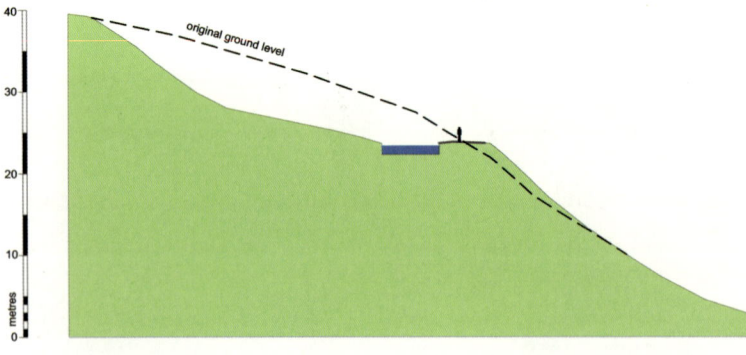

Above: A cross section through the huge terrace embankment at Chirk Bank.

Right: A south-facing cross-section through Canal Wood Cutting indicating the large volume of earth that was moved to create the canal and towing-path.

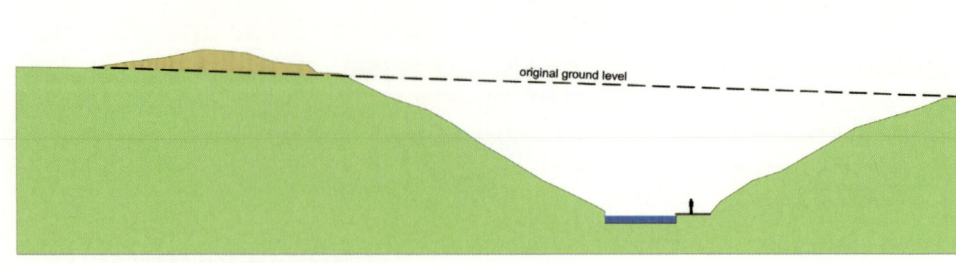

2.a.7 Tunnels

The canal, after being here carried above the earth, is shortly afterwards, near Chirk, carried under ground.... For this purpose, a tunnel has been cut through a hill which opposed it, to allow the canal to pass under it. Curiosity induced me to examine more particularly this wonderful structure; I therefore entered it, and found at first the wandering unseen in this manner under every thing living, exceedingly interesting. A wooden rail which runs by the edge of the canal and along the open space left between it and the arch for a foot-path, serves to prevent any unfortunate accidents. The walk however soon lost the charm of novelty, and with the light of day all my pleasure disappeared. I soon found myself in utter darkness, with the aperture at the end of the tunnel, appearing at a distance like a dim star.

S. Heinrich, *Travels through England, Wales and Scotland in the year 1816 by Dr. S.H. Spiker, Librarian to His Majesty the King of Prussia*; translated from the German (1820)

The two tunnels within the Nominated Site – Chirk and Whitehouses – exemplify the use of major engineering features to build more efficient waterways. The historian of world canals, Charles Hadfield, calculated that some 36 miles/58 kilometres of canal tunnels had been constructed in Britain by the time that the network reached its peak in the mid-nineteenth century, and that this was far more than the total in the rest of the world at that time. Earlier canals had driven tunnels to pass through unavoidable obstacles; but Telford and Jessop invested in them here to optimise a route. Both tunnels are shallow and were wholly or partly built by cut-and-cover methods: excavating a trench from the surface and erecting an arch before back-filling. They were among the first British canal tunnels to have towing-paths. Their predecessors were built more cheaply with narrow bores and boats had to be 'legged' by boatmen or labourers who walked boats through on the tunnel sides, a slow process that disrupted navigation.

Pedestrians still have the thrill of walking through both tunnels on the original horse-path, clutching the handrail to guide them in the gloom, with boats passing them in the adjacent channel, just as contemporary visitors experienced, such as the librarian

The interior of Chirk Tunnel, showing the brick arch construction and the towing-path.

Left: Whitehouses Tunnel from the north.

Below: Chirk Tunnel north portal set in its high retaining wall. The sloping handrail avoided snagging of towing ropes.

to the King of Prussia in 1816. The towing-paths are built on arches to allow movement of the water as boats pass, with handrails on vertical iron posts similar to those in the parapets of the two aqueducts. The brick arches of both tunnels are in good condition. The portals are set in high rubble-stone walls that hold back the ground behind. The tunnel bores are flared outwards, enabling boats to be funnelled to the centre and creating a grander impression of scale. The architectural details are boldly functional: parabolic arches with emphasised keystones, string-courses and parapets.

Chirk Tunnel, at 1,378 feet / 420 metres, is the longer of the two and one of the principal engineering works on the canal. Its striking situation at the end of Chirk Aqueduct expresses visibly the vigour with which the new canal leapt valleys and pierced hills to cut its course. The remains of a shaft connecting the tunnel roof to the ground surface suggest that part of it was built by conventional tunnelling methods, but most of it was cut-and-cover. A report to the canal company on 25 November 1801 described the work: 'At the north end of the aqueduct there is a tunnel 460 yards in length which (except for a final proportion of towing-path) is also completed - to form this tunnel, the ground, though deep, was cut open in different lengths, which afforded an opportunity of making the brickwork very perfect, and securing the top of the arch with clay and loose stones, to prevent the waters of the upper strata from injuring the work'. There is evidence that the shorter and shallower Whitehouses Tunnel was built

in preference to a deep cutting partly to preserve the amenity of the polite landscape in the approach to Chirk Castle.

2.a.8 Over-bridges

Canal bridges are perhaps the most beautiful and interesting of canal structures, and have the charm not only of the regional variety of types, but also of local variety within those types. Thus, within a regional standard, as for example Telford's little stone bridges on the Shropshire Union Canal, you will find homogenous style, but never mechanical repetition. Purely functional, quite unselfconscious, perfectly proportioned and fitting snugly into the landscape, these bridges have a fine monumentality which few engineering structures have since achieved, except perhaps the modern reinforced concrete bridges of Robert Maillart. They are perfect examples of the functional tradition.

Eric de Maré, *The Canals of England* (1950)

The canal within the Nominated Site has thirty-one over-bridges. The majority, twenty-three in all, are original to the construction of the canal and nineteen of these remain virtually unaltered. Five original bridges have been lost or replaced over the last two centuries. Most bridges served to accommodate adjacent landowners

Top: A typical masonry over-bridge on the canal at Plâs-Ifan (bridge number 40).

Bottom: Scotch Hall Bridge (29) with its flanking arches for horse-worked railways serving Trevor Basin.

whose property was split by the canal, while others were for road crossings or to aid the operation of the canal. Telford and Jessop appear where possible to have resisted building bridges on the busy main line, as they would be pinch-points to traffic.

The original over-bridges are of several types to suit different functions and situations. The 'standard' bridges follow the traditional form found on British canals: sweeping, hump-backed bridges with single spans wide enough for the towing-path and a narrow channel. However, Telford's early training as a stonemason attuned him more than most engineers to the beauty of fine masonry, and he produced some of the most elegant examples of the canal bridge-builders art. In most cases a three-centred arch is set in spandrels that batter gently upwards and is flanked by curving wing walls. Fourteen standard over-bridges are listed in the Gazetteer below, beginning at the eastern boundary of the Nominated Site at Gledrid (bridge number 19).

The design subtly alters to suit local circumstances. The stone varies according to local availability, and brick is used for some wider arch rings. Irish Bridge (bridge number 27), has very high abutment walls to maintain the level of a public road across the cutting - a precursor of Telford's tall over-bridges on the deep cuttings of his Birmingham and Liverpool Junction Canal three decades later. Bridges at curves in the canal are wider to give room for boats to turn, for example Millars Bridge (number 35). The form is also varied where the lie of the land requires longer approach ramps, as at Plâs-Ifan (40). Tŷ-craig Bridge (48A) springs directly from a rock face and has no towing-path as it is at the head of navigation of the Llangollen Branch.

Among the innovative features of the canal are three over-bridges of composite construction, using masonry strengthened with cast-iron beams. The use of supporting iron allowed a strong but flat arch, reducing the gradients of the approaches on public road crossings where the lie of the land was not conducive. The three composite bridges contain members cast from the same

patterns. The earliest is Chirk Bank (bridge 21), dating from around 1795-1801. The other two are at Trevor Basin – Scotch Hall Bridge (29) and Rhos-y-coed Bridge (31) – and date from about 1800-1805. All three have cambered cast-iron girders supporting ashlar voussoirs. Scotch Hall Bridge has two flanking arches over the lines of former horse-worked railways that served the wharves.

Two lift bridges of traditional form are in the Nominated Site, at Froncysyllte (number 28) and Llanddyn (44), providing a crossing at the level of the canal banks. They are drawbridges, hinged to one abutment with an overhead balance beam to raise the deck. Both have been rebuilt with new materials and automated lift mechanisms for safety reasons. A swing-bridge crosses the entrance to Trevor Dry Docks, of a pattern later followed by Jessop and Telford on the Caledonian Canal in Scotland.

Telford designed three footbridges in the Nominated Site with masonry piers and approach ramps and decks in timber

Top: Bryn Howel Bridge (bridge number 38).

Above: The small bridge over the water feeder at Tŷ Craig (48A).

A digital model showing the construction of the three masonry bridges with shallow arches supported by cast iron girders.

Llanddyn Lift Bridge (44).

or wrought iron. The spans were wide enough to cross the canal and towing-path with the channel remaining at full width. A dressed-stone pier of Woodlands Bridge (22) survives. The masonry of White Bridge footbridge (33) and Postles Bridge (32) is complete, but the decks were replaced in modern materials in the twentieth century. Postles Bridge is a 'roving bridge', a characteristic type of canal crossing to take horses from one bank to the other where the towing-path changed sides. The sturdy ramps to the deck are both on the same elevation so that horses would both cross and pass under the bridge, ensuring that the tow rope did not have to be disconnected.

Ten later bridges that also cross the canal within the Nominated Site are listed in the Gazetteer for completeness, but most are recent foot or road bridges. Two are of some interest near Horseshoe Falls. Chain Bridge incorporates remnants of wrought-iron chain believed to be from an iron suspension bridge of 1814 that carried coal from the canal wharf to the Holyhead Road. The five-arch Kingsbridge Viaduct (49A), of 1906, carries a road over the canal and river and under the Llangollen to Corwen Railway.

Horseshoe Falls Weir.

2.a.9 *Horseshoe Falls Weir and water control features*

The best engineers of 1790 to 1835 had the simple ability to design one thing after another. Rennie and Telford attended to everything from aqueducts to gudgeon pins…. There was a desire to get things right and make them look right too. There is the same delight in clarity and order on the pages of Telford's Atlas as in a Wedgwood pot catalogue. There is the same tendency, too, to standardisation linked with an unerring instinct for quality.

Nigel Crowe, *Canals* (1994)

The crescent-shaped iron weir at Horseshoe Falls draws water for the whole canal. The elegance of the weir and its pleasant environs have made it a popular beauty spot, well-used by local people and visitors for two centuries. The Nominated Site includes the whole visual setting. The provision of water was a vital component in the design of canals, and many built during the Canal Mania in Britain suffered from water shortages that crippled their operation. Jessop was determined to avoid such problems and in 1795 proposed that the River Dee at Horseshoe Falls be the water source for the canal. He also recommended a dam to raise the level of the lake at Bala – Llyn Tegid – so as to conserve supplies and regulate the flow into the river 25 miles / 32 kilometres upstream.

The weir is placed in the braided bed of the Dee at a sharp bend above rapids. The

An aerial view of the head of the feeder at Horseshoe Falls.

width creates a substantial reservoir. The weir was designed by Telford. It is J-shaped rather than a horseshoe, though this is not readily apparent from most viewpoints. The crescent form improves the resistance of the structure to the flow of water and distributes pressure across its length. It also reduces the impact of debris and aids its collection as it is driven to the ends. The structure is 460 feet/ 140 metres long, with a sloping upstream face and a vertical fall limited to just 4 feet/ 1.22 metres to reduce the risk of damage by floods. It is constructed of masonry with a capping of bull-nosed cast iron in 9 feet/2.75 metres sections which maintain a perfect level across the width of the river. This was a new application of cast iron, and it became widely used later in the nineteenth century as a durable and adaptable material for weirs. Water is drawn off through a sluice and under two footbridges into the feeder watercourse. The fine meter house, built in 1947, is a symbol of the survival of the canal in the mid twentieth century, when it found new importance as a supplier of drinking water to north-west England.

The ability to control water levels in the canal and drain sections is crucial to its safe operation and maintenance. There are eight overflow weirs or sluices in the Nominated Site, varying in form from simple sluice gates set in the towing-path to elegantly-constructed overflow weirs. Although easily overlooked, and frequently renewed over the years for operational reasons, many exhibit craftsmanship and attention to detail. Their masonry was completed with care to avoid the risk of earthwork erosion; the quality of much of this work is hidden below ground. At Wenffrwd an outlet passes through a culvert before reaching a flagstoned cascade 46 feet/14 metres down the side of the embankment. The waste water weir at Trevor Basin is almost invisible passing under the towing-path, but it is then carried into a stone-lined channel all the way down the hill to the River Dee, ensuring that gushing water in times of heavy rainfall does not undermine the piers of Pontcysyllte Aqueduct. Pentre-felin sluice is an example of ongoing renewal: the sluice wall rebuilt

in engineering brick in about 1900 is set between the original curved ashlar wing walls.

At over-bridges, tunnels and on the steeply-sloping valley-sides, slots constructed in masonry on either side of the waterway allow temporary stop-plank dams to be installed. These can be used to drain sections of canal for maintenance or to isolate sections if a bank is breached.

2.a.10 Basins and wharves

The Ellesmere Canal… will pass thro' or near to many extensive and valuable Collieries & Lime Stone, Slate and other Quarries, Iron Works, Lead Mines etc… will open a safe and easy communication for the carriage of Goods and Merchandice by water… and will be of great publick utility.

Ellesmere Canal Prospectus (c.1793)

Some twenty wharves and basins identified in the Gazetteer are testament to the ways in which canals were used during the Industrial Revolution. Many appear today simply as flat, grassy verges where carts were once loaded or horse-drawn railway wagons brought slate, coal or lime to the canal bank, but below the turf there is invariably evidence of the material that was stockpiled. The wharves are often associated with a broadening of the canal into a basin or a turning point for narrow boats.

The channel to carry overflow water near Pontcysyllte Aqueduct.

The basin and wharf at the northern end of Chirk Aqueduct in 1977 with a typical narrowboat and a small holiday cruiser.

The short space between Chirk Tunnel and Chirk Aqueduct is a diamond-shaped basin on a shelf cut from the hillside. This was the northern terminus of the canal for a year until Chirk Tunnel opened in 1802, and it continued to provide a waiting point for boats entering the tunnel or crossing the aqueduct and a wharf close to Chirk village. Between Chirk and Whitehouses Tunnels, Black Park Basin was one of the busiest trading points on the canal. There is an oval widening to allow boats to turn into an interchange dock which served an early nineteenth-century horse-worked railway from Black Park Collieries and later the Glyn Valley Tramway from slate quarries at Glyn Ceiriog. The dock is currently buried, but the former entrance can be detected in the edge of the towing-path.

At Froncysyllte a large basin signifies that this was the terminus of the canal for three years before Pontcysyllte Aqueduct was completed, and it continued to be an important place of interchange. A public wharf communicated with the Holyhead Road and two private wharves brought traffic from nearby limestone quarries to banks of limekilns that originated when the canal was completed and were extended throughout the nineteenth century.

The most important complex of basins, wharves and associated buildings is at Trevor, extending for a sixth of a mile / 0.34 kilometres at the terminus of the main line, with wharves formerly served by horse-worked railways on both banks. On the west side an early nineteenth-century warehouse is now in use as a café and shop. On the east, two early nineteenth-century dry docks remain in use for their original purpose of repairing boats, one covered by a later building and workshop. The dry docks are rare survivors of hundreds that existed on British canals. Beyond Scotch Hall Bridge, with its secondary railway arch, are two terminal arms for the Ruabon Brook railway, separated by a pier and with a dock to one side. This arrangement permitted interchange between canal boats and five horse-worked railways; three on the pier and one on each bank. Next to this is the blocked junction bridge to a former private branch canal to Plas Kynaston foundry, completed in about 1830.

The Llangollen Branch was recognised soon after its construction as a picturesque route for pleasure boating. At Bryn-Howel an Edwardian boat house accommodated a pleasure boat owned by the terracotta manufacturer J.C. Edwards. Llangollen town wharf was used for pleasure boats and for general trade, represented by an attractive rubble-stone warehouse that is now a café and horse-drawn boat centre.

Below: An aerial view of the terminus of the main line of the canal at Trevor Basin. The pier for the Ruabon Brook railway interchange, with an arm of the canal on either side, is at the bottom left.

Bottom: The entrance to the dry docks at Trevor Basin, designed by Telford in 1805.

2.a.11 Canal houses

The custom of housing canal staff in purpose-built cottages began slowly in the late eighteenth century and lasted until the mid-twentieth century. By far the largest number of cottages were built in the early to mid nineteenth century, when commercial activity was intense and restructuring and improvements took place on many waterways.

Nigel Crowe, *Canals* (1994)

Scotch Hall at Trevor Basin.

The vast numbers of labourers and skilled craftsmen needed to build the canal lived in temporary encampments and barracks, lodged with local families or were drawn from the local workforce. However, several purpose-built houses were provided for the engineers during the construction of the canal. Scotch Hall, in an imposing position beside the canal at Trevor Basin looks towards Pontcysyllte Aqueduct over what was originally the construction yard. This is believed to have been built for the supervising engineer, Matthew Davidson, and would have been where Telford stayed during his visits. Now the Telford Inn public house, its elegant proportions and hipped slate roof with overhanging eaves are characteristic of Telford's work as an architect. The adjacent building is believed to have been the accounts house throughout the construction project. Nearby, another two-storey Georgian house, Wood Bank, was probably the drawing office. It was still owned by the Canal Company in 1838 and

Wood Bank Cottage, Pontcysyllte, NPRN 308392, SJ 26814 42158

A plan of Wood Bank at Trevor, probably the drawing office during the construction of Pontcysyllte Aqueduct, with malt kilns behind.

Cartref, a detached canal cottage at Chirk Bank, probably for a foreman.

was described as 'house and offices, malt kiln and croft'. The symmetrical facade has large sash windows which would have provided ample light and views across the whole length of Pontcysyllte Aqueduct. A similarly-placed building at Chirk Aqueduct, Telford Lodge, was probably a resident engineer's house up to 1801.

Most maintenance workers on the completed canal lived in neighbouring communities, and boatmen had accommodation on their narrow boats. Nevertheless, key workers' cottages for operational staff can be seen at several locations. Most were built by the Shropshire Union Canal Company in the late nineteenth century. The largest group, containing four houses and maintenance buildings, is at the south end of Chirk Aqueduct, built on the 60 feet/18.3 metres high spoil mound from the adjacent cutting. (Workers' houses were often placed on land rendered otherwise unusable by tipping.) The nearest house to the Aqueduct is detached and was probably for the foreman. Canal houses at Chirk Bank Bridge are still occupied by canal workers and maintenance boats are often moored outside.

An over-bridge on the Llangollen Branch of the canal.

2.a.12 Gazetteer

For if ever a canal could be said to show virtually every aspect of the engineer's craft, then the Llangollen is that canal.

Anthony Burton, *The Waterways of Britain* (1983)

The following Gazetteer lists all the features of the Nominated Site in geographical order from east to west. Each is located by its distance in kilometres from the water source at Horseshoe Falls and its National Grid Reference (NGR), relating to the official map base for the United Kingdom maintained by Ordnance Survey. The number next to each site name is its National Principal Record Number in the National Monuments Record of Wales. Further information and images of each feature can be found on-line at www.coflein. gov.uk.

The Gazetteer also shows the current State of Conservation, ownership and protective designation for each feature, which are discussed in more detail in Sections 4 and 5. State of Conservation categories (column headed SoC in Gazetteer), are defined as: **Good, Fair, Fair*** and **Poor.** Where features are shown as '-' they have not been assessed at this time. This may be because the structure was not accessible or because assessment is not applicable (e.g. for areas of land or for wholly modern structures).

Designation is denoted as **Scheduled** (Scheduled Ancient Monument), **Listed** (Listed Building), and **Conservation Area**. See Section 5.b for details of these protections. Features not specifically designated but protected by proximity to a designated structure are labelled **In Setting**. The designation of some features was in progress at the time of going to press: this is denoted by an asterisk (*).

GAZETTEER

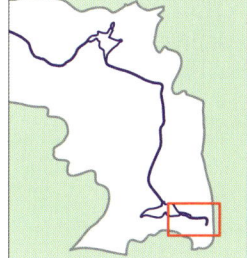

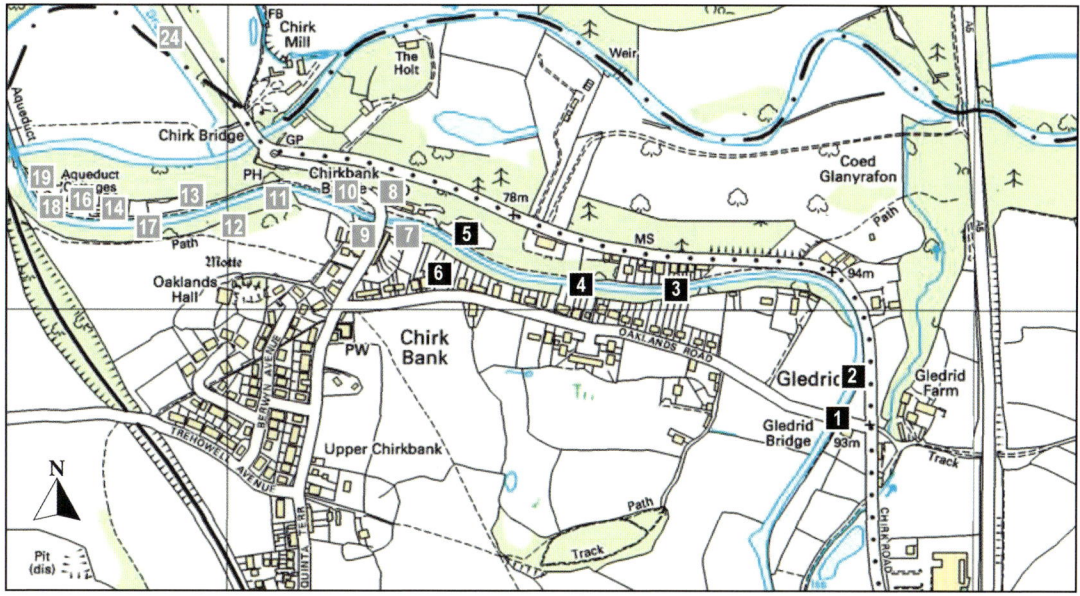

	Distance	Grid Reference	Description	Date and designers	SoC	Ownership	Protection
1. Main line canal formation							NPRN 405725
	17.64km	SJ 29811 36854- SJ 27241 42464	Channel of main line of the Ellesmere Canal within the Nominated Site for the 5 miles (8km) from Gledrid Bridge to the terminus at Trevor Basin	1795-1805, William Jessop and Thomas Telford	Fair / Good	British Waterways	*Scheduled
2. Gledrid Bridge (19)							NPRN 405775
	17.64km	SJ 29811 36854	Brick canal over-bridge similar to the typical design used on the main line; with stop-plank grooves to isolate sections of the canal in case of a breach or for maintenance	1795 or after 1815, Thomas Telford	Poor	Shropshire CC	*In Setting
3. Chirk Bank Embankment (15)							NPRN 405776
	17.48-16.93km	SJ 29596 37031	Large embankment on the south side of the Ceiriog Valley; the start of the section of highly-engineered canal through difficult terrain to Trevor	1795-1801, William Jessop and Thomas Telford	Fair	British Waterways and private	*Scheduled
4. Remains of Quinta Bridge (20)							NPRN 406641
	17.1km	SJ 29467 37035	Narrowing at the site of the former Bridge No 20, with stop-plank grooves to isolate sections of canal in case of a breach or for maintenance	1795-1801, William Jessop and Thomas Telford	Fair	British Waterways	*Scheduled
5. Chirk Bank spoil tip							NPRN 406642
	16.93km	SJ 29326 37103	Bank projecting into the valley north-eastwards from the canal towing-path for spoil probably from one of the early canal side collieries	Nineteenth century	-	British Waterways and private	*In Setting
6. Quinta Colliery and Brickworks railway wharf							NPRN 406643
	16.92km	SJ 29279 37090	Industrial wharf in a terraced area in the hillside with a low retaining wall to south, now gardens	Nineteenth century	Poor	British Waterways and private	*In Setting

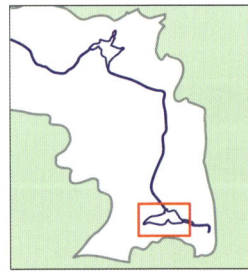

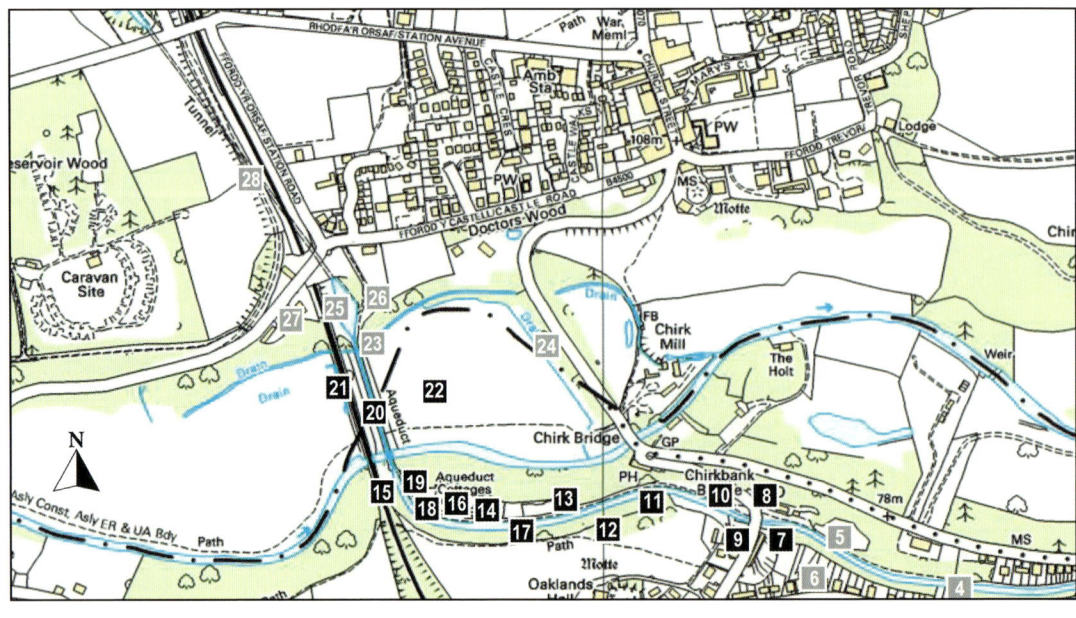

	Distance	Grid Reference	Description	Date and designers	SoC	Ownership	Protection
7. Chirk Bank public wharf							NPRN 406644
	16.86km	SJ 29230 37122	Level wharf area for general trade on the canal, alongside what was to become the Holyhead Road	Probably 1795-1801	Fair	British Waterways	*Scheduled
8. Canal View Cottages							NPRN 405777
	16.83km	SJ 29225 37141	Row of canal-side cottages and a former public house alongside the canal and the Holyhead Road	Early and late nineteenth century	Fair	private	*In Setting
9. Chirk Bank Bridge (21)							NPRN 405778
	16.81km	SJ 29202 37119	Bridge of innovative design with a flattened stone arch supported by curved cast-iron beams to reduce the gradients on the approaches for traffic crossing	1795-1801, William Jessop and Thomas Telford	Fair *	Shropshire CC	Listed
10. Chirk Bank Bridge wharf							NPRN 406662
	16.79km	SJ 29186 37133	Wharf to west of Chirk Bank Bridge; site of a warehouse and stables demolished in 1933	Nineteenth century	Fair	British Waterways	*Scheduled
11. Remains of Woodlands Bridge (22)							NPRN 405779
	16.69km	SJ 29086 37155	Fine ashlar pillar on the south side of the canal that once supported a typical canal footbridge; footings of the northern support are buried	1795-1801, William Jessop and Thomas Telford	Fair	British Waterways and private	*Scheduled
12. Chirk Aqueduct building-stone quarry							NPRN 406645
	16.69km	SJ 29021 37127	Quarry excavated from the level of the canal on its south side for stone to build Chirk Aqueduct	1795-1801, William Jessop and Thomas Telford	Fair	British Waterways and private	*In Setting

	Distance	Grid Reference	Description	Date and designers	SoC	Ownership	Protection
	13. Cartref						NPRN 405781
	16.54km	SJ 28945 37145	Worker's cottage on canal-owned spoil bank	After 1891	Good	private	*In Setting
	14. 4-5 Aqueduct Cottages						NPRN 406599
	16.43km	SJ 28830 37133	Pair of red-brick, semi-detached houses for canal maintenance workers; joined privy and pigsty block at garden end	After 1891, Shropshire Union Railway and Canal Company	Fair	private	*In Setting
	15. Chirk Aqueduct construction yard platform						NPRN 406663
	16.43-16.34km	SJ 2873 3714	Huge earthwork platform believed to have been created as a yard for dressing stone and preparing materials to construct Chirk Aqueduct	1795-1801, William Jessop and Thomas Telford	Fair	British Waterways and private	*In Setting
	16. Aqueduct Cottages maintenance depot hut						NPRN 405783
	16.4km	SJ 28814 37133	Corrugated-iron maintenance depot shed in a yard between Aqueduct Cottages	Twentieth century	-	British Waterways	
	17. Chirk Bank West Cutting (23-24) and embankments (16-18)						NPRN 405780
	16.39km	SJ 28906 37130	Considerable rock cutting in hillside to accommodate the canal as it swings north to cross the Ceiriog Valley, with a large earthwork bank opposite	1795-1801, William Jessop and Thomas Telford	Fair	British Waterways	*Scheduled
	18. 2-3 Aqueduct Cottages, Chirk Bank						NPRN 405782
	16.38km	SJ 28784 37140	Semi-detached houses built for canal maintenance workers	Late nineteenth or early twentieth century, Shropshire Union Railway and Canal Company	Fair	Private / BW (No3)	*In Setting
	19. 1 Aqueduct Cottages, Chirk Bank						NPRN 406598
	16.34km	SJ 28764-37157	Red-brick, detached house built for a canal maintenance foreman at the south end of Chirk Aqueduct; privy and pig-sty at garden end	After 1891, Shropshire Union Railway and Canal Company	Fair	private	*In Setting
	20. Chirk Aqueduct						NPRN 344016
	16.28-16.1km	SJ 28700 37283	Ten-arch masonry aqueduct, the tallest navigable aqueduct in the world before Pontcysyllte; it tested and developed methods of using voids in masonry and iron-plates in the trough; outlet sluice 9; stop-plank grooves	1795-1801, William Jessop and Thomas Telford	Fair*	British Waterways	*Scheduled Listed
	21. Chirk Railway Viaduct						NPRN 87002
	16.31-16.07km	SJ 28669 37286	Tall masonry railway viaduct which demonstrates the era of transport engineering following the canals, built by Telford's former assistant, Thomas Brassey; originally ten spans with pedimented piers and timber side spans; timber replaced with six additional spans in 1858	1846-48, Henry Robertson and Thomas Brassey as contractor	Good	Network Rail	Listed
	22. Land to east and west of Chirk Aqueduct						
	16.12km	SJ 28695 37364	Meadow land in the floor of the Ceiriog Valley of importance to the visual surroundings of Chirk Aqueduct	-	-	private	*In Setting

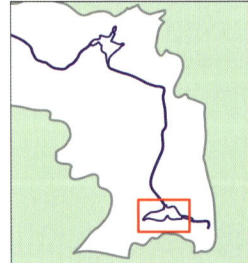

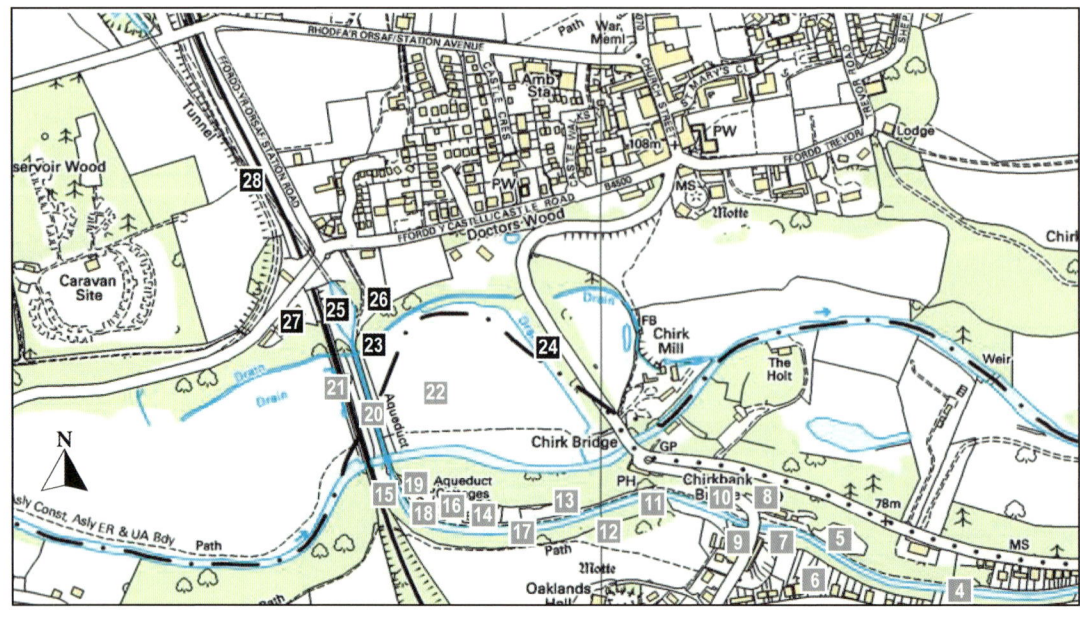

	Distance	Grid Reference	Description	Date and designers	SoC	Ownership	Protection
23. Chirk Mill leat							NPRN 406646
	16.12km	SJ 28695 37364	Mill leat passing under Chirk Aqueduct, now dry; part of the pre-canal water economy; supplied a medieval corn mill and a turbine generating electricity for Chirk 1924-30	By 1506, Chirk Castle estate	Poor	British Waterways and private	*In Setting
24. Holyhead Road Embankment, Chirk							NPRN 406698
	16.1km	SJ 28950 37368	Large, straight and evenly-graded earthen embankment; one of the major works on the Holyhead Road designed by Telford following his commission by Parliament in 1811 to improve the route from London to Dublin	1815-20, Thomas Telford	-	Wrexham CBC and Private	*Scheduled
25. Chirk Basin and cutting 25-6							NPRN 405784
	16.06km	SJ 28657 37410	Basin constructed in a cutting and shelf on the steep hillside between Chirk Aqueduct and Chirk Tunnel, used for waiting boats and wharf traffic; briefly the terminus of the canal, 1801-02	1795-1801, William Jessop and Thomas Telford	Fair	British Waterways	*Scheduled
26. Site of Chirk Basin wharf buildings							NPRN 406665
	16.06km	SJ 2867 3741	Site of probable weighbridge and wharfinger's hut, with archaeological potential	Nineteenth century	Fair	British Waterways	*Scheduled
27. Telford Lodge / Min-y-waen, Chirk							NPRN 406597
	16.04km	SJ 28599 37409	Hip-roofed villa, probably the resident engineer's house overlooking the major works at Chirk	Probably c.1795, William Jessop and Thomas Telford	Poor	private	*In Setting
28. Chirk Tunnel							NPRN 405785
	16.01-15.59km	SJ 28522 37613	One of the first British canal tunnels with a towing-path, supported on arches; brick-lined and built by cut-and-cover but with centre section excavated from two shafts, one still open from below; maximum depth 46ft 7ins (14.23m); stop-plank grooves	1795-1802, William Jessop and Thomas Telford	Fair	British Waterways	*Scheduled Listed

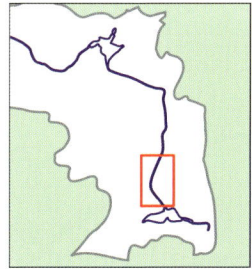

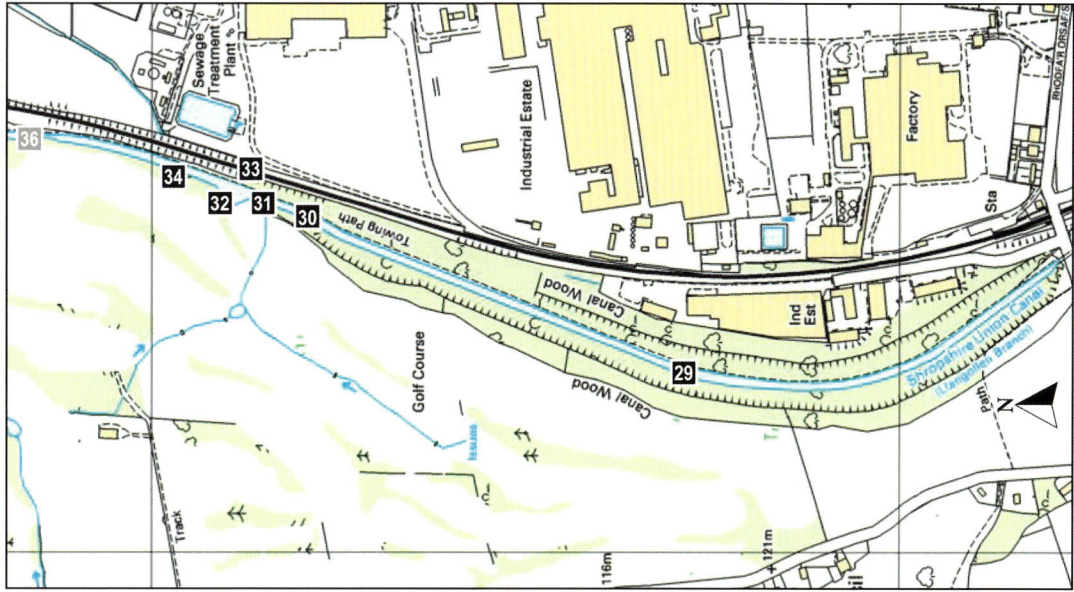

	Distance	Grid Reference	Description	Date and designers	SoC	Ownership	Protection
29. Canal Wood Cutting, Chirk							NPRN 405790
	15.59-14.43km	SJ 28241 38264	Long cutting to permit a straight route for the canal, the sides probably planted for stability, exemplifying cut-and-fill earth-moving developed on the canal	1795-1802, William Jessop and Thomas Telford	Fair	British Waterways	*Scheduled
30. Glyn Ceiriog Tramway wharf							NPRN 406666
	14.44km	SJ 28477 38822	Masonry quay wall on the towing-path side of the canal for unloading rail wagons	1888	Poor	British Waterways	*Scheduled
31. Afon Bradley feeder							NPRN 406667
	14.43km	SJ 28470-38843	Substantial stream diverted into the canal to gather water	1795-1802, William Jessop and Thomas Telford	-	British Waterways	*Scheduled
32. Black Park Collieries railway dock turning-basin							NPRN 405986
	14.39km	SJ 28479 38887	Turning basin for boats serving the railway-canal interchange	c.1805, for T. E. Ward	Fair	British Waterways	*Scheduled
33. Black Park Collieries railway dock							NPRN 405791
	14.39km	SJ 28505 38863	Entrance to a former loading dock, with blocking visible under the towing-path; buried loading dock at right-angles beyond	c.1805, for T. E. Ward	Fair	British Waterways and corporate	*Scheduled (part)
34. Afon-Bradley overflow, culvert 91, and sluice 10							NPRN 405792
	14.28km	SJ 28509 38965	Complex of water-control features to avoid flooding of the canal	Twentieth century	-	British Waterways	*Scheduled

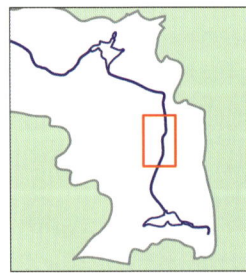

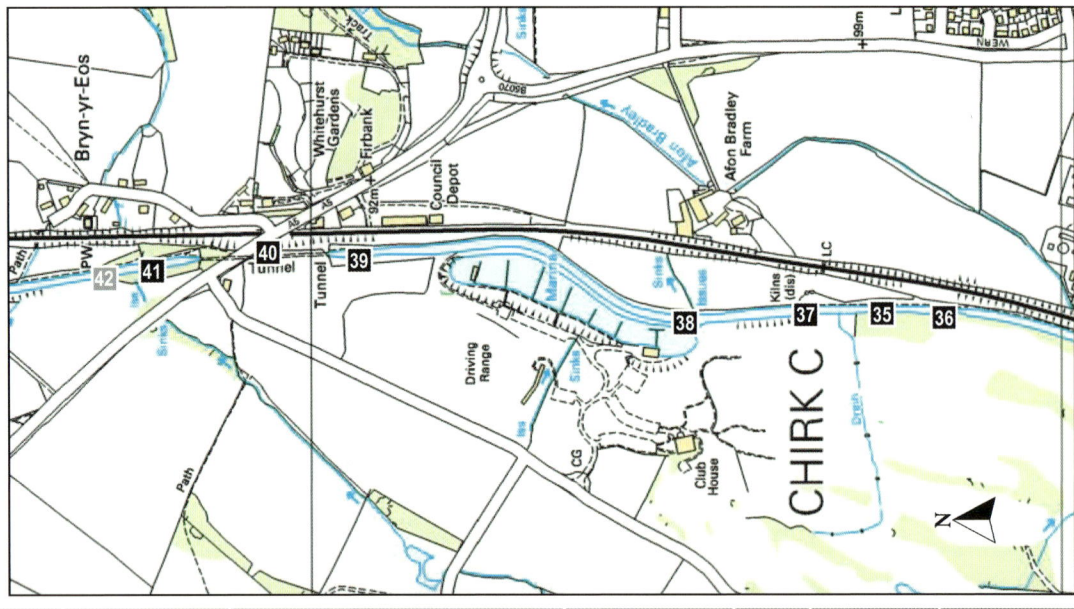

Distance	Grid Reference	Description	Date and designers	SoC	Ownership	Protection
35. Red Bridge Cutting (29-30)						NPRN 406695
14.15-13.96km	SJ 28563 39241	Shallow cutting on both sides of the canal to facilitate a straight course	1795-1802, William Jessop and Thomas Telford	Fair	British Waterways	*Scheduled
36. Red Bridge abutments (24)						NPRN 405793
14.11km	SJ 28561 39144	Narrowing of the canal for a former arched over-bridge of which the masonry abutments remain; stop-plank grooves	1795-1802, William Jessop and Thomas Telford	Poor	British Waterways	*Scheduled
37. Afon-Bradley limekilns						NPRN 405795
13.92km	SJ 28586 39335	Two limekilns built into the towing-path side of the canal; brick drawing arch in a rubble-stone kiln; indicative of lime production for building the canal and later trade	1795-1802, William Jessop and Thomas Telford	Poor	British Waterways	*Scheduled
38. Afon-Bradley Farm Culvert (92)						NPRN 406721
13.77km	SJ 28550 39486	Culvert to take a small stream under the canal	1795-1802, William Jessop and Thomas Telford	Fair	British Waterways	*Scheduled
39. Whitehouses Tunnel south approach cutting						NPRN 406591
13.45-13.26km	SJ 28634 39971- SJ 28628 39842	Deep cutting leading up to Whitehouses Tunnel; exemplifying cut-and-fill earth-moving developed on the canal	1795-1802, William Jessop and Thomas Telford	Fair*	British Waterways	*Scheduled
40. Whitehouses Tunnel (25)						NPRN 405796
13.26-13.09km	SJ 28633 40059	One of the first canal tunnels in Britain with a towing-path, built by cut-and-cover; portals at each end of ashlar arches set in battered brick retaining walls, curved for strength; stop-plank grooves	1795-1802, William Jessop and Thomas Telford	Fair	British Waterways	*Scheduled *Listed
41. Whitehouses Tunnel north approach cutting						NPRN 406590
13.09-13.01km	SJ 28613 40272 to SJ 28631 40148	Deep cutting leading up to Whitehouses Tunnel; exemplifying cut-and-fill earth-moving developed on the canal	1795-1802, William Jessop and Thomas Telford	Fair*	British Waterways	*Scheduled

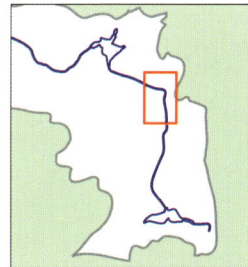

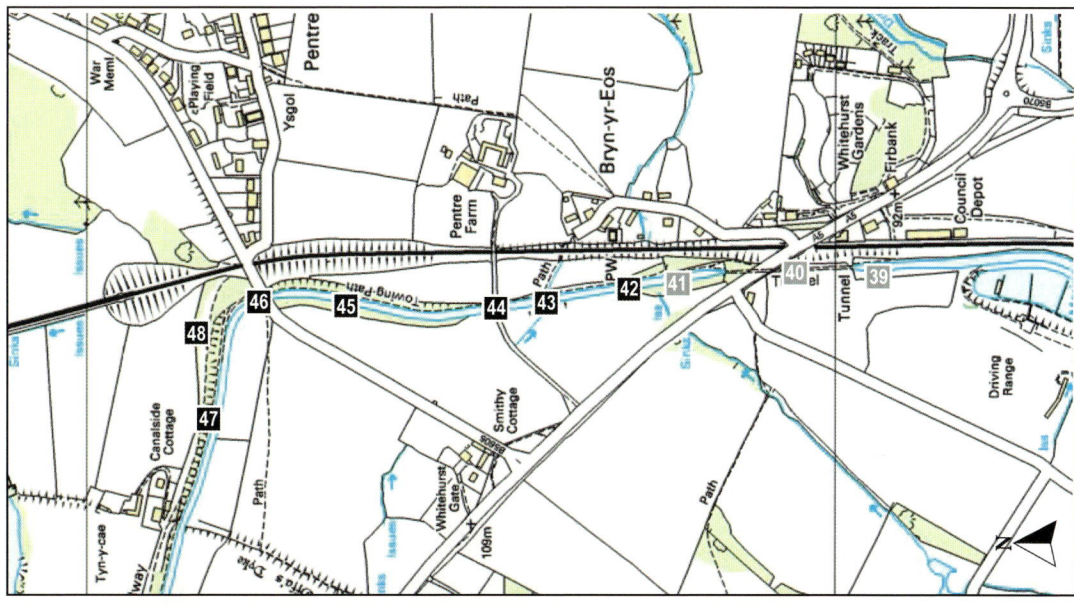

Distance	Grid Reference	Description	Date and designers	SoC	Ownership	Protection
42. Pen-y-bryn Embankment and culvert 93						NPRN 406722
13.0km	SJ 28621 40242	Embankment and stone-arched stream culvert	1795-1802, William Jessop and Thomas Telford	Fair	British Waterways	*Scheduled
43. Pentre Embankment (19) and Bryn-yr-oes Culvert (94)						NPRN 406723
12.84km	SJ 28596 40388	Embankment and stone-arched stream culvert	1795-1802, William Jessop and Thomas Telford	Fair / Poor	British Waterways	*Scheduled
44. Whitehouse Bridge (26)						NPRN 405797
12.77km	SJ 28584 40455	Original arched masonry bridge with stop-plank grooves	1795-1802, William Jessop and Thomas Telford	Fair*	British Waterways	Listed
45. Irish Bridge Cutting (33-4)						NPRN 405993
12.75-12.41km	SJ 28594 40657	Deep cutting, 1,213ft (370m) long exemplifying the development of cut-and-fill earth-moving; spoil was used in the Pontcysyllte Aqueduct approach embankment	1795-1802, William Jessop and Thomas Telford	Fair	British Waterways	*Scheduled
46. Irish Bridge (27)						NPRN 405798
12.46km	SJ 28595 40764	Tall masonry bridge near the north end of Irish Bridge Cutting, with high abutments of a type used to cross deep cuttings on later canals	1795-1802, William Jessop and Thomas Telford	Poor	Wrexham CBC	Listed
47. Irish Bridge Embankment (20)						NPRN 406696
12.4-11.84km	SJ 28433 40838	Valley-side embankment	1795-1802, William Jessop and Thomas Telford	Fair	British Waterways	*Scheduled
48. Pen-y-bont Brick and Tile Works wharf						NPRN 406701
12.36km	SJ 28576 40811	Wharf for a railway from Pen-y-bont Brick and Tile Works	Early twentieth century	Fair	British Waterways	*Scheduled

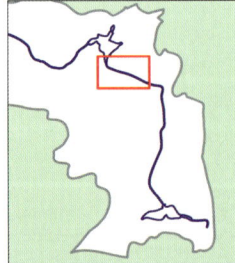

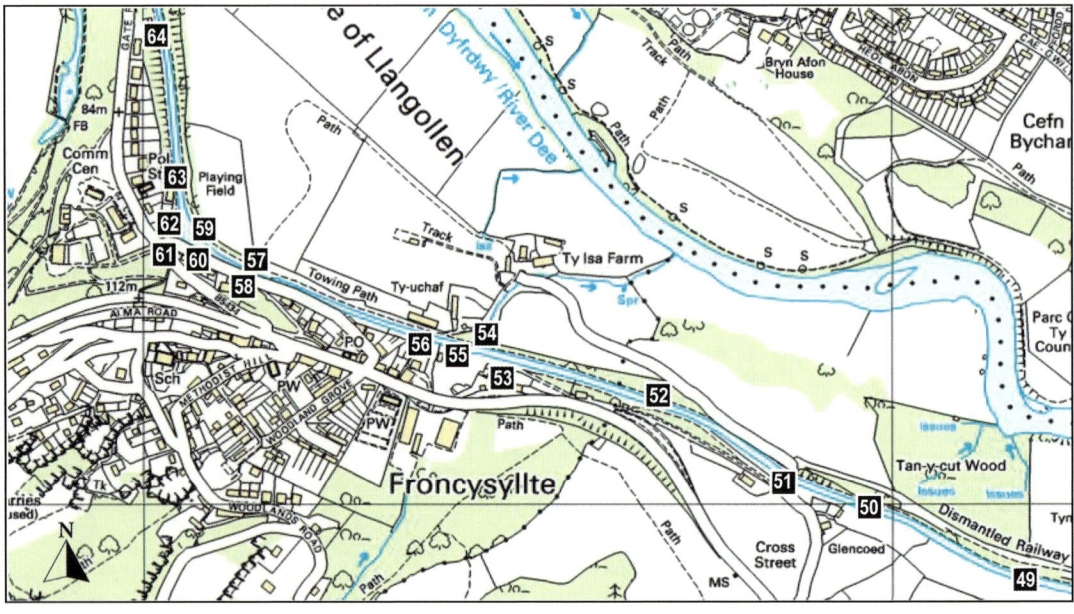

	Distance	Grid Reference	Description	Date and designers	SoC	Ownership	Protection
49. Cross Street Farm Cutting (36)							NPRN 406647
	11.86-11.1km	SJ 28169 40892	Low cutting on the south-west side of the canal	1795-1802, William Jessop and Thomas Telford	Fair	British Waterways	*Scheduled
50. Cross Street stop-plank grooves							NPRN 406648
	11.77km	SJ 27965 41001	Narrowing of the canal with masonry facing and slots for stop-planks to retain water in the event of a breach or to drain sections for maintenance	Probably 1795-1802, William Jessop and Thomas Telford	Fair	British Waterways	*Scheduled
51. Cross Street Aqueduct and Embankment							NPRN 405799
	11.66km	SJ 27861 41038	Embankment with small, single-arch aqueduct of traditional masonry and puddled clay design; originally an accommodation crossing for farmland; later used by a horse-drawn railway	1795-1802, William Jessop and Thomas Telford	Poor / Good	British Waterways	*Scheduled Listed
52. Fron Embankment (21)							NPRN 406649
	11.59-11.19km	SJ 27688 41157	Large embankment on the valley-side of the canal using spoil from the Irish Bridge and Chirk Wood cuttings exemplifying the development of cut-and-fill earth-moving	1795-1802, William Jessop and Thomas Telford	Fair	British Waterways	*Scheduled
53. Froncysyllte east limekiln bank / Pen-y-Bryn wharf							NPRN 405808
	11.25km	SJ 27486 41180	Tall bank of six masonry kilns, showing the growth of the lime industry; wharf for Pen-y-Bryn limestone quarries railway	Late nineteenth century	Fair	private	*In Setting
54. Tŷ-uchaf culvert (95) and sluice (11)							NPRN 405811
	11.19km	SJ 27455 41228	Tall masonry-arched culvert to take a stream under the canal, linked to a sluice to drain the canal for maintenance	1795-1802, William Jessop and Thomas Telford	Fair	British Waterways	*Scheduled

	Distance	Grid Reference	Description	Date and designers	SoC	Ownership	Protection
	55. Froncysyllte limekilns dock						NPRN 406651
	11.18km	SJ 27423 41205	Loading dock formed in an indent in the hillside where a stream entered the canal, now buried	Early nineteenth century	Fair	private	*Scheduled
	56. Froncysyllte west limekiln bank and wharf						NPRN 405809
	11.13km	SJ 27373 41211	Two banks of masonry limekilns of early nineteenth-century type and a wharf for canal trade, originally owned by William Hazledine; served by railway from Froncysyllte Limestone Quarries	Early nineteenth. century, William Hazledine	Fair	private	*In Setting
	57. Fron footbridge						NPRN 406703
	10.89km	SJ 27151 41313	High-level steel and masonry footbridge for use when the lift bridge is open	Twentieth century	-	British Waterways	*In Setting
	58. Fron Lift Bridge (28)						NPRN 405810
	10.89km	SJ 27146 41313	Modern bascule bridge to traditional design for low-level canal crossings but with hydraulic power; stop-plank grooves	Twentieth century	-	British Waterways	*In Setting
	59. Froncysyllte canal cottage						NPRN 406526
	10.78km	SJ 27022 41365	Former canal lengthman's house, indicative of developing provision for maintenance workers on the canal	Late nineteenth century, Shropshire Union Railway and Canal Company	Fair	private	*In Setting
	60. Froncysyllte Basin culvert (96)						NPRN 406704
	10.78km	SJ 27063 41362	Typical arched culvert carrying a stream under the basin; stream now diverted and culvert abandoned	1795-1802, William Jessop and Thomas Telford	-	British Waterways	*Scheduled
	61. Froncysyllte public wharf						NPRN 406706
	10.78km	SJ 27042 41370	Level wharf area for general trade, with road access; at the terminus of the canal from1802 until Pontcysyllte Aqueduct was completed in 1805	1795-1802, William Jessop and Thomas Telford	Fair	British Waterways	*Scheduled
	62. Froncysyllte Basin						NPRN 406708
	10.78km	SJ 27066 41364	Widening of the canal for boats to wait before entering the Pontcysyllte Aqueduct approach embankment; the terminus of the canal from1802 to 1805	1795-1802, William Jessop and Thomas Telford	Fair	British Waterways	*Scheduled
	63. Froncysyllte mess and Old Institute						NPRN 406527/406528
	10.73km	SJ 27032 41388	Mess building for canal maintenance workers and a former workers' institute which provided education for boat children	Late nineteenth century, Shropshire Union Railway and Canal Company	Good	British Waterways	*In Setting
	64. Pontcysyllte Aqueduct south embankment (23)						NPRN 405812
	10.78-10.27km	SJ 27012 41739	Earth embankment bringing the canal up to Pontcysyllte Aqueduct, 2,000ft (610m) long and 75ft (23m) high, planted with trees to increase stability; one of the largest civil earthworks of its era	1795-1805, William Jessop, Thomas Telford and William Davies	Fair	British Waterways	*Scheduled Conservation Area

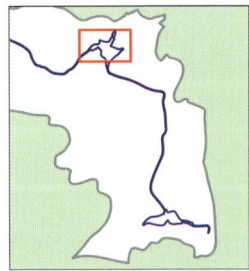

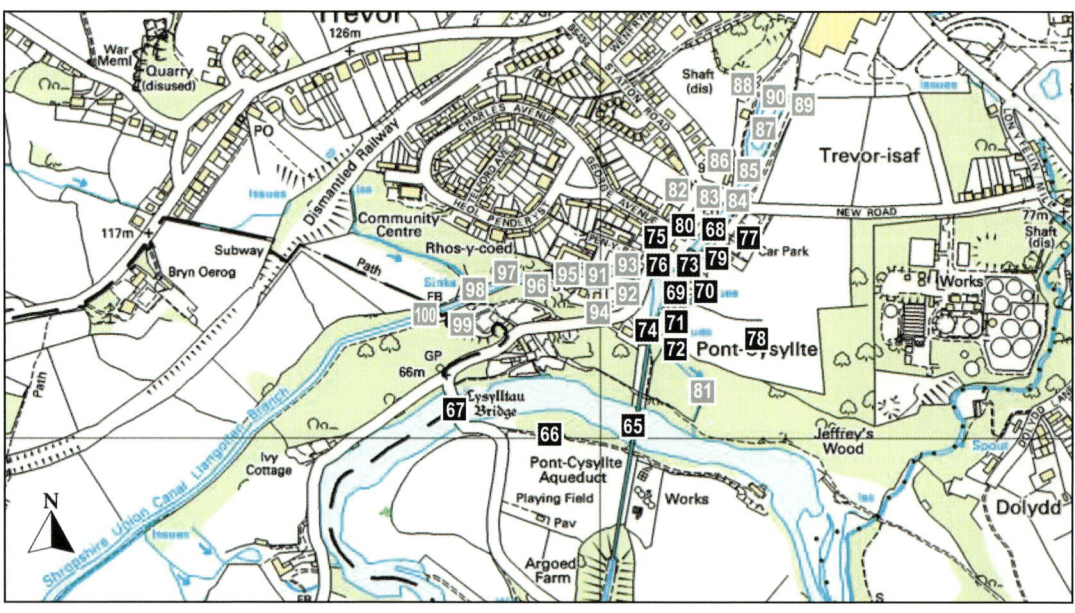

	Distance	Grid Reference	Description	Date and designers	SoC	Ownership	Protection
65. Pontcysyllte Aqueduct							NPRN 34410
	10.2km	SJ 2705 4203	Nineteen-span cast-iron aqueduct supported on tapering masonry piers; a pioneering work of the heroic phase of British canal engineering and the central feature of the Nominated Site	1795-1805, William Jessop and Thomas Telford	Good	British Waterways	Listed Scheduled Conservation Area
66. Land to the west and east of Pontcysyllte Aqueduct							
	10.2km	SJ 2705 4203	Meadows and woods around the River Dee of importance to the immediate visual setting of Pontcysyllte Aqueduct		-	private / corporate	Conservation Area (part) *In Setting
67. Cysylltau road bridge over the River Dee							NPRN 23989
	10.19km	SJ 2681 4204	Post-medieval three-arched bridge over the River Dee providing historical comparisons with the engineering of the canal and important views of Pontcysyllte Aqueduct, which derives its name from the bridge	South arch and pier 1697, widened in eighteenth century	Fair	Wrexham CBC	Listed Scheduled
68. Trevor Basin							NPRN 402309
	10.3-10km	SJ 2714 4228	Basin 0.2 miles (0.34km) long forming the terminus to the main line of the canal, on an artificial terrace retained by a stone wall to the south-east; ending in an interchange point for an early horse-worked railway	1795-1805, William Jessop, Thomas Telford and Matthew Davidson	Fair	British Waterways	*Scheduled Conservation Area
69. Trevor Basin dry docks swing-bridge							NPRN 406627
	10.01km	SJ 27093 42207	Timber swing-bridge carrying the towing-path over the entrance to dry docks; similar to large swivel bridges later used by Telford and Jessop on the Caledonian Canal	Probably originally c.1805, Thomas Telford and Matthew Davidson	-	British Waterways	Conservation Area
70. Trevor Basin dry docks							NPRN 405831/406530
	10.01km	SJ 27106 42199	Twin dry docks with a partial cover building that is a rare example of canal dry docks still in operation; double wrought-iron basins on a masonry hearth to boil pitch; drainage culvert along the foot of Trevor Basin platform	c.1805 by Thomas Telford; cover building later	Poor	British Waterways	Listed Conservation Area

	Distance	Grid Reference	Description	Date and designers	SoC	Ownership	Protection
71. Trevor Basin interpretation centre							NPRN 406713
	10.03km	SJ 27106 42183	Red-brick stores building south of the dry dock, now an interpretation centre for the Nominated Site	Late nineteenth century	Good	British Waterways	Conservation Area
72. Trevor Basin building platform retaining wall							NPRN 406652
	10.03km	SJ 27099 42159	Coursed rubble-stone wall at south-east of the building platform on which Trevor Basin is constructed	1795-1805, William Jessop, Thomas Telford and Matthew Davidson	Fair	British Waterways	*Scheduled Conservation Area
73. Trevor Basin dry dock manager's house							NPRN 406700
	10.04km	SJ 27133 42216	House close to the north-east corner of the dry dock for canal-related workers; later a public house	Before 1879	Good	British Waterways	Conservation Area
74. Trevor Basin waste-water weir and culvert							NPRN 406529
	10.05km	SJ 27077 42159	Masonry weir on the eastern side of the canal with a culvert under the towing-path and Trevor Basin platform	1801-05, Thomas Telford and Matthew Davidson	Fair *	British Waterways	*Scheduled Conservation Area
75. Trevor Basin warehouse							NPRN 405832
	10.06km	SJ 27093 42258	Stone-built warehouse or store for general trade on the canal, built into the west wall of the terrace created for the basin; now offices, shop and cafe	Early nineteenth century	Fair *	British Waterways	Conservation Area
76. Trevor Basin footbridge							NPRN 406532
	10.06km	SJ 27121 42253	Modern concrete beam footbridge on masonry supports	Twentieth century	-	British Waterways	Conservation Area
77. Car park and toilets							
	10.06km	SJ 27185 42269	Modern visitor facilities for the Nominated Site	2000	-	Wrexham CBC	Conservation Area
78. Land to east of Trevor Basin							
	10.06km	SJ 27196 42144	Land near the interpretation centre of importance to views of Pontcysyllte Aqueduct		-	private	Conservation Area
79. Trevor Basin stores							NPRN 406654
	10.08km	SJ 27150 42253	Wide corrugated-iron shed on the wharf, typical of twentieth-century canal-side stores buildings	Twentieth century	Fair	British Waterways	Conservation Area
80. Ruabon Brook Railway branch at Trevor Basin							NPRN 406707
	10.10km	SJ 27141 42290	Narrow-gauge railway track and siding on the west side of Trevor Basin for a railway-canal interchange	c.1805, originally Thomas Telford and Thomas Denson	Fair	British Waterways	Conservation Area

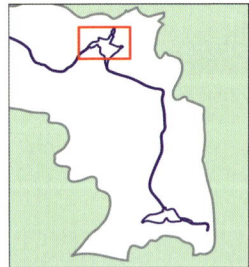

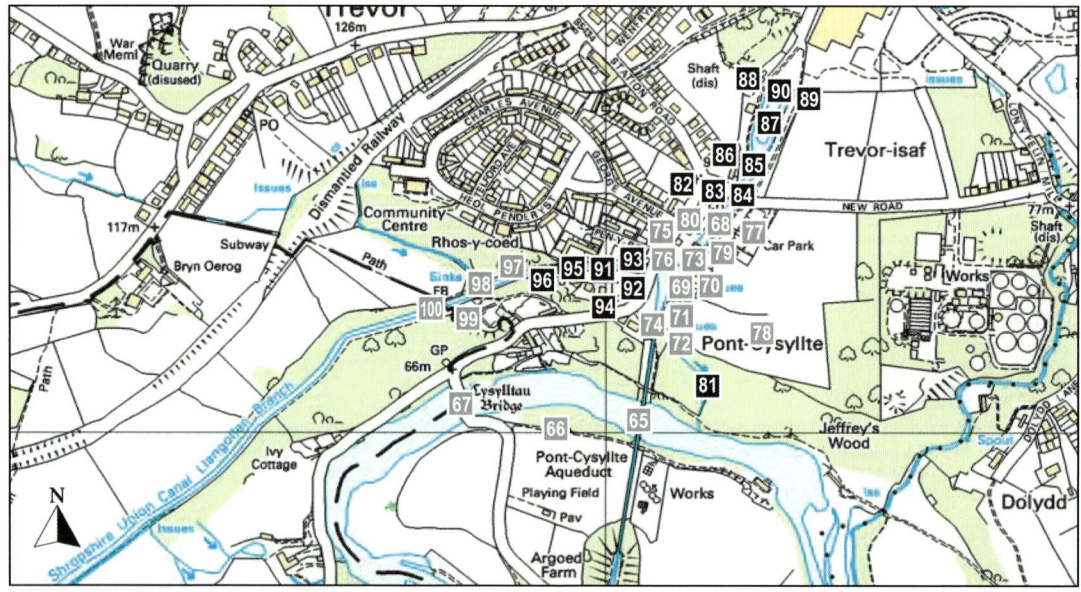

	Distance	Grid Reference	Description	Date and designers	SoC	Ownership	Protection
81. Trevor Basin waste-water channel							NPRN 406714
	10.11km	SJ 27137 42064	Long and steep masonry overflow channel from the canal to the River Dee, diverted obliquely south-eastwards to avoid any danger of scouring the piers of Pontcysyllte Aqueduct	1795-1805 and later, Thomas Telford, and Matthew Davidson	Fair	British Waterways	Conservation Area
82. Scotch Hall / Telford Inn							NPRN 27905
	10.13km	SJ 2714 4232	Believed to be the house of the resident engineer Matthew Davidson and where Telford stayed during the building of Pontcysyllte Aqueduct; now a public house	1795-1803, Thomas Telford and Matthew Davidson	Fair *	private	Listed Conservation Area
83. Scotch Hall account house outbuilding							NPRN 405996
	10.14km	SJ 27151 42319	Single-storey building on the south-west side of Scotch Hall Bridge, believed to be the accounts house and coach house during construction of Pontcysyllte Aqueduct; now a house	1795-1805, Thomas Telford and Matthew Davidson	Fair	private	Listed Conservation Area
84. Scotch Hall Bridge (29)							NPRN 34411
	10.15km	SJ 27173 42317	Masonry bridge of an innovative design with a flattened stone arch supported by curved cast-iron beams; two later side arches, one spanning an extension of the Ruabon Brook; stop-plank grooves	1795-1805, Thomas Telford and Matthew Davidson	Fair *	Wrexham CBC	Listed Conservation Area
85. Trevor Basin culvert (1)							NPRN 406709
	10.16km	SJ 27181 42329	330ft (100m) long diagonal culvert under Trevor Basin and its earthwork platform from the south of Scotch Hall to discharge east of the platform	1795-1805, Thomas Telford and Matthew Davidson	-	British Waterways	*Scheduled Conservation Area
86. Rose Cottage wharfinger's house							NPRN 406534
	10.19km	SJ 27165 42351	House typical of canal wharf workers' accommodation	Nineteenth century, possibly circa 1805 by Thomas Telford and Matthew Davidson	Fair	private	Conservation Area
87. Ruabon Brook Railway pier							NPRN 405833
	10.31km	SJ 27216 42425	Masonry pier projecting into Trevor Basin which carried three lines of tracks allowing wagons on the horse-worked railway to discharge into boats on either side	1803-05, Thomas Telford and Thomas Denson	Poor	British Waterways	*Scheduled Conservation Area

	Distance	Grid Reference	Description	Date and designers	SoC	Ownership	Protection
88. Ruabon Brook Railway buildings							NPRN 406653
	10.32km	SJ 27200 42478	Buildings serving the horse-worked Ruabon Brook Railway at the canal terminus; then houses, now demolished	Early nineteenth century	Poor	British Waterways	Conservation Area
89. Plas Kynaston Canal Bridge (29A)							NPRN 406531
	10.32km	SJ 27255 42461	Narrow masonry over-bridge at the north-east corner of Trevor Basin, crossing the blocked entrance to the former Plas Kynaston branch canal	1820s, for Exuperius Pickering	Poor	British Waterways	Conservation Area
90. Ruabon Brook Railway transfer dock							NPRN 406705
	10.33km	SJ 27241 42464	Single-boat dock at the north-east corner of Trevor Basin originally enclosed in a railway-canal transfer warehouse	Early nineteenth century	Poor	British Waterways	*Scheduled Conservation Area
91. Llangollen Branch formation							NPRN 405725
	10.0-0.67km	SJ 27056 42214- SJ 19588 43283	Channel of the Llangollen Branch for 5.8 miles (9.32km) from the main line at Trevor to the feeder watercourse; built to a narrower specification on steep slopes, subject to breaches and preventative re-lining	1804-8, Thomas Telford and Thomas Denson	Fair * / Good	British Waterways	*Scheduled
92. Site of Rhôs-y-coed railway bridge (30)							NPRN 406699
	10.00km	SJ 27065 42212	Site of a flat-decked movable bridge for an extension of the Ruabon Brook Railway, adjacent to the junction bridge at the entrance to the Llangollen Branch	Nineteenth century	Fair	British Waterways	*Scheduled Conservation Area
93. Rhôs-y-coed Bridge (31)							NPRN 405835
	9.99km	SJ 27056 42214	Junction bridge at entrance to the Llangollen Branch, of an innovative design with a flattened stone arch supported by curved cast-iron beams; stop-plank grooves	1804, Thomas Telford and Thomas Denson	Fair	Wrexham CBC	Listed Conservation Area
94. Western construction yard for Pontcysyllte Aqueduct and site of Trevor Forge							NPRN 406689/406686-7
	9.98km	SJ 27032 42177	High masonry wall supporting a platform levelled for the construction of Pontcysyllte Aqueduct and later occupied by Exuperius Pickering's Trevor Forge and coking kilns and a wharf for Ruabon Brook Railway; now houses and gardens	Earthworks 1795-1805, William Jessop, Thomas Telford and Matthew Davidson; forge after 1808, Exuperius Pickering	Fair	British Waterways and private	Conservation Area (part)
95. Bont Wood Cutting (37)							NPRN 406710
	9.88km	SJ 26991 42221	Cutting on the hill side of the feeder canal as it branches west	1804-8, Thomas Telford and Thomas Denson	Fair	British Waterways	*Scheduled
96. Postles Roving Bridge (32)							NPRN 405868
	9.86km	SJ 26936 42217	A bridge for carrying the towing-path from one side of the canal to the other, with both approaches on the same side to allow the towing rope to pass through; original masonry supports with later steel deck	1804-8, Thomas Telford and Thomas Denson, deck replaced	Fair	British Waterways	*In Setting

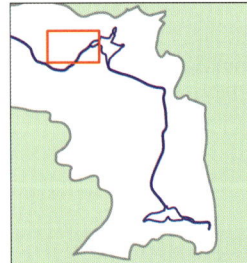

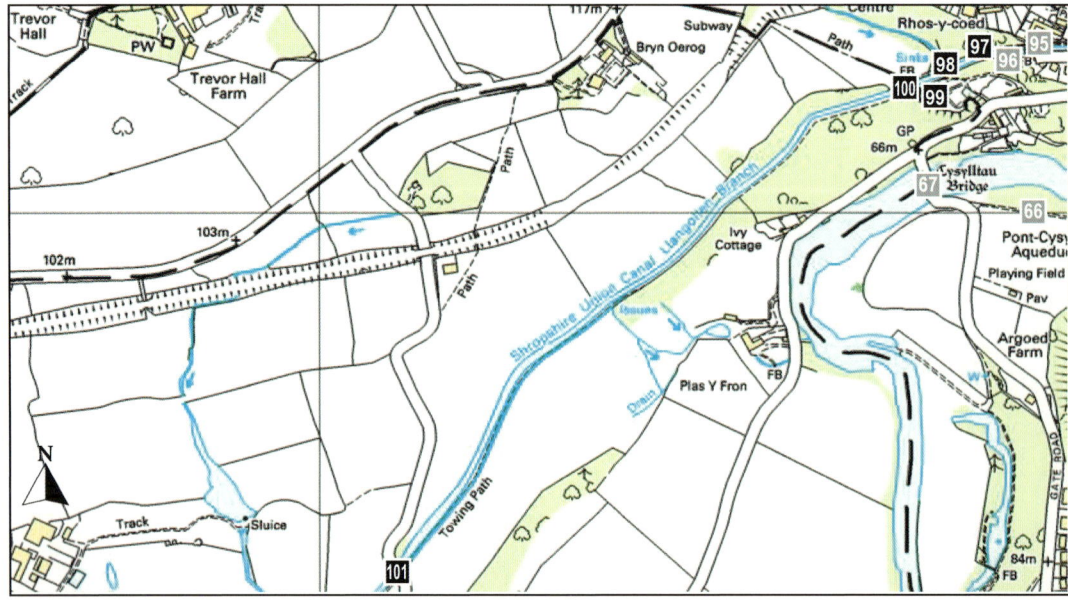

	Distance	Grid Reference	Description	Date and designers	SoC	Ownership	Protection
97. Detached part of western construction yard for Pontcysyllte Aqueduct							NPRN 406702
	9.85km	SJ 26883 42224	Earthwork platform largely untouched since the time of the Pontcysyllte Aqueduct construction and likely to have archaeological potential, cut by the Llangollen Branch c.1805; later used for forge slag tipping	1795-1805, William Jessop and Thomas Telford	Fair	British Waterways and private	*In Setting
98. Wood Bank culvert (97) and embankment							NPRN 406535
	9.77km	SJ 26835 42191	Culvert and substantial embankment	1804-8, Thomas Telford and Thomas Denson	Fair	British Waterways	*Scheduled
99. Wood Bank and malt kilns							NPRN 308392/405837
	9.74km	SJ 26814 42158	House overlooking Pontcysyllte Aqueduct, formerly owned by the canal company and reputed to be the drawing office during construction; associated malt kilns built into the canal bank	1795-1805, William Jessop and Thomas Telford	Fair	private	Listed
100. White Bridge footbridge (33)							NPRN 405867
	9.72km	SJ 26785 42171	Footbridge with stone abutment; timber deck replaced in steel	Abutments 1804-8, Thomas Telford and Thomas Denson	Fair	British Waterways	*In Setting
101. Plas-yn-y-pentre Bridge (34)							NPRN 405866
	8.74km	SJ 26103 41522	Original arched masonry bridge and stop-plank grooves	1804-8, Thomas Telford and Thomas Denson	Fair *	Denbighshire CC	Listed

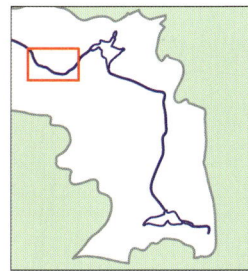

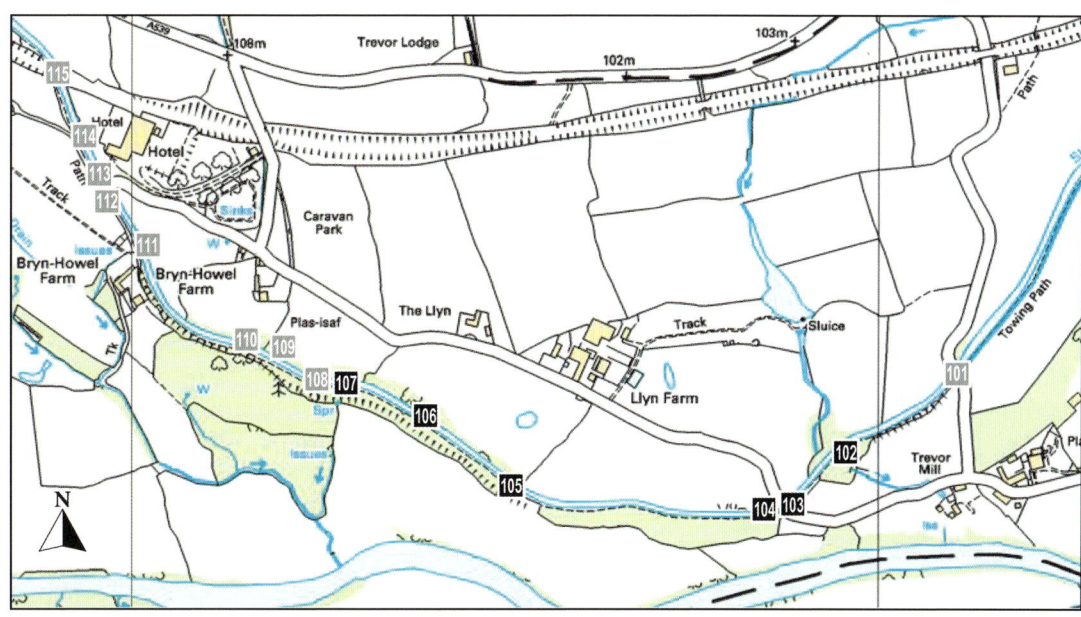

	Distance	Grid Reference	Description	Date and designers	SoC	Ownership	Protection
102. Trevor Mill culvert (98) and Millars Embankment (24–25)							NPRN 405865
	8.52km	SJ 25960 41387	Masonry stream culvert and very large embankment on the site of an earlier mill-pond; later the site of a large breach	1804-8, Thomas Telford and Thomas Denson	Fair	British Waterways	*Scheduled
103. Millars Bridge wharf							NPRN 406614
	8.49km	SJ 25885 41340	Site of a crane and store on a small road-side wharf along the towing-path, probably for Trevor corn mill	Nineteenth century	Fair	British Waterways	*Scheduled
104. Millars Bridge (35)							NPRN 405864
	8.44km	SJ 25868 41335	Original arched masonry bridge for a road diverted during construction, with unusually wide brick arch to improve visibility and manoeuvrability on a curve	1804-8, Thomas Telford and Thomas Denson	Fair *	Denbighshire CC	Listed
105. Bryn-ceirch Cutting (38), and embankment							NPRN 406613/406623
	8.1-7.68km	SJ 25389 41457	Shelf into the hillside with cutting and bank; a gravel pit excavated into the cutting was probably a source of materials for construction	1804-8, Thomas Telford and Thomas Denson	Fair	British Waterways	*Scheduled
106. Bryn-ceirch Bridge (36)							NPRN 405863
	8.06km	SJ 25506 41365	Original arched masonry bridge	1804-8, Thomas Telford and Thomas Denson	Fair	British Waterways	Listed
107. Plâs-isaf culvert (99)							NPRN 406679
	7.8km	SJ 25269 41505	Masonry culvert under the canal	1804-8, Thomas Telford and Thomas Denson	Fair	British Waterways	*Scheduled

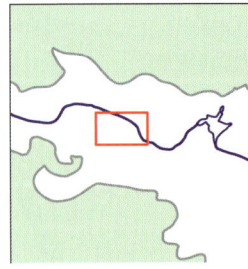

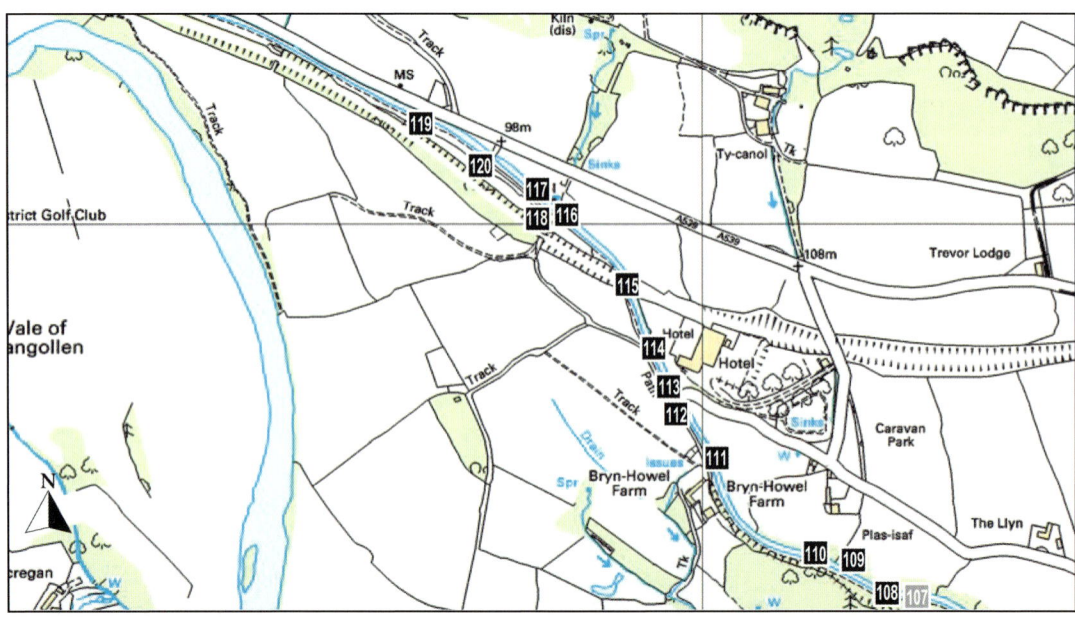

	Distance	Grid Reference	Description	Date and designers	SoC	Ownership	Protection
	108. Plâs-isaf Bridge (37)						NPRN 405861
	7.77km	SJ 25257 41511	Original arched masonry bridge with unusually wide brick arch to improve manoeuvrability and visibility at a curve	1804-8, Thomas Telford and Thomas Denson	Fair	British Waterways	Listed
	109. Trevor Limestone Railway wharf						NPRN 406607
	7.58km	SJ 25201 41553	Wharf with a railway siding at the foot of a gravity-operated incline from Trevor Hall Wood Quarry, superseded in the late nineteenth century by the Plâs-ifan inclined railway	Early nineteenth century, Exuperius Pickering	Fair	British Waterways	*Scheduled
	110. Plâs-isaf limekilns and wharf						NPRN 406611
	7.52km	SJ 25151 41562	Site of a wharf and canal-side limekilns using road and canal transport, surviving as an earthwork	Early nineteenth century, probably Exuperius Pickering	Fair	British Waterways and private	*In Setting
	111. Bryn-Howel boat-turning basin						NPRN 406606
	7.45km	SJ 25027 41684	Natural indent in the hillside developed as a basin for turning boats, serving Plâs-isaf limestone wharf	1804-8, Thomas Telford and Thomas Denson	Fair	British Waterways	*Scheduled
	112. Bryn-Howel Cutting (39)						NPRN 406605
	7.38-7.29km	SJ 24969 41786	Short, small cutting on the hill side of the canal	1804-8, Thomas Telford and Thomas Denson	Fair	British Waterways	*Scheduled
	113. Bryn-Howel Bridge (38)						NPRN 406021
	7.35km	SJ 24965 41769	Typical arched canal bridge with stop-plank grooves	1804-8, Thomas Telford and Thomas Denson	Good	Denbighshire CC	Listed

	Distance	Grid Reference	Description	Date and designers	SoC	Ownership	Protection
114. Bryn-Howel boat-house							NPRN 85085
	7.2km	SJ 24942 41842	Edwardian brick pleasure-boat house for the adjacent mansion of J.C. Edwards of the terracotta works at Trefynant, Trevor	Between 1879 and 1900, for J.C. Edwards	Fair	private	*In Setting
115. Bryn-Howel railway bridge (39)							NPRN 405862
	7.18km	SJ 24896 41927	Bridge for the Vale of Llangollen Railway, originally a steel-girder bridge by Telford's former assistant, Thomas Brassey; deck replaced in reinforced concrete	1860s, Thomas Brassey, altered 1960s	-	private	*In Setting
116. Plâs-Ifan Limestone Railway wharf							NPRN 406675
	7.07km	SJ 24812 42020	Wharf for a limestone railway from Trevor Hall Wood Quarry, superseding that to the canal at Plâs-Isaf	Mid nineteenth century	Fair	British Waterways	*Scheduled
117. Plâs-Ifan outlet sluice (13)							NPRN 406677
	7.04km	SJ 24797 42030	Sluice to drain the canal for maintenance	-	Fair	British Waterways	*Scheduled
118. Plâs-Ifan Culvert (100)							NPRN 405860
	7.04km	SJ 24784 42007	Stone-arched culvert taking a stream under the canal	1804-8, Thomas Telford and Thomas Denson	Fair	British Waterways	*Scheduled
119. Plâs-Ifan Embankment							NPRN 406675
	6.97-6.6km	SJ 24633 42129	Embankment on the valley-side of the canal, partially re-built following breach	1804-8, Thomas Telford and Thomas Denson	Fair	British Waterways	*Scheduled
120. Plâs-Ifan Bridge (40) and stop-plank shelter							NPRN 405859/406676
	6.93km	SJ 24719 42088	Original masonry bridge incorporating a road diversion 394ft (120m) from the east to lessen the gradients; stop-plank grooves and roofed shelter for stop planks	1804-8, Thomas Telford and Thomas Denson	Good	Denbighshire CC British Waterways	Listed

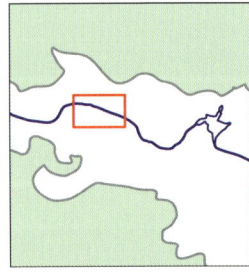

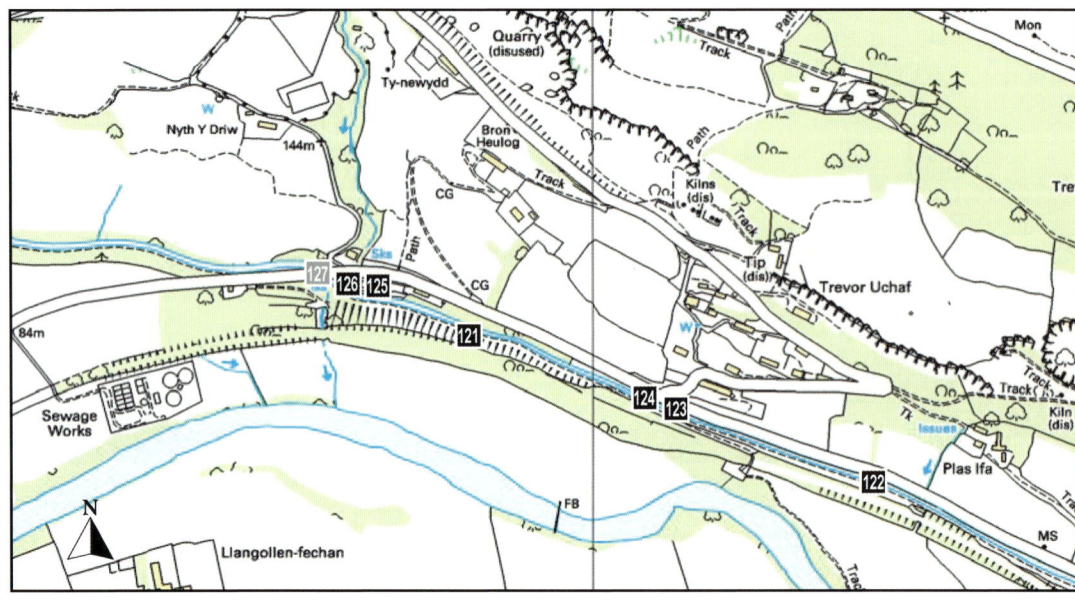

	Distance	Grid Reference	Description	Date and designers	SoC	Ownership	Protection
121. Sun Trevor Embankment (26) and site of breach							NPRN 406674/406657
	6.6–5.79km	SJ 23821 42477	Considerable embankment on the valley-side of the canal; site of a serious early breach (at SJ 23899 42460) which demonstrated the need for re-lining works on mountainside sections of channel	1804-8, Thomas Telford and Thomas Denson	Fair	British Waterways	*Scheduled
122. Trevor / Plâs-Ifan railway wharf							NPRN 406716
	6.48km	SJ 24373 42277	Wharf for the inclined railway from Trevor Limestone Quarries	Early nineteenth century	Fair	British Waterways	*Scheduled
123. Sun Trevor limestone railway wharf							NPRN 406655-6
	6.26km	SJ 24082 42380	Wharf for the limestone railway from Trevor Quarry	Early nineteenth century	Fair	British Waterways	*Scheduled
124. Sun Trevor Bridge (41)							NPRN 34762
	6.22km	SJ 24061 42369	Original arched masonry bridge incorporating a second, smaller arch to the north for the Trevor limestone railway; stop-plank grooves	1804-8, Thomas Telford and Thomas Denson	Good	British Waterways	Listed
125. Wenffrwd culvert (101), and embankment							NPRN 406537
	5.78km	SJ 23664 42539	Masonry culvert and embankment	1804-8, Thomas Telford and Thomas Denson	Good	British Waterways	*Scheduled
126. Wenffrwd outlet sluice (14)							NPRN 406536
	5.77km	SJ 23655 42538	Outlet to drain the canal to the adjacent culvert for maintenance	1804-8, Thomas Telford and Thomas Denson	Fair *	British Waterways	*Scheduled

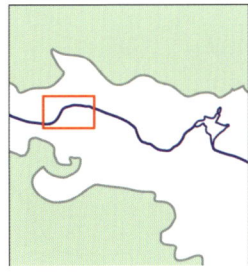

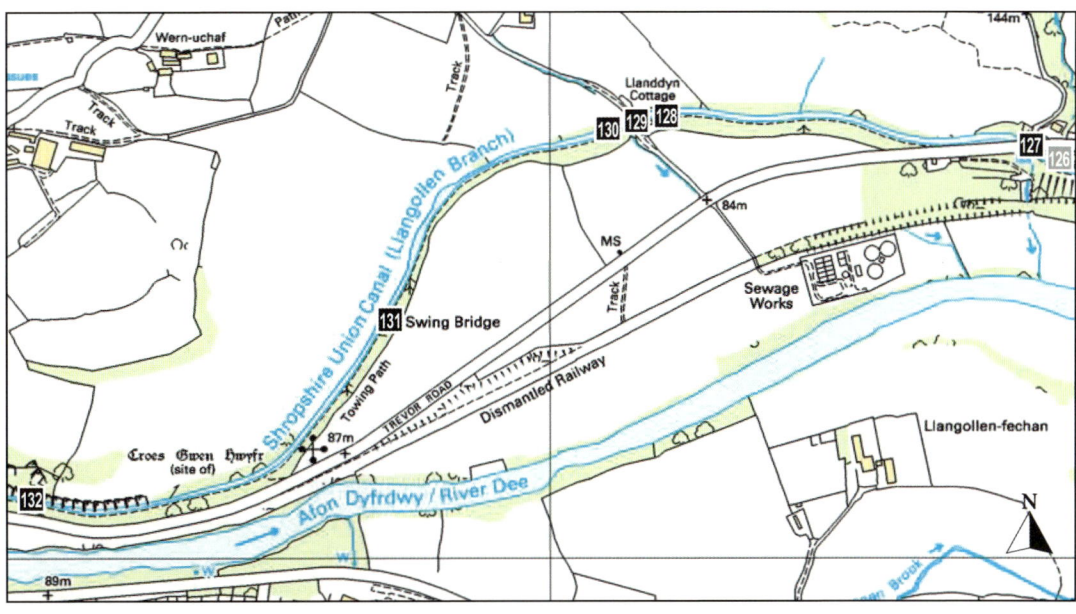

	Distance	Grid Reference	Description	Date and designers	SoC	Ownership	Protection
127. Wenffrwd Bridge (42)							NPRN 405858
	5.75km	SJ 23650 42550	Modern concrete road bridge	Mid twentieth century	-	Denbighshire CC	*In Setting
128. Llanddyn Cottage							NPRN 406538
	5.2km	SJ 23131 42583	Lengthman's house, representing the increasing level of organisation of canal maintenance	Late nineteenth century, Shropshire Union Railway and Canal Company	Fair *	British Waterways	*In Setting
129. Llanddyn Bridge (43) and stop-plank store							NPRN 405857/406612
	5.19km	SJ 23115 42584	Original arched masonry bridge; stop-plank grooves and small timber-built store for stop planks	1804-8, Thomas Telford and Thomas Denson, plank store twentieth-century	Good	Private British Waterways	Listed *Scheduled
130. Llanddyn Culvert (102)							NPRN 406544
	5.17km	SJ 23097 42584	Masonry culvert to take a stream under canal	1804-8, Thomas Telford and Thomas Denson	Fair *	British Waterways	*Scheduled
131. Llanddyn Lift Bridge (44)							NPRN 405856
	4.73km	SJ 22777 42327	Lift bridge of traditional form for a low-level crossing, with hydraulic operation, and stop-plank grooves	Twentieth century	-	British Waterways	*In Setting
132. Wern-isaf Rock Walls cutting and embankment and culvert 103							NPRN 405855/406670-3
	4.34-3.32km	SJ 22308 42082	Rock cutting on the hill-side, the deepest on the canal, and a large embankment on the valley-side with frequent stop-plank grooves to close off water in the event of a breach; masonry culvert to take a stream under canal	1804-8, Thomas Telford and Thomas Denson	Fair	British Waterways	*Scheduled

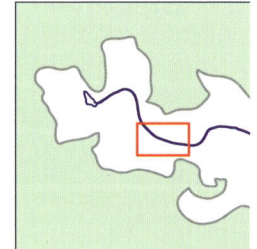

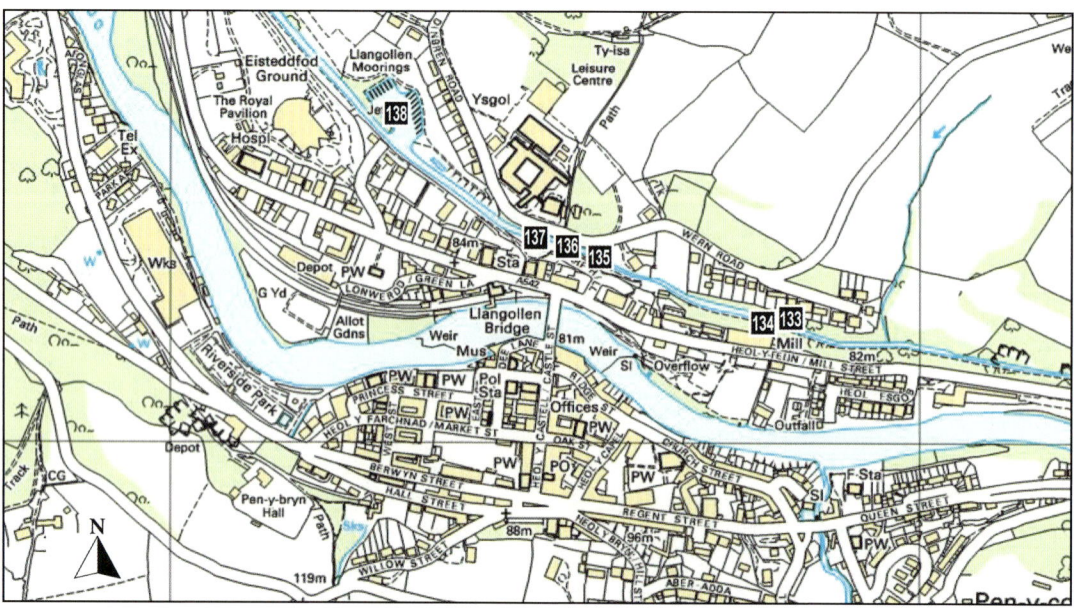

	Distance	Grid Reference	Description	Date and designers	SoC	Ownership	Protection
133. Upper Dee Flannel Mills water intake							NPRN 406589
	3.31km	SJ 21801 42162	Water intake under the canal towing-path to a textile mill powered by canal water, now converted to secondary uses	Late nineteenth century	Fair	British Waterways	*Scheduled
134. Siambr-wen stream culvert (104)							NPRN 406669
	3.19km	SJ 21693 42190	Typical masonry culvert taking a stream under the canal	1804-8, Thomas Telford and Thomas Denson	Fair	British Waterways	*Scheduled Conservation Area
135. Wharf Cottage							NPRN 405852
	3.04km	SJ 21547 42247	Typical wharfinger's cottage of stone and brick, built into the retaining wall of the canal owing to the difficult terrain	Early and late nineteenth century	Good	private	Listed Conservation Area
136. Siambr-wen Bridge (45)							NPRN 405850
	3.0km	SJ 21522 42274	Twentieth-century replacement of an earlier bridge; stop-plank grooves	Mid twentieth century	-	private	Conservation Area
137. Llangollen Wharf and warehouse							NPRN 405851
	2.98km	SJ 21489 42268	Public town wharf and warehouse, stone-built with a brick extension, for the general goods trade on the canal	Early nineteenth century, possibly Thomas Telford and Thomas Denson	Fair	British Waterways and private	Listed Conservation Area
138. Llangollen turning hole							NPRN 406587
	2.78km	SJ 21337 42391	Original turning hole now used as part of a mooring basin	1804-8, Thomas Telford and Thomas Denson	Fair	British Waterways	*Scheduled

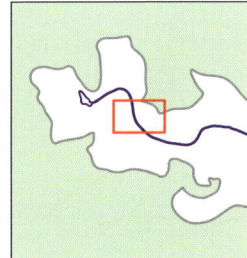

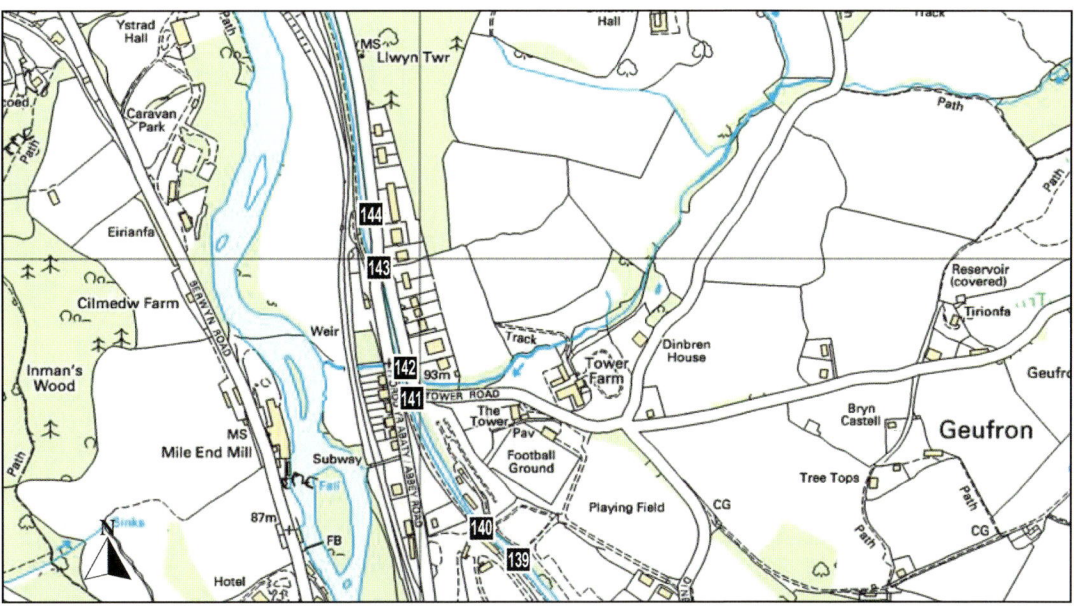

	Distance	Grid Reference	Description	Date and designers	SoC	Ownership	Protection
139. Pen-y-ddol cutting (40) and embankment (27)							NPRN 406588
	2.5km	SJ 21124 42609	Cutting on the hill-side and an embankment on the valley-side, exemplifying the engineering of the Llangollen Branch	1804-8, Thomas Telford and Thomas Denson	Fair	British Waterways	*Scheduled
140. Pen-y-ddol Bridge (46)							NPRN 405849
	2.4km	SJ 21077 42637	Original arched masonry bridge	1804-8, Thomas Telford and Thomas Denson	Fair	British Waterways	Listed
141. Penddol culvert							NPRN 406668
	2.22km	SJ 20976 42839	Typical masonry culvert taking a stream under the canal, now silted	1804-8, Thomas Telford and Thomas Denson	-	British Waterways	*Scheduled
142. Tower stream culvert (106)							NPRN 406545
	2.2km	SJ 20976 42843	Typical masonry culvert taking a stream under the canal	1804-8, Thomas Telford and Thomas Denson	Fair	British Waterways	*Scheduled
143. Tower Bridge (47)							NPRN 405845
	2.05km	SJ 20943 42989	Concrete-decked road bridge	Late twentieth century	-	Denbighshire CC	*In Setting
144. Tower Bridge Cutting (41)							NPRN 406659
	2.0km	SJ 20931 43053	Hill-slope cutting exemplifying the engineering works needed for the Llangollen Branch	1804-8, Thomas Telford and Thomas Denson	Fair	British Waterways	*Scheduled

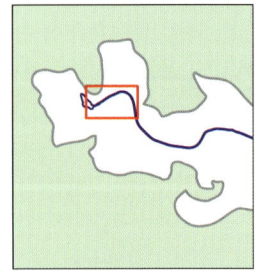

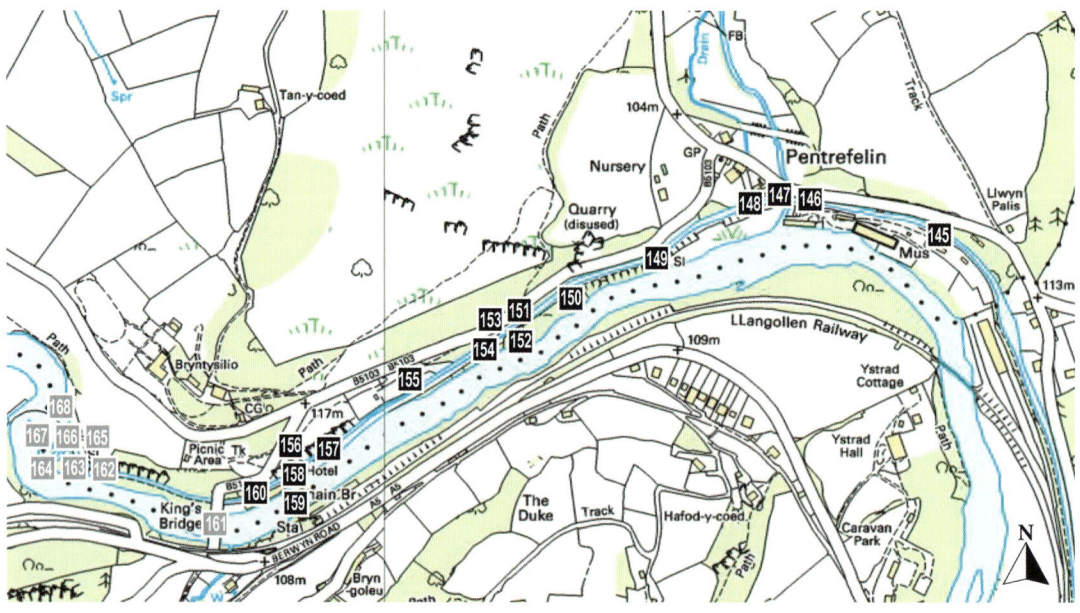

	Distance	Grid Reference	Description	Date and designers	SoC	Ownership	Protection
145. Pentrefelin Bridge (48)							NPRN 43125
	1.37km	SJ 20729 43601	Typical, original arched masonry bridge; stop-plank grooves	1804-8, Thomas Telford and Thomas Denson	Poor	private	Listed
146. Site of Pentrefelin Slate Mill railway bridge							NPRN 406658
	1.18km	SJ 20543 43635	Site of a lift or swing-bridge for a railway crossing the canal to take slate to the slab mill from the quarries	1852, Henry Dennis	Fair	British Waterways	*Scheduled
147. Afon Eglwyseg Aqueduct, Pentrefelin							NPRN 405843
	1.07km	SJ 20539 43639	Masonry aqueduct of traditional design and a causeway embankment supported by long masonry retaining walls	1804-8, Thomas Telford and Thomas Denson	Fair	British Waterways	*Scheduled Listed
148. Pentre-felin Corn Mill culvert (107)							NPRN 24892
	1.04km	SJ 20515 43635	Culvert under the canal for the tail-race of Pentre-felin Corn Mill, indicating the canal engineers' provisions for the pre-existing water economy	1804-8, Thomas Telford and Thomas Denson	-	British Waterways	*Scheduled
149. Pentre-felin outlet sluice (15)							NPRN 405840
	0.87km	SJ 20362 43558	Deep sluice set in masonry wing-walls through the substantial retaining bank carrying the canal above the River Dee	1804-8 with later patching, Thomas Telford and Thomas Denson	Poor	British Waterways	*Scheduled
150. Tŷ Craig limekilns							NPRN 406586
	0.74km	SJ 20244 43500	Bank of four limekilns set into the river bank to be charged with coal and limestone from the canal	Early nineteenth century, built for Exuperius Pickering	Fair	private	*In Setting

	Distance	Grid Reference	Description	Date and designers	SoC	Ownership	Protection
	151. Tŷ Craig stop-lock						NPRN 405842
	0.67km	SJ 20176 43479	Masonry abutments flanking a narrowing of the canal, formerly housing a gate to restrict boats from entering the feeder watercourse	Early nineteenth century, Thomas Telford and Thomas Denson	Poor	British Waterways	*Scheduled
	152. Feeder watercourse formation						NPRN 406724
	0.67-0km	SJ20176 43479- SJ19588 43283	Watercourse leading from the navigable section of the Llangollen Branch to Horseshoe Falls, 0.4 miles (0.66km) long	1804-8, Thomas Telford and Thomas Denson	Fair / Good	British Waterways	*Scheduled
	153. Tŷ Craig limekiln-manager's house and kiln ramp						NPRN 406584
	0.66km	SJ 20183 43458	House for limekiln manager and a ramp down to the drawing-holes of kilns; demonstrating the coal and lime trade on the canal	Early nineteenth century, built for Exuperius Pickering	Fair	private	*In Setting
	154. Tŷ Craig Bridge (48A)						NPRN 405841
	0.63km	SJ 20149 43454	Smaller variant of Telford's standard arched bridge abutted directly to the rock face, without a towing-path as the watercourse was not intended for regular navigation	1804-8, Thomas Telford and Thomas Denson	Poor	Denbighshire CC	Listed
	155. Canal Cottage, Llantysilio						NPRN 406583
	0.5km	SJ 20031 43393	Lengthman's cottage purchased by British Waterways in 1947 to house maintenance workers	Early nineteenth century, built for Llantysilio Hall estate	Fair	British Waterways	*In Setting
	156. Chain Bridge rock cutting and retaining wall						NPRN 405886
	0.48-0.23km	SJ 19862 43270	Rock cutting into the valley side and a retaining wall above the River Dee	1804-8, Thomas Telford and Thomas Denson	Fair	British Waterways	*Scheduled
	157. Llantysilio Footbridge (49)						NPRN 406546
	0.33km	SJ 19897 43286	High-level steel footbridge giving access to Horseshoe Falls as part of the long-established use of the watercourse and weir for leisure and amenity	Twentieth century	-	private	*In Setting
	158. Chain Bridge Wharf						NPRN 406718/406719
	0.3km	SJ 19871 43260	Location of an early nineteenth-century wharf at the canal's head of navigation and a weighbridge for lime and coal with probable below-ground remains	Early nineteenth-century, built for Exuperius Pickering	Fair	British Waterways and private	*Scheduled (part)
	159. Chain Bridge, Llantysilio						NPRN 24054
	0.27km	SJ 19868 43224	Suspension footbridge re-using chains from an earlier suspension bridge by Telford, probably made by William Hazledine at Plas Kynaston Forge	Early nineteenth century and early twentieth century, parts by Thomas Telford	Fair*	private	*In Setting
	160. Chain Bridge Hotel western footbridge						NPRN 406601
	0.21km	SJ19811 43232	Footbridge	Pre 1870s	Poor	private	*In Setting

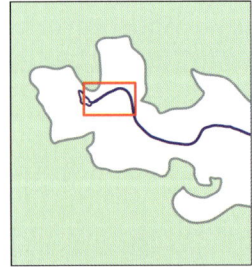

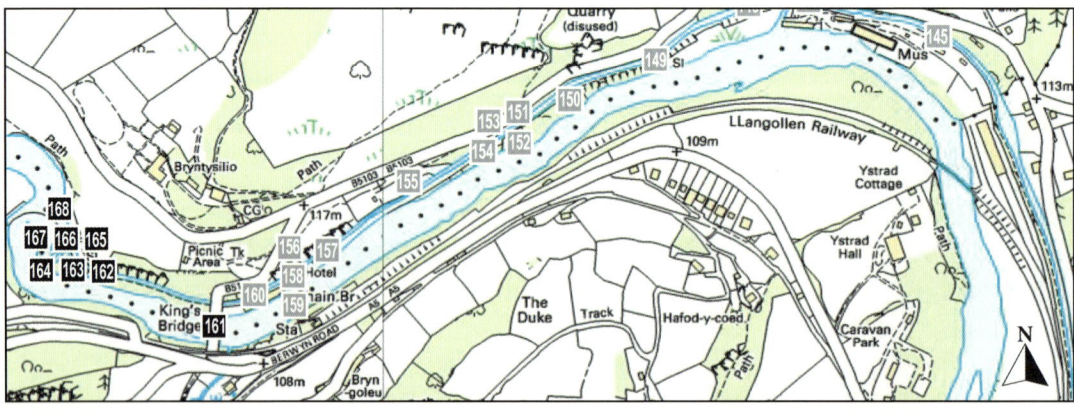

	Distance	Grid Reference	Description	Date and designers	SoC	Ownership	Protection
161. King's Bridge Viaduct (49A)							NPRN 405839/43123
	0.18km	SJ 19772 43235	Five-arched masonry road viaduct crossing the River Dee and the canal in a visually impressive grouping, demonstrating the commonplace use of large multi-span structures a century after the canal	1902-06	Fair	Denbighshire CC	Listed
162. Horseshoe Falls mess, maintenance hut and stop-plank shelter							NPRN 405730/406585
	0.029km	SJ 19622 43258	Maintenance hut and mess room building of typical late nineteenth-century design with a substantial, gabled, timber structure for storing planks to stop the canal in the event of a breach	Late nineteenth and twentieth century	Fair	British Waterways	*In Setting
163. Horseshoe Falls meter house							NPRN 405729
	0.006km	SJ 19612 43279	Fine, dressed-stone building for the water measuring gauge added as part of the secondary use of the canal for domestic water supply	1947	-	British Waterways	*In Setting
164. Horseshoe Falls footbridge							NPRN 406717
	0.005km	SJ 19604 43280	Footbridge crossing the feeder watercourse	Twentieth century	-	private	*In Setting
165. Horseshoe Falls overflow sluice and bridge							NPRN 406610
	0.002km	SJ19593 43274	Overflow and sluice for water management, crossed by a footbridge	Modern	-	British Waterways	*Scheduled
166. Horseshoe Falls intake gate and footbridge							NPRN 406725
	0.001km	SJ19588 43283	Sluice taking water from Horseshoe Falls into the feeder watercourse and later footbridge	Nineteenth and twentieth centuries	-	British Waterways	*Scheduled
167. Horseshoe Falls weir							NPRN 403685
	0km	SJ 19560 43345	Elegant, curved weir with a cast-iron curb supplying water to the whole canal, representative of water management and the innovative use of cast iron	1804-8, Thomas Telford and Thomas Denson	Fair	British Waterways	Listed *Scheduled
168. Land around Horseshoe Falls							
	0km	SJ 19560 43345	Land around Horseshoe Falls of importance to its visual setting	-	-	private	In Setting

2.b History and development

2.b.1 Introduction: Canals and the Industrial Revolution

the Industrial Revolution was ushered in by the canal age and led to the railway age.

Christopher Hill, *Reformation to Industrial Revolution* (1967)

Pontcysyllte Aqueduct and Canal comprise an outstanding example of a transport system of the Industrial Revolution. Internationally, the timescale, causes and form of industrialisation varied, but it may be summarised as a quickening of technical, economic and social change that began with the British Industrial Revolution in the late eighteenth and early nineteenth centuries and spread to Europe, North America and the entire globe. Fernand Braudel, in his masterly survey of world history, *Le Temps du Monde* (1979), referred to the Industrial Revolution as 'massive, all-pervasive and innovatory'. It fundamentally changed the economic and social basis of life. Many of its characteristics are evident within the Nominated Site. Its physical assets are directly expressive of the improvement of transport, the use of new technologies, the development of new means of investment and increasing levels of capitalisation. The purposes for which it was built are reflective of increased inter-regional trade, accelerating growth in output and the shift to fossil fuels that provided the life-blood of canal traffic.

Braudel wrote concerning the factors that led to growth so early in Britain: 'perhaps most of all, there was the proliferation of new means of transport, something which preceded the demands of trade, and then helped it expand'. Pontcysyllte Aqueduct and Canal exemplify the construction of a network of efficient canals to link the British coalfields, connecting sources of raw materials with processing locations and markets. Inland water was the foremost mode of industrial transport throughout the British Industrial Revolution, and it was pivotal in opening up the coalfields to economic exploitation. England and Wales were served by some 5,340 miles / 8,600 kilometres of navigable inland waterways, an industrial transport system unsurpassed until the rapid expansion of locomotive railways in the subsequent phase of industrialisation.

Philip James de Loutherbourg's evocation of the shock of the Industrial Revolution and its transformation of society, a depiction of the iron furnaces of Coalbrookdale in Shropshire, painted in 1801.

Even while it was under construction, the unprecedented aqueduct at Pontcysyllte captured the imagination of artists: this painting by John Ingleby shows the trough being erected on top of the completed arches, with the construction decks still in place at the level below.

The construction of the canals in Britain represented an important new phase in the history of inland navigation internationally. Over 1,180 miles/1,900 kilometres of the waterways network were built in just two decades from 1790 to 1810, during which the nominated canal was built. The achievement was made possible by the development of joint-stock companies to raise capital from numerous small investors, the creation of effective contracting teams, and the development of new engineering techniques and materials. All of these developments would later be applied to other construction needs. Such intensive and ambitious canal-building also depended on the profession of civil engineering that was maturing in Britain in the late eighteenth and early nineteenth centuries, and on the creative genius of a generation of individuals, among whom William Jessop and Thomas Telford were the most prolific and influential.

The history of navigable canals extends over many centuries before the building of Pontcysyllte Aqueduct and Canal. They were built in ancient Egypt. The magisterial Grand Canal in China, the first to cross a watershed, was begun between 581 and 617 BC, and the Romans built several artificial waterways. Important navigations were constructed in Italy, France, Saxony and elsewhere in the Middle Ages. The *trekvaarten* canals of the Netherlands, mostly dug for drainage purposes, were intensively used for passenger transport by the seventeenth century. The first major canal in Europe built primarily for navigation was the Canal du Midi, completed in 1681 to link the Atlantic and Mediterranean coasts of France and now a World Heritage Site. Navigable canals were built in the early and mid-eighteenth century in Russia, Prussia, France and Ireland, and more followed throughout Europe.

The waterways system that developed in Britain between the 1760s and the 1830s can be regarded as a new beginning in inland transport that was driven by the needs of industrialisation and private enterprise, springing from the canal built at Manchester by the Duke of Bridgewater in 1761. During the next thirty years, canals linked the four principal river estuaries of southern Britain. The feverish speculation in shares of the Canal Mania in the 1790s resulted in many more projects, Pontcysyllte Aqueduct and Canal among them. Within twenty years networks of canals had been completed in all the main British coalfields, a direct link had been made to London and three routes crossed the Pennine hills, the 'spine' of England. Schemes were completed even after the introduction of locomotive railways, and by 1850 Britain had added to its 620 miles / 1,000 kilometres of naturally navigable rivers roughly 680 miles / 1,100 kilometres of improved river navigations and 4,000 miles / 6,500 kilometres of artificial canals. The role of the vast manual labour teams who built these navigations was carried forward into the words 'navigator' and 'navvy', used in English to describe earthwork builders on railways and roads for the next two centuries.

A series of innovations made possible this extraordinary provision of a new transport network. The Duke of Bridgewater's Canal set the legal precedent of compulsory purchase of land by Act of Parliament, assisting canals to cross the lands of multiple owners. Popular shareholding by many small investors was spearheaded by canal companies, enabling a scale of capital investment that otherwise would have been inconceivable: canals introduced the better-off to the marketable company share and became by far the largest concentrations of capital in the Industrial Revolution. The canals were seedbeds for organisational developments such as contract management, the professionalisation of engineering and the recognition of economies of scale. They also called for technical innovations such as improved earthwork calculations, the use of construction railways and the structural use of iron. All these innovations, later carried forward into the development of railways, roads and industrial projects,

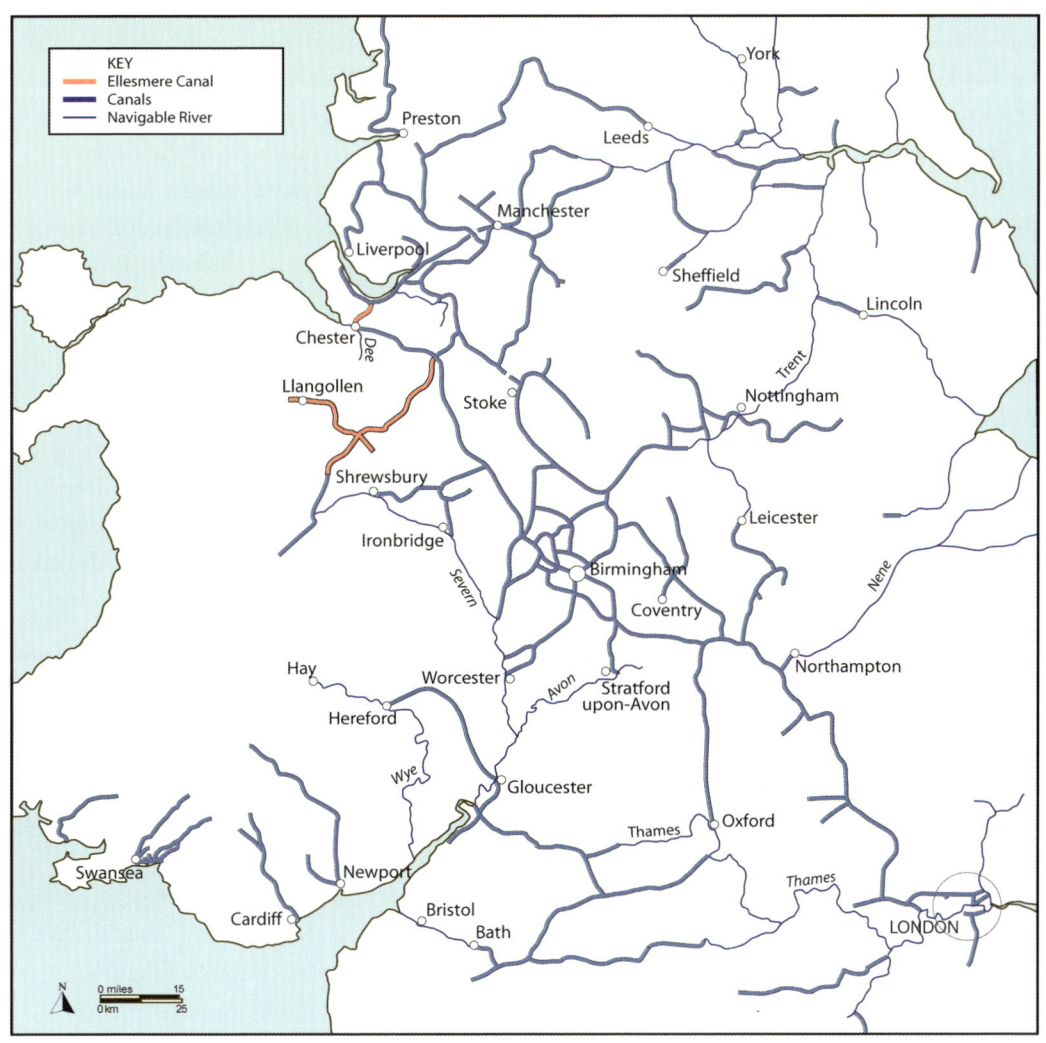

Map 8. A simplified map showing the inland waterways network of central Britain.

are manifested in Pontcysyllte Aqueduct and Canal. They were also influential in other countries. The historian of world canals, Charles Hadfield, observed that Britain 'became a showpiece… engineers from all over Europe visited her to learn what they could, and then went home to apply the lessons learned… in the New World also her influence was felt'. In Belgium, the Ruhrgebiet, the Pas de Calais and Burgundy, Pennsylvania and New England, canals became a similarly essential component of industrialisation.

Overall, British canals were prodigiously successful in their economic effects: distributing coal to regions without their own supplies, stimulating economic growth by making available cheap energy, delivering minerals from mines and goods from factories, and distributing agricultural produce to growing centres of population. Canals dramatically enhanced the efficiency of the whole economy. Their construction provided well-paid employment for tens of thousands of men and stimulated demand for bricks, building stone, lime, clay, timber and iron.

It was said at the opening of Pontcysyllte Aqueduct that it was 'destined to convey the riches of the mineral Kingdom into the World of Industry and thence to every part of the universe.' Telford observed that the Duke of Bridgewater had been, 'the model and root of the canal navigation of England… by his exertions and example (he) turned a great portion of British talent and capital into a direction which has in a few years pervaded and improved the whole kingdom and been a principal means of extending its commerce and manufactures'.

The heavily-engineered length of canal in the Nominated Site is an outstanding example of the canals that linked British coalfields with their markets and is one of the greatest achievements of this phase of transport engineering. Its nomination complements those of other sites of the first Industrial Revolution, already inscribed onto the World Heritage List, that bear witness to the development of the textile, coal and iron industries and international trade.

2.b.2 The evolution of the canal project

It is the greatest Works, I believe, that is in hand in the kingdom and will not be completed for many years to come.

Thomas Telford in a letter to Andrew Little, 1793

The project that was to produce Pontcysyllte Aqueduct and Canal grew from discussions among interested parties in 1789. These were endorsed enthusiastically at a public meeting in 1791 at Ellesmere, a market town in Shropshire from which the new canal company took its name. The declared objective was to make a strategic connection between the Atlantic ports of Liverpool and Bristol by cutting a canal from the River Mersey to the River Severn. When shares were put on offer on 10 September 1792 there was a stampede to invest. A local newspaper, *The Chester Courant*, reported dramatic scenes as people travelled from all over the country: 'Shrewsbury, about 16 miles from Ellesmere, was so crowded on the nights before and after the meeting that many people found very great difficulty in getting accommodated: several gentlemen being obliged to take care of their own horses, cook their own victuals, and sleep two or three in a bed.' Between noon and sunset 1,234 speculators offered almost a million pounds.

An Act of Parliament conferring legal powers for construction was obtained in 1793. With William Jessop as their engineer, the proprietors began with those parts of their intended network that would offer instant revenue and be simplest to build. The line from Chester to the River Mersey was opened to bring coal from Lancashire and imported goods from Liverpool, and was well used by passenger boats. By the end of 1795, the Ellesmere system consisted of three lines from Welsh Frankton, near Ellesmere, and one from the River Mersey, where the new settlement of Ellesmere Port came into existence.

The strategic linking of the Severn and the Mersey was always a dubious aim. The Severn was a notoriously uncertain river navigation, and large ships already

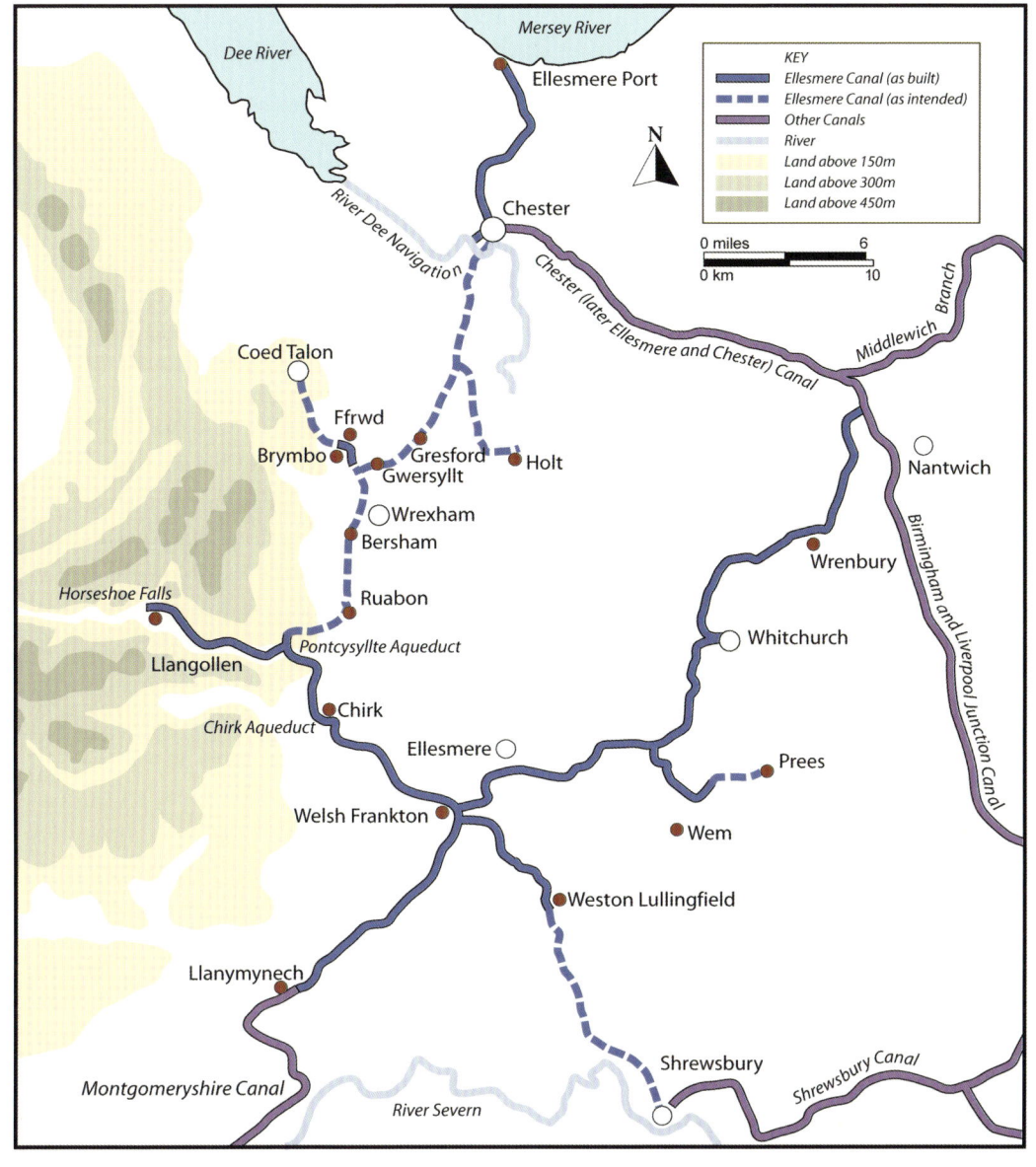

KEY
- Ellesmere Canal (as built)
- Ellesmere Canal (as intended)
- Other Canals
- River
- Land above 150m
- Land above 300m
- Land above 450m

Map 9. A map showing the Ellesmere Canal and its connections as proposed and built.

sailed between Liverpool and Bristol by sea. The company quickly decided that its prime focus should be to connect to the Mersey, but it was divided into factions regarding how this should be achieved. One faction favoured a direct line from Chirk northwards; the other saw the main benefit of the canal as linking the Denbighshire coalfield and the countryside of north Shropshire and preferred a more circuitous route. Work on the direct line began, but in 1800 Jessop advised that it would be 'wholly inadvisable to execute a canal between Pontcysyllte and Chester'. The eastern line prevailed, and in 1805 it was completed through Shropshire to join the older Chester Canal. Much later this gave direct access to the heart of the canal network in the English Midlands through Telford's Birmingham

and Liverpool Junction Canal, completed in 1835, and the two merged as the Shropshire Union Canal Company.

Serving the coalfields was the most momentous function of British canals, and the great crossings of the Ceiriog and Dee valleys were shaped in part by the desire for the direct line to the Mersey and in part by the need for access to coal reserves and iron-making enterprises. Consideration was given to carrying coal over the Dee valley by a horse-worked railway on a viaduct, but it was decided to complete the aqueduct and serve the areas further north by railways. The opening of the structure on 26 November 1805 represented the completion of the main line of the canal as it was now intended. Symbolically, the inaugural procession included two empty barges to be filled with coal at Trevor Basin.

As the ambition of some proprietors to reach Chester directly was never realised, Pontcysyllte Aqueduct has sometimes been portrayed as a magnificent structure that did not fulfil an economic purpose. However, the link to the nascent industrial area on the north side of the Dee remained a vitally-important strategic goal. The proprietors had decided not to complete the direct line before work on the aqueduct had much progressed, but they observed the direct economic benefits that the crossing of the valley would bring to the coalfield. The area's economic growth during more than forty years between 1805 and the building of main-line railways was enabled by the canal. The company's Chairman, Rowland Hunt, perceived its economic benefits in his oration at the opening, quoting a writer's observation: 'Wherever the Spirit of Commerce has touched the mountains on the whole borders of Wales, they began to smoke'.

Over a decade later, with trade growing rapidly, the French engineer and commentator Charles Dupin watched the boats coming and going across Pontcysyllte Aqueduct laden with coal and iron. He saw the canal as exemplary for having created a regional system connected to a national network that could link different sources of minerals and products and give access to Liverpool, Manchester, Ireland and London: 'The Ellesmere canal is perhaps the only example that can be produced in the three kingdoms, of a system of canals, combined in this manner for the special wants of the works in the mines, and of agriculture, while the supply of the manufactories and towns is an object of secondary importance; hence, the principal landholders of the valleys with which the canal of Ellesmere now opens a communication, were the persons who, as early as 1792, formed the company to which this noble enterprise owes its origin. This is an example which should especially interest the provinces in the centre of France, the landholders in which may acquire an entirely new source of territorial riches, by combining a similar system of internal communication for the disposal of their agricultural produce.'

2.b.3 The builders of Pontcysyllte Aqueduct and Canal

The early nineteenth century was the age of the polymath virtuoso engineer, of Telford, Rennie, Fairbairn, the Jessops, the Brunels and the Stephensons. In no other period of English history were there so many engineers in private practice whose names are still recognized.

Barrie Trinder, *The Making of the Industrial Landscape* (1982)

Thomas Telford (1757-1834) was the most famous engineer of his generation, a design genius whose influence on civil engineering was manifold and permanent. Pontcysyllte Aqueduct was the earliest of his internationally recognised achievements and the work he chose to be depicted with in his portrait as first President of the Institution of Civil Engineers. William Jessop (1745-1814) is less celebrated, but he was the most prolific engineer of the early Canal Age and was revered by his contemporaries; Pontcysyllte Aqueduct was also his greatest monument.

Jessop was 48 when he was appointed engineer to the Ellesmere Canal in 1791. He had already built the Cromford Canal and the Leicester Navigation, had carried out improvements on the River Trent and worked extensively on the canals of Ireland. He was to become the dominant canal engineer of the ensuing years. As Charles Hadfield and Professor A.W. Skempton wrote in their biography of him, 'Then came Jessop – alone – to tower over the period from 1785 to 1805. On his shoulders fell the weight of the canal mania.' Jessop's expertise was wide. In 1792 he had become a founder-partner in the Butterley Company, an iron-working concern in Derbyshire, and he was regarded as an authority on the structural use of iron. He was building railways as early as 1790. While working on the Ellesmere Canal he was responsible for the construction of the West India Dock in London and the massive floating harbour in Bristol, for the Croydon, Merstham and Godstone Iron Railway, and the Grand Junction Canal, which linked the Midlands directly with London.

Far left: A marble bust of Thomas Telford by Peter Hollins at the Institution of Civil Engineers.

Left: William Jessop around the time that work started on the Ellesmere Canal, after a drawing by George Dance, 1796.

He was influential on the generations that followed. The *Edinburgh Encyclopaedia* said of him in a biographical article of 1817, 'Totally free of all envy and jealousy of professional rivalship, his proceedings… were free from all pomp and mysticism, and persons of merit never failed in obtaining his friendship and encouragement.' He was one of the earliest members of the Smeatonian Society, which first gave recognition to civil engineering as a profession distinct from military engineering. Jessop joined the Society in 1773, two years after its foundation, and he was its Secretary for eighteen years.

Jessop had four assistants to lay out the Ellesmere Canal, Thomas Dadford junior, William Turner, John Duncombe and Thomas Denson. However, on 23 September 1793 Thomas Telford was appointed as 'General Agent, Surveyor, Engineer, Architect and Overlooker of the Works'. Sir Neil Cossons has written, 'Thomas Telford was one of the giants of

PONT Y CYSSYLLTE,
IN THE VALE OF LLANCOLLEN, DENBIGHSHIRE.

Left: An engraving looking across the canal at Froncysyllte towards Pontcysyllte Aqueduct, published in 1830 after a drawing by Henry Gastineau.

his age, a man of boundless energy and intellectual curiosity who helped to define the nineteenth century as the heroic age of engineering.' Yet he was only 36 and had no experience of waterways when he was appointed to the Ellesmere Canal. This was to be the turning point of his career. It gave him the opportunity to tackle a substantial engineering project and show the innovatory powers of design and management that would make him world famous.

Telford's life is one of the great stories of advancement from lowly origins to international influence. It was recounted famously by Samuel Smiles in his *Lives of the Engineers* (1867), and numerous biographies have been written since. He was born the son of a shepherd in lowland Scotland, who died when he was three months old. He was apprenticed as a stonemason aged 13, then gained work in Edinburgh, London and Portsmouth and in 1787 arrived in Shrewsbury to rebuild the medieval castle as a fashionable town house for his patron, William Pulteney. He began to practise as an architect with great success, but his appointment to the part-time post of county surveyor involved him with bridge design. Telford came to be part of an informal grouping of Enlightenment intellectuals in Shropshire that included the polymath ironmaster William Reynolds, the agricultural improver Joseph Plymley, the philosopher Archibald Alison, and Charles Bage, designer of the iron-framed Ditherington Mill at Shrewsbury. Men like Reynolds and Bage knew more than any of their contemporaries about the structural properties of iron. Telford was also close to the poet Robert Southey and wrote poetry himself. He was politically radical, demonstrating his Enlightenment thinking by distributing tracts to Scottish peasants and writing in 1791 in favour of 'some single revolution' in Britain.

Telford quickly developed knowledge of the use of iron in construction. In 1795 he completed an iron bridge across the River Severn at Buildwas and in 1796, as engineer for the Shrewsbury Canal, he designed the Longdon Aqueduct in iron. In 1801, with breathtaking foresight, he proposed an iron bridge to cross the Thames in London in a single span. He went on to design the most modern and efficient canals of the Canal Age, taking the ideas pioneered with Jessop on the Ellesmere Canal to their logical conclusions in waterways such as the Birmingham and Liverpool Junction Canal, the Caledonian Canal and the Gloucester and Berkeley Ship Canal. In Sweden he worked on the 118 miles / 190 kilometres long Göta Canal from 1809 to 1833 and was knighted for his services to the country. As a road and bridge engineer he was responsible for over 900 miles / 1,450 kilometres of road and 1,000 bridges, including the Holyhead Road to link London and Dublin through north Wales. His majestic Menai suspension bridge from the north Wales mainland to Anglesey in 1826 was justly regarded as one of the wonders of the age. Telford became known in his own lifetime as 'Pontifex Maximus' and his work was extensively published. He is recognised internationally as one of the outstanding figures in the rise of civil engineering as a profession.

The responsibility for the daring innovation of Pontcysyllte Aqueduct must be shared between Telford, the inspired younger man, and Jessop, the responsible consulting engineer. Rowland Hunt, in his oration at the opening of Pontcysyllte Aqueduct praised, 'our General Agent, Mr Telford, who with the advice and judgement of our eminent and much respected Engineer, Mr Jessop, invented and with unabating diligence carried the whole into execution'. The project was an early example of the shared professional responsibility that became a hallmark of engineering practice and involved not one but two of the great civil engineers of the Industrial Revolution.

One of the achievements of Jessop and Telford was to create around them a team of highly-skilled and trusted engineers and craftsmen: the division of labour between these individuals became the preferred model for future practice. Members of their teams continued to work together. John Simpson, 'the accurate mason who erected the pillars', was a contractor for masonry at both aqueducts and other work on the tunnels and cuttings. Telford regarded him as a 'treasure of talents and integrity'. He went on with Telford and Jessop to their great Caledonian Canal project in Scotland. Matthew Davidson, who acted as the clerk of works at Pontcysyllte, supervised bridges for Telford in Shropshire and went to the Caledonian Canal. John Wilson, a stonemason for Chirk and Pontcysyllte, proceeded to the Caledonian Canal, the Göta Canal and the Menai Bridge. William Davies was responsible for the main cuttings and most of the embankment at Froncysyllte and also went on to the great Caledonian venture. Hunt called William Hazledine 'the spirited founder of the Duct itself'. He came from a family in the Shropshire iron trade and established a foundry at Plas Kynaston from which he supplied the cast iron for Chirk and Pontcysyllte. He later developed a substantial local business in coal and lime and continued to supply components for Telford's major civil engineering projects.

2.b.4 The construction of Pontcysyllte Aqueduct and Canal

Pontcysyllte aqueduct… perhaps the greatest monument in stone of English canal engineering, is over a thousand feet long and 121 feet above the river. On the same canal may be seen the Chirk aqueduct and tunnel. Telford's canals took a much more direct course than Brindley's, and so involved much more dramatic engineering…

W.G. Hoskins, *The Making of the English Landscape* (1955)

The challenging landscape of the Welsh uplands stimulated the canal's engineers to consider new methods through a constant exchange of ideas and practice between previous engineering achievements and current investigations. The dynamic relationship between Jessop, the prolific master canal-builder, and Telford, the younger engineering genius, was highly productive. The designs for the canal and its features were revised constantly in the light of the problems encountered

A contemporary drawing of the partially-completed piers of Pontcysyllte Aqueduct, showing one of the several levels of temporary construction decks.

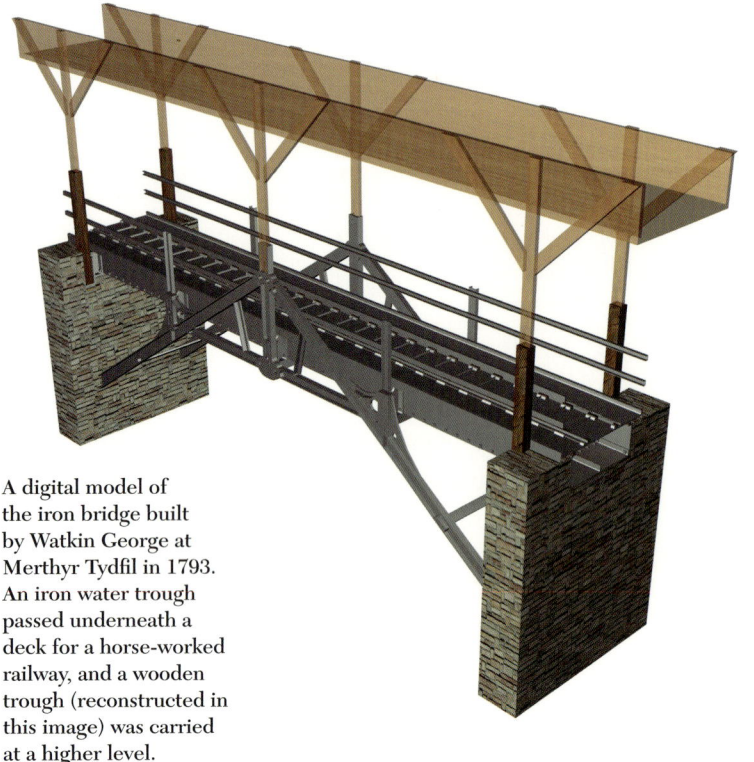

A digital model of the iron bridge built by Watkin George at Merthyr Tydfil in 1793. An iron water trough passed underneath a deck for a horse-worked railway, and a wooden trough (reconstructed in this image) was carried at a higher level.

Robert Fulton, the American inventor, engraved after a portrait by Chappel in 1800.

A digital model of the Vyrnwy Aqueduct on the Montgomeryshire Canal, showing the traditional construction of aqueducts with masonry waterproofed with heavy puddled-clay, a source of instability in larger or higher spans.

and new solutions devised. It became the testing ground for ideas that were carried forward into subsequent engineering and management practice internationally. In organisation, innovations included principles of contract management, delegation of duties within engineering teams and the professional independence of engineers. In technology, they included hollow masonry and new waterproofing methods to reduce weight, composite use of cast iron and stone, earthwork calculations, multiple construction railways, barrow-inclines and cut-and-cover tunnels.

Construction within the Nominated Site began at the eastern end in 1795. Contracts were let for the terraced rock cutting and embankment at Chirk Bank, a massive earthwork in its own right. Telford identified a suitable source of building stone and began a quarry in the hillside next to the canal, opening onto the terrace for ease of transport. He made detailed cut-and-fill calculations to minimise the movement of spoil and permit the creation of a large, level platform to act as the construction yard for the aqueduct. Telford and Jessop had originally planned a relatively small structure across the River Ceiriog, to be built traditionally with stone and puddled clay, in the middle of an earthwork embankment. The proposal was vetoed by Richard Myddleton of Chirk Castle, who was an influential shareholder in the canal company, on the grounds that the views in his estate would be spoiled. The initial response was to detour upstream, where a less obtrusive embankment and aqueduct could be built, but in due course a more monumental aqueduct was preferred.

The projected crossings of both the Ceiriog and Dee became part of the debate on iron structures that pervaded engineering thinking in Britain in the 1790s. Jessop ordered a complete reassessment of the existing proposals for Chirk Aqueduct when serious structural defects in conventional puddled-clay aqueducts being built on other canals began to come to light. The Iron Bridge at Coalbrookdale of 1781 had been a spectacular demonstration of the potential of cast iron and had become justly famous as the starting point of iron construction in Britain. In 1793 an ironworks engineer at Merthyr Tydfil in south Wales, Watkin George, had constructed Pont-y-Cafnau, an iron bridge carrying a horse-worked railway and a trough for water power. This had been recorded by the ironmaster William Reynolds, beginning an exchange that informed work on the Ellesmere Canal.

Both of the engineers of Pontcysyllte Aqueduct and Canal were also aware of a wider contemporary interchange of ideas about iron structures. The political philosopher of the American and French Revolutions, Tom Paine, had exhibited parts of an iron bridge in London in 1790-1. Two iron bridges designed by John Rennie were sent to the island of Nevis in 1791 and 1794. In 1795, the architect John Nash threw an iron bridge over the River Teme, and Rowland Burdon built a 236 feet / 72.7 metre bridge of iron voussoirs near Sunderland that became celebrated, leading to similar structures over the River Thames, in Jamaica and elsewhere. Also in 1795, the American Robert Fulton proposed a 90 feet /27.5 metres high iron aqueduct on the Peak Forest Canal that stimulated new thinking, though it was never built.

Such consideration of the possibilities of iron was the milieu of Jessop and Telford's decision-making at Chirk. In March 1794, Telford made a sketch of an iron trough supported on iron towers in a location that could be Pontcysyllte (page 87). Jessop reported in 1795 to the canal committee, 'It was originally proposed to cross the Chirk valley a little above Chirk Bridge… it would still be desirable to adopt the first idea, and if instead of an embankment of earth, which would shut up the view of the valley, it should be crossed by an iron aqueduct I should hope the objection might be removed, as instead of an obstruction it would be a romantic feature in the view.'

An opportunity for Telford to try out an iron aqueduct came in the same year, when the partially-built masonry aqueduct on the Shrewsbury Canal at Longdon was destroyed by floods. Telford worked with Reynolds to carry out experiments to test to destruction various structural elements. The resulting, low iron trough supported by bracing struts was opened on 14 March 1796. At the same time Telford built his first iron bridge, at Buildwas, and undertook a detailed study of the Iron Bridge at

Telford's Longdon Aqueduct of 1796 on the Shrewsbury Canal.

Detail of one of the composite masonry and iron bridges at Trevor Basin.

Coalbrookdale, noting that the arch was deflecting through abutment pressures and criticising its architectural embellishments. At Chirk Bank he designed the first of the three innovative composite bridges in the Nominated Site, which have flat masonry arches supported on cast-iron beams – probably completed sometime between 1795 and 1800. Jessop, too, was assessing iron aqueducts and was involved with his partner in the Butterley Iron Company, Benjamin Outram, in completing a 44 feet / 16.7 metre long cast-iron aqueduct on the Derby Canal in 1795-6.

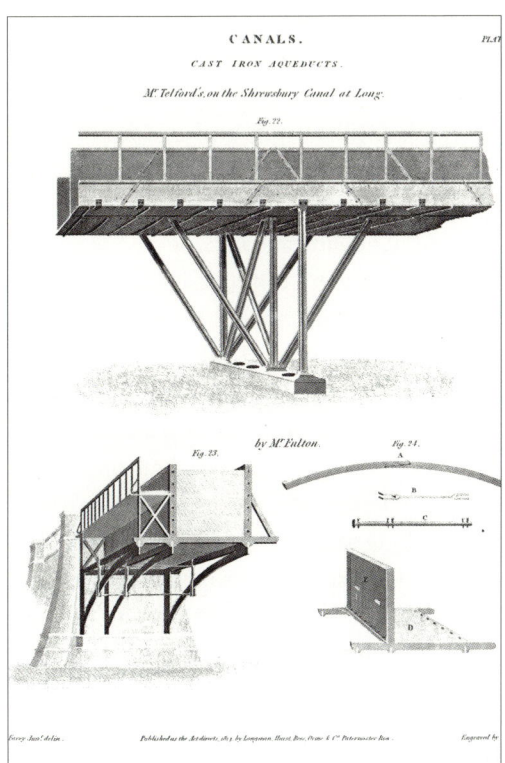

CANALS.

CAST IRON AQUEDUCTS.

Mr Telford's, on the Shrewsbury Canal at Longd.

Fig. 22.

by Mr Fulton.

Fig. 23.   Fig. 24.

A plate from Rees's *Cyclopaedia* illustrating thinking on iron aqueducts at the time that Pontcysyllte Aqueduct was being built.

Chirk Aqueduct, with a construction deck and six of the ten arches completed, in a watercolour drawn by Sir Richard Colt Hoare on 6 June 1799, when he wrote in his diary that he 'stopped to take a view of the noble aqueduct forming across the valley'. The resident engineers' house Telford Lodge is in the distance.

The foundation stone at Chirk was laid in June 1796, but before construction began Telford altered the proposal to replace the iron trough with stone arches, lightened by having hollow spandrels strengthened by cross walls. Longdon Aqueduct had shown signs of flexing, and the time may have not seemed right for an all-iron trough to be tried at Chirk, which was to be the tallest navigable aqueduct ever built. Chirk's design was still a breakthrough compared with conventional aqueducts in its reduced breadth and lighter foundation loading – essential qualities in an aqueduct of such height. Costs were estimated for a trough of stone slabs with brick side walls, similar to Roman aqueducts. However, it was eventually decided to reintroduce cast iron in the form of one-inch thick plates bolted together to form the base of the trough. These could straddle the arches and cross walls and tie together the sides, preventing the structural spreading that had distorted recent puddled-clay aqueducts. The sides of the trough were constructed of hard-burnt bricks, sealed with the newly-patented hydraulic mortar known as Parker's Cement and faced with stone blocks.

Chirk Aqueduct was opened with complete success in 1801. It was both physically and visually light. The balanced proportions were made possible by the new methods, permitting a shallow deck above the arches. Telford believed that the beauty of an object depended on its fitness for purpose and was conscious of the serene effect of high multi-arch Roman aqueducts. He commented with satisfaction on the noble qualities of the new structure. Unlike the Iron Bridge at Coalbrookdale, or the contemporary stone aqueducts of John Rennie, it offered a clear, functional design without architectural embellishment.

By the time that Chirk Aqueduct was completed, the long line of cuttings and tunnels to the north was still underway. Telford was responsible for the first substantial canal tunnels in Britain to have towing-paths – Berwick Tunnel on the Shrewsbury Canal, opened in 1797, and Chirk, completed in 1801. The wider bore needed to accommodate the path was a major investment, but horse-towing removed the congestion otherwise caused by 'legging' the boats through. Considerable attention was given by Telford to the surest methods for constructing the tunnels, and the use of cut-and-cover techniques, rather than boring and lining, contributed to the quality of the wide arches and reduced the risks of damage by percolating water. The cuttings were made exceptionally wide in comparison to previous practice, so that they did not form bottle-necks to traffic. Vast quantities of spoil had to be removed and Telford was responsible for introducing 'cut-and-fill calculations' to obviate any waste of effort, which could be substantial on such colossal works. The importance of this was recognised at the time. At the opening of the canal, Rowland Hunt praised the 'well-computed labours' of the contractor, William Davies.

Within a year of Chirk Aqueduct being opened the canal had been extended onwards to Froncysyllte. Here, the great approach embankment towards Pontcysyllte was being built with the aid of construction railways that brought spoil from the cuttings and tunnels. Froncysyllte was to remain the canal terminus for three years while the aqueduct was completed.

While they were learning lessons at Chirk Aqueduct, the engineers developed their plans for the even more demanding challenge of the Dee Valley. Jessop had always advised a high-level crossing but by the time that Telford was appointed in 1793 the proprietors had agreed to the more feasible solution, given the technology of the moment, of a three-span aqueduct at a low level, approached by flights of locks on either side. Telford was dissatisfied, foreseeing that the water supply would be insufficient to support a large volume of traffic through the locks. His sketch of 1794 for an iron aqueduct revitalised the high-level crossing by removing the thick walls and puddled-clay that would have been unsustainable at such a height. Telford wrote to his friend Andrew Little in March 1795 that he had recommended an iron aqueduct, and on 14 July Jessop reported, 'I must now recommend to the Committee to make this saving by adopting an Iron Aqueduct at the full height originally intended…'. He proposed a cast-iron trough on eight stone piers, 50 feet / 15.2 metres apart between

John Rennie's Lune Aqueduct, a substantial masonry structure with architectural detailing that contrasted strongly with the functionalism of Chirk.

long earthen embankments. Support was provided on the canal committee by the ironmasters William Reynolds and John Wilkinson and on 25 July 1795 the foundation stone was laid by Richard Myddleton MP.

Telford prepared detailed specifications and drawings during 1796 and tenders were sought for the ironwork, but in 1799 work at Pontcysyllte was suspended to expedite completion of the aqueduct at Chirk. Construction of the abutments and piers

Telford's sketch of March 1794 representing an idea for an all-iron aqueduct in a location that could be Pontcysyllte.

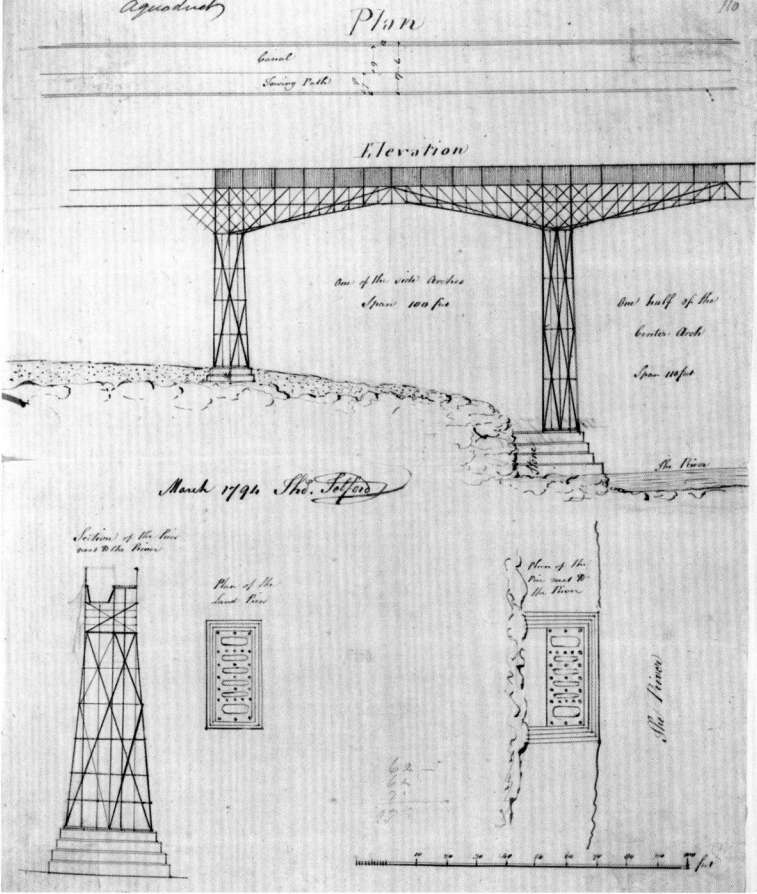

Telford's wooden scale model to test the fitting of the component of Pontcysyllte Aqueduct, now in the National Waterways Museum.

resumed early in 1800. Jessop observed that '…the columns without any exception, are executed in a more masterly manner than anything of the kind that I have seen before'. Telford doubled the length of the design to nineteen spans.

The work on the piers was radical in several ways. First, they were designed to minimise weight by tapering and having hollow upper sections with strengthening cross-walls. Second, they were erected using temporary gangways, allowing materials to be brought from the construction yard, probably on railways, at successive levels as the piers were raised. Third, the engineers gave unusual attention to the safety of the workforce. Jessop had written to Telford in 1795, 'In looking forward to the time when we shall be laying the Iron Trough on the Piers I foresee some difficulties that appear to me formidable – In the first place I see the men giddy and terrified in laying stones with such an immense depth underneath them with only a space of 6 feet wide and 10 feet long to stand upon.' He recommended that the piers be widened. In 1800 he proposed the hollow upper sections: 'it will save five or six hundred pounds in the expence; and what to me appears most material, it will afford safety to the workmen.' Telford

recalled in his autobiography, '…one man only fell during the whole of the operations in building the piers, and affixing the iron work upon their summit, and this took place from carelessness on his part.'

In November 1801 the committee resolved that the columns should carry an iron trough (rather than a railway, as considered for a time after the canal to Chester had been rejected), and in March 1802 a contract was signed with Hazledine to supply the ironwork and fix it in place. Telford commissioned a wooden model of one span, now in the National Waterways Museum, to test the arrangements. By November 1804 the arches and trough had been erected over nine spans and further components were at Trevor Basin awaiting erection. The workmen gained such familiarity with the methods that the aqueduct was completed in 1805. The total cost was £47,018. In November, the main line of the canal was opened in a meticulously arranged ceremony. A procession of boats crossed Pontcysyllte Aqueduct to the accompaniment of music and gunfire and the cheers of 8,000 spectators. The canal was already serving to promote a continuing exchange of ideas and it was immediately recognised as a spectacular achievement.

Work shifted from 1804 to the construction of the Llangollen Branch, now essential to provide a safe supply of water to the canal. Telford was the principal engineer for this project, with Thomas Denson as his assistant. The techniques developed on the main line were carried forward into the branch canal, most importantly in the construction of terrace embankments. The junction was marked by another composite iron and masonry over-bridge. Work was also carried out to control the flow of water into the River Dee by raising the level of Llyn Tegid at Bala: an important early example of a large water control scheme. Cutting proceeded rapidly, and the line and the weir at Horseshoe Falls were opened in 1808, completing the Ellesmere Canal network as it was to be built and providing it with a sure supply of water.

Analysis of the piers at Pontcysyllte Aqueduct shows evidence of the construction decks.

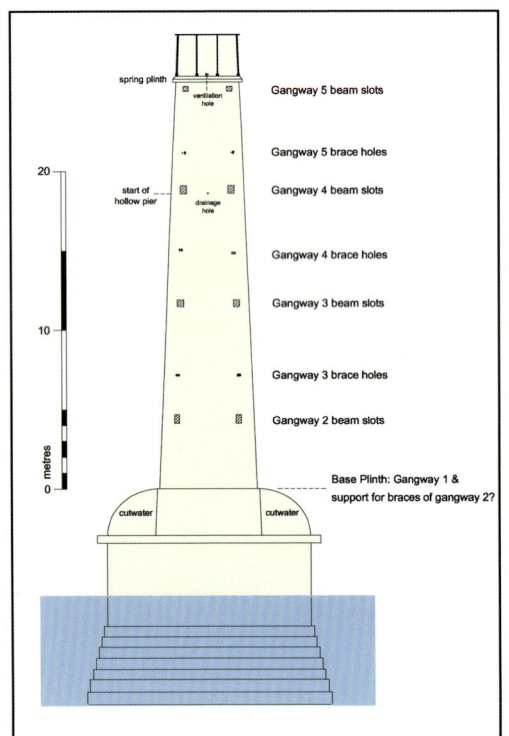

2.b.5 Contemporary perceptions of Pontcysyllte Aqueduct and Canal

The approach from Llangollen presents a most delightful scenery of hill and valley, terminated by these lofty pillars supporting their well-turned arches; the whole affords a view of beauty and grandeur, rarely exceeded by nature or art.

Oliver Oldschool, *The Port Folio*
(Philadelphia, 1809)

Throughout the period of the canal's construction, the area was visited by artists, poets, architects and other influential people taking the tour of Wales. Pontcysyllte Aqueduct made a powerful impression on the contemporary imagination and was perceived as something more than a component of an inland navigation system. The first generation of visitors regarded it as a work of art, in its broadest sense, and a masterpiece of human ingenuity as well as a utilitarian structure. Early visitors to the canal included the Duke of Wellington and writers of the Romantic movement such as Sir Walter Scott, Percy Bysshe Shelley, Robert Southey and William Wordsworth. After war with France ended in 1815 foreign visitors were drawn by both the Romantic impulse and a fascination with the new world of technology and industry that Britain embodied. The north Wales tour, through Llangollen, continued to be favoured during the nineteenth century: later visitors to the area included Felix Mendelssohn, John Ruskin, Charles Darwin, Queen Victoria and the Austrian diplomat Prince Paul Esterházy.

Chirk Aqueduct, the first major structure to be completed, was praised by all who saw it. In the eyes of contemporaries Jessop's ambition to create a Romantic feature in the view had been fulfilled. Even before it was finished the antiquarian and artist Sir Richard Colt Hoare wrote, 'From the length of this building, the straight lines and light piers which intersect the valley it has a pleasing effect even in its imperfect state. When finished it will have the most grand and picturesque appearance.' John Sell Cotman, one of the greatest British

John Sell Cotman's glowing depiction of Chirk Aqueduct after his visit in 1801.

landscape painters, visited it in 1801. In a now-famous watercolour (probably done from memory, given its discrepancies of detail) he captured the grandeur of the structure and depicted it as though a work of antiquity entirely sympathetic to the natural beauty of its setting. The art historian Francis Klingender noted that Cotman's depiction 'demonstrates how profoundly his classical sense of design was stirred by the massive simplicity of that great engineering work.'

All visitors to the area were drawn to Pontcysyllte Aqueduct, and all commented on it favourably. Many ranked it with the great works of antiquity. The words most often used to describe it underline the general perception of it as a masterpiece: supreme, magnificent, beautiful, wonderful, and stupendous. Southey wrote of,
'Telford who o'er the vale of Cambrian Dee
  Aloft in air at giddy height upborne
  Carried his Navigable road.'

Pontcysyllte viewed as a grand work of man in a Claudian landscape, in a painting by James Gibb.

The American writer Washington Irving called it 'that stupendous work'. Numerous drawings and engravings were produced of the aqueduct, emphasising above all its delicacy and rhythm against the backdrop of wild scenery.

A report written in 1804 declared Pontcysyllte Aqueduct 'one of the most extraordinary efforts of human art', and William Mavor, who saw it in 1805, considered it 'one of the most stupendous works of art that was ever accomplished by man'.

Engineers and scientists who visited were equally impressed. Charles Dupin, visiting from France in 1816, called it 'something enchanted' and 'a supreme work of architecture, elegant and unadorned' (see page 35). Michael Faraday, the great scientist, crossed the aqueduct in 1819, noting that it was 'too grand a thing to be hastily passed' and observing as he viewed it from the ancient road bridge below that 'it seemed light as a cloud'. The great Prussian architect Karl Friedrich Schinkel saw the significance of the aqueduct in the context of

Chirk Aqueduct in an engraving after a drawing by Henry Gastineau, 1830.

the canal when he visited in 1826: 'We first saw Pontcysyllte, where a beautiful valley is crossed by a canal on 19 arches of cast iron supported by 90 feet high piers; a section of the canal goes across an embankment of heaped-up earth. A mile or so further on the canal goes through a cutting through a hill, and then crosses another valley on a series of great arches' (translated by Barrie Trinder).

The Canal Company Chairman, Rowland Hunt, had travelled extensively but saw Pontcysyllte Aqueduct as comparable with the great monuments of Classical civilisations. 'Antiquity', he said in his opening oration, 'has produced no structure as an Aqueduct, which can compare with Pontcysyllte', and went on to describe the Pont du Gard. He compared the new structure with the great aqueduct at Lisbon, the engineering works constructed by Louis XIV in connection with fountains at Versailles, and the reservoir of St Ferriol on the Canal du Midi. He argued that while the aqueducts of antiquity were designed either for amusement or for domestic uses,

'Pontcysyllte is destined to convey the Riches of the mineral Kingdom into the World of Industry, and thence to every part of the Universe'.

Hunt perceived the achievement in several contemporary contexts. He saw the canal as part of the waterways system that had developed from the pioneering enterprises of the Duke of Bridgewater, 'our great national commercial patron'. He saw Pontcysyllte Aqueduct as a structure made possible by Britain's flourishing iron industry, and acknowledged that it continued a sequence of notable structures that began with the Iron Bridge at Coalbrookdale. In a wider engineering context he placed Pontcysyllte alongside the works of James Watt and Matthew Boulton, makers of steam engines, and John Smeaton, the earlier engineering genius. He perceived it as part of those contemporary developments in manufacturing and transport that later generations were to call the Industrial Revolution.

Chirk Aqueduct viewed as an eye-catching monument in a mountain landscape: a painting by John Varley (1778-1842).

2.b.6 The influence of Pontcysyllte Aqueduct and Canal

Great civil engineers leave their own monuments; they are remembered for what they build. These three have further claims on posterity [Thomas Telford, Eugène Freyssinet and Karl Terzaghi]. Each of them was responsible for great works that alone were sufficient to establish his reputation; but in addition, each changed, on a world-wide basis, the practice of his profession.'

John. H. Stephens, *Structures* (1976)

The canal within the Nominated Site exemplifies a number of waterways that were significantly more ambitious than those which preceded them. New ideas were developed or brought together in response to the particular challenges of the Welsh uplands to create what may be understood to be the first canal of the 'heroic', rather than the 'pioneering', age. It symbolises the transition from transport routes that followed the landscape to those that commanded it. Such canals affected the course of transport development and future thinking about construction and design. The ensuing interchange of values extended between countries and across time by several means.

The canals of the Industrial Revolution in Britain were visited and studied by engineers from many countries and British canal engineers took their skills overseas. Having adopted ideas initially from waterways in Europe, by the early nineteenth century Britain could demonstrate the potential of canals in industrialising countries. Its industrial transport system drew statesmen, entrepreneurs and engineers from many parts of Europe and America to study it, and many took away knowledge to apply elsewhere. One visitor, for example, was the American engineer Canvass White, who was sent to Europe in 1817 by the New York State Governor to study canal construction. He walked 2,000 miles / 3,387 kilometres along British canals and returned with notes, drawings and instruments to assist work on the Erie Canal. The features within the Nominated Site were among the greatest sources of such inspiration.

The transfer of canal technology to North America began with the decision of improvers in Pennsylvania to seek advice from William Jessop. On Jessop's recommendation, William Weston, who had worked under him on plans for the Ellesmere Canal, sailed for the United States in 1792 to spend several years designing canal schemes and training American engineers (including Benjamin Wright, who took charge of the Erie Canal). One of Telford's assistants, Hamilton Fulton, was appointed on his advice as state engineer to North Carolina and Georgia. In Canada, the British engineers Colonel John By and N.H. Baird designed the Rideau Canal. British engineers also designed the great Ganges Canal in India.

The British model was influential in many parts of Europe in the crucial stages of industrialisation. Schinkel was among a multitude of influential people from Germany who saw Pontcysyllte, including Prince Hermann von Pückler-Muskau, who described it as 'a work which would have done honour to Rome', and the librarian to the King of Prussia, who referred to 'the magnificent aqueduct'. Count Baltzar von Platen of Sweden toured Britain with Telford for several months in preparation for work on the Göta Canal. The Canal du Berry and Canal de l'Ourcq in France both followed the British model and in 1818 Francois Becquey, the director of the Bureau des ponts et chausées, sent three engineers to Britain for several months, one of whom, J.M. Dutens, travelled 1,800 miles / 2,900 kilometres. The result was Becquey's influential report to the King to provide France with a comprehensive network in the manner of the British system, with canals of a yet larger scale. Important canals built in the Dutch-Belgian kingdom after 1815 learned from Telford's Caledonian and Gloucester and Berkeley ship canals.

The influence was also disseminated in print. Publications in French to draw lessons from British canals included Dutens' *Mémoires sur les travaux publiques de l'Angleterre* and *Atlas de la Navigation Intérieure de l'Angleterre et de la France,* both published in 1819, and *Des canaux navigables considérés d'une manière générale, avec des recherches comparatives sur la navigation intérieure de la France et celle de l'Angleterre* (1822). Charles Dupin provided detailed descriptions of many British canals in his six-volume *Voyages dans la Grande-Bretagne* (1820-24). His work was published in English as *The Commercial Power of Great Britain* (1825). Dupin recognised the success of the Ellesmere Canal in particular in creating a regional system and commended it for application in France (see above, page 80). He continued with regard to the engineering aspects of the Nominated Site: 'The Ellesmere canal, so remarkable for its object and extent, is no less so for the beauty of several works of art, the merit of which we were the first to make known to the engineers of the Continent. It must claim the attention of scientific men…'. He included descriptions of the aqueducts, cuttings, tunnels and basins and elevations and sections of Chirk and Pontcysyllte aqueducts

British publications included John Phillips's *General History of Inland Navigation, Foreign and Domestic* (1803) and Abraham Rees's thirty-nine volume *Cyclopaedia or Universal Dictionary of Arts, Sciences and Literature* – in which the 150-page article on canals, dated 1806, identified the 'most stupendous work' at Pontcysyllte. Information about Pontcysyllte was published in journals such as *The Mechanics Magazine* and *The Edinburgh Encyclopaedia*, and in Telford's autobiography and *Atlas*. In the United States of America, the architect and engineer William Strickland was commissioned by the Pennsylvania Society for the Promotion of Internal Improvement in 1825 to visit Britain for his influential *Reports on Canals, Railways, Roads and Other Subjects*. James Renwick of Columbia University wrote about cast iron construction in 1822, 'Cast iron has, of late years, been used in Great Britain for the construction of aqueducts, and with much advantage. The most magnificent work of this sort is on the Ellesmere Canal, in

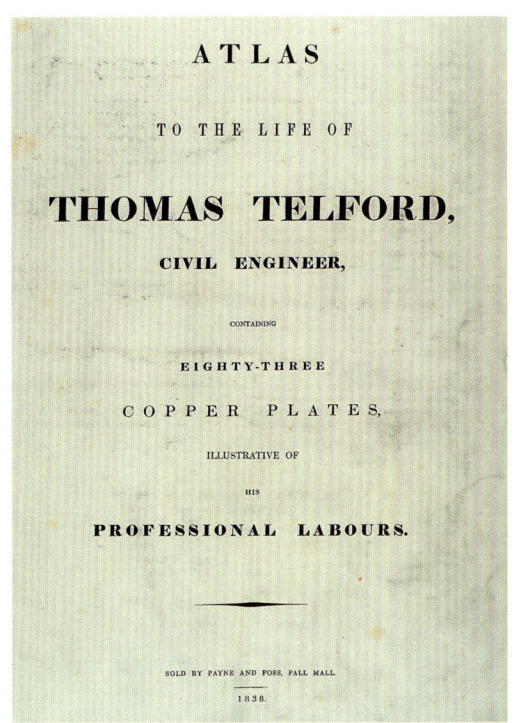

ATLAS

TO THE LIFE OF

THOMAS TELFORD,

CIVIL ENGINEER,

CONTAINING

EIGHTY-THREE

COPPER PLATES,

ILLUSTRATIVE OF

HIS

PROFESSIONAL LABOURS.

SOLD BY PAYNE AND FOSS, PALL MALL.
1838.

The Atlas accompanying the Life of Telford made drawings of all his major works widely available when it was published in 1838.

the Vale of Llangollen, Wales.' Renwick enlarged on this in his *Applications of the Science of Mechanics to Practical Purposes* (New York, 1844).

Their experience of innovation on the Ellesmere Canal informed Telford and Jessop's later projects for canals, docks, roads, railways and bridges, thereby influencing others in Britain and overseas. Jessop's reputation resulted in contact with canal promoters from several countries. Telford became the most prolific engineer of the age – in the 1820s it was said that there was no civil engineering project in Britain in which he was not involved. He advised on canal-building in Nova Scotia, India and Russia and on projects in Sweden for twenty years from 1808. The protégés of both engineers went on to influence future generations in many countries. Through their pivotal roles in the two early institutions for civil engineering they helped numerous individuals and permanently established the profession: the Institution of Civil Engineers now has 80,000 members worldwide. Many who worked for Jessop and Telford on the Ellesmere Canal followed them to the Caledonian Canal in Scotland, built from 1803 to 1822, where many techniques developed at Pontcysyllte

Telford and Jessop took their new ideas of bold engineering to the Caledonian Canal in Scotland, 1803-22, which was capable of carrying ocean-going ships.

were applied to a waterway that would accommodate ocean-going warships. Several went with Telford to Sweden to plan the Göta Canal and set up the workshops at Motala, which were acknowledged as the main training ground for engineers in that country. Key figures in the first generation of locomotive railway builders were influenced directly by Telford: John and William Hughes, contractors on the Ellesmere Canal, worked on the London and Birmingham Railway in the 1830s; William Cubitt designed some of the major railways of England and undertook projects in Germany and France; Thomas Brassey went on as a contractor to build a high proportion of the railways of England, France, Canada, Australia, South America and India.

Through all these means, a continuing interchange took place with regard to ideas that had been developed or brought together in the Nominated Site. The dynamic relationship between Jessop, the prolific master canal-builder, and Telford, the younger engineering genius, made the canal a testing ground for new ideas. Among many technical developments, several of particular importance were carried forward into future projects.

- **Boldly-engineered routes that commanded the landscape:** The section of canal in the Nominated Site was among the earliest transport routes to emphasise the intensive use of cuttings, tunnels, aqueducts and embankments to create a wide, level and direct route. It contrasted strongly with earlier canals and represented a significant increase in construction cost and effort in order to permit efficient operation. With other heroic era canals it set new standards and Telford went on to design others that took absolutely straight routes. The principles of such engineering were fundamental to the ability to build railways and later roads and became normal practice internationally.

- **Metal aqueducts:** Pontcysyllte's success inspired over forty cast-iron aqueducts during the rest of the canal age in Britain. Six years after its completion, Benjamin Bevan designed an iron aqueduct on the Grand Junction Canal after visiting Chirk and Pontcysyllte. Three large aqueducts were built on the Edinburgh and Glasgow Union Canal in 1817-22: their engineer, Hugh Baird, consulted Telford and was referred to the iron founder of Pontcysyllte. Metal aqueducts continued

to evolve in the late nineteenth century with wrought iron and steel, in Britain, Sweden, France, Belgium, Canada, the United States of America and elsewhere. They became essential as approach structures to vertical boat lifts in many countries after 1875. In 1896 a 2,172 feet /662-metres steel structure on the Canal latéral à la Loire in France became the longest aqueduct yet built.

- **Iron in construction:** The achievements in the Nominated Site were part of a sequence of innovations and developments that led to the general acceptance of iron and then steel as ubiquitous construction materials and enabled ever-greater achievements. Britain in the late eighteenth and early nineteenth centuries was the leading centre of innovation in the iron industry and pioneered new uses of the material in bridges and buildings. According to the ICOMOS/TICCIH *Context for World Heritage Bridges* (1997) Pontcysyllte represented 'extraordinarily innovative arrangements in which the cast iron had real structural value'. The prefabrication of lightweight elements that could be slid into position was revolutionary. The composite over-

bridges in the Nominated Site were also innovatory, paralleling methods used in the first iron-framed buildings, and Telford illustrated them in his *Atlas*. His work on the canal led to Telford's breathtaking but unfulfilled proposal in 1801 to cross the Thames in London with a single iron span, and his prodigious achievements with iron bridges became internationally renowned. For engineers and investors generally, Pontcysyllte proved potently the potential of iron. It promoted ongoing development in bridges and buildings in many countries: Robert Stephenson built a cast-iron railway viaduct at Newcastle, high wrought-iron viaducts by Wilhelm Nordling and Gustave Eiffel were features of railway-building in France, and the Forth Bridge in Scotland of 1890 had an influence on

Pontcysyllte Aqueduct and Cysyllte Bridge in 1826 by G. Arnold.

A cut-away drawing of a typical, small iron aqueduct following the model established by Pontcysyllte, on the Montgomeryshire Canal, 1819.

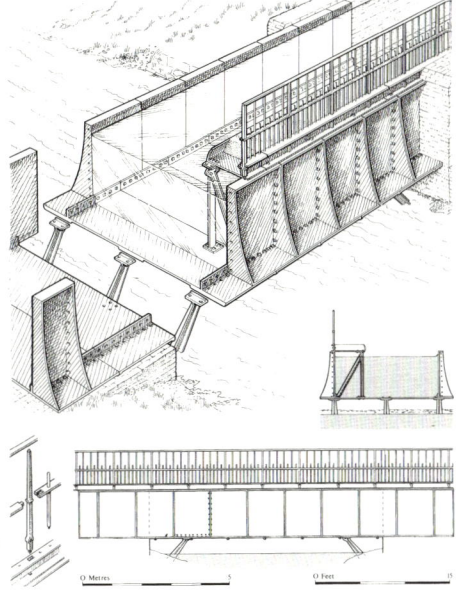

The clarity of design of Chirk Aqueduct achieved through its use of new materials.

civil engineering that paralleled that of Pontcysyllte almost a century earlier. Use of iron in buildings continued to be developed through American innovations in steel-frame construction, culminating in the commonplace structural use of steel beams and steel-reinforced concrete.

- **Functionalist design:** The French art historian Pierre Francastel, in the *Larousse Encyclopedia of Modern Art* (1961), identified the significance of a small number of architects, engineers and inventors who developed early iron construction, including Abraham Darby, François Brunet, Marc Seguin, Tom Paine, Rowland Burdon and Telford - 'these were the real initiators of an intellectual revolution that led to the idea of functionalism, and started the whole complicated evolution of modern architecture.' The acceptance of notable early iron structures that were true to their materials, such as Pontcysyllte, changed the aesthetics of engineering and architecture. Nikolaus Pevsner, in *Pioneers of Modern Design* (1960), asked when iron first became an aesthetic asset: 'One is inclined to say in iron bridges, because to us their resilience and elegance, made possible only by the use of iron, are aesthetically

so irresistible.' The new thinking was influential in a wider design context: as the architectural critic J.M. Richards wrote in connection with the structures of the Nominated Site in *The Functional Tradition in Early Industrial Buildings* (1958), the 'geometrical simplicity derived from the closest and most economical relationship between form, structure and materials, is the essence of the functional tradition'. Telford and Jessop consciously sought forms that would achieve nobility through simplicity and truth to materials rather than embellishment, in contrast to many contemporary designers. Their canal as a whole combined rigour of design with sensitivity to its impact on a valued landscape and set an example relevant to major civil engineering projects today.

- **Tunnels with towing-paths:** Telford's tunnels on the Shrewsbury Canal and the Ellesmere Canal were the first substantial tunnels on British canals to have towing-paths, though the Malpas Tunnel on the Canal du Midi had one earlier. Telford designed broader-bore tunnels with towing-paths that allowed water to circulate under them as boats passed. In the nineteenth century this became the norm internationally. In 1827

Telford designed the 2,926 yards / 2,676 metres Second Harecastle Tunnel on the Trent and Mersey Canal with a towing-path, supplementing a precursor that had become a bottleneck for increasing traffic. Chirk and Whitehouses Tunnels were built through an early use of cut-and-cover techniques, enabling more stable construction of wide bores. These were used subsequently in canal, railway and road construction wherever no great depth was required.

- **Construction railways:** The use of construction railways to move spoil for the earthworks of the canal and deliver materials for Pontcysyllte Aqueduct was not new but had never been carried out at this scale before. The practice was followed on the Caledonian Canal and published by Telford in his *Atlas*. Jessop and Telford also pioneered the use of animal-assisted barrow-run inclines to move spoil. These techniques were to be widely used in subsequent civil engineering projects internationally.

- **Double-tracked railways:** The extension of the transport route from Trevor Basin as a horse-worked railway in 1804-05 was part of a pattern followed by many contemporary canal companies. The idea of investing in double track to maximise efficiency was published by Telford in the *Edinburgh Encyclopaedia* and was to be copied many times in the succeeding three decades. Jessop built the Surrey Iron Railway in London and the Kilmarnock and Troon Railway in Scotland with double track.

The complexity and scale of engineering on the canal was made possible by a number of organisational innovations. New techniques were evolved for the organisation and resourcing of large engineering projects. Many of these were carried forward into subsequent management practice.

- **Division of responsibility between specialists:** Telford and Jessop created clear divisions that enabled them to delegate effectively to trained personnel, as evidenced in the houses built to accommodate the engineers who supervised the construction of the

A painting by Moses Griffiths, who observed Pontcysyllte Aqueduct under construction. Telford said that only one man lost his life during the work.

Whitehouses Tunnel, showing the path that permitted continuous towing by horses.

Cut-and-fill calculations and multiple construction railways enabled vast earthworks, such as the Froncysyllte Embankment, which was built with spoil brought from the cuttings and tunnels to the south.

Ellesmere Canal. This was elaborated further on the Caledonian Canal where, as at Pontcysyllte, Jessop was Consulting Engineer and Telford Chief Engineer. Both made an annual six-week tour to examine the work in progress. Two resident engineers there had previously been employed on the Ellesmere Canal, Matthew Davidson and John Telford. William Davies, who built the Froncysyllte embankment, was responsible for overseeing earthworks and John Simpson and John Wilson, who built the piers at Pontcysyllte, were in charge of the stonework. Such divisions of labour spread internationally and permitted the achievement of large engineering projects that are among the essential requirements of modern society.

- **Principles of contract management:** The system of management used to deliver the canal project made a separation between the design team and the contractors and employed detailed specifications, proven tenderers and rigorous monitoring. Telford was to develop this further on the Caledonian Canal and the Holyhead Road, which were Government-financed projects. The practices were open, transparent and accountable and became fundamental to large-scale projects. Sidney Pollard wrote in *The Genesis of Modern Management* (1965), 'It was the canal builders, and Thomas Telford in particular, who first called into being the large contracting firm, responsible, resourceful, and

pioneering in its own managerial solutions…'. Sir Alexander Gibb wrote in *The Story of Telford: the Rise of Civil Engineering* (1935), 'Telford introduced or elaborated the system of monthly payments; of the retention of definitive sums as guarantee of satisfactory workmanship and punctual completion; of a period of maintenance during which the contractor is responsible for the state of the new work…'. John H. Stephens (1976) considered that Telford 'established the professional ethos of the civil engineer – the Engineer with a capital E in the contract documents, not himself a party to the contract between client and contractor, but administering it, giving advice in the interest of his client, yet in a position of independence, and arbitrator in matters of dispute. British civil engineers have followed this tradition to the letter, and the strength of British consulting engineers over more than a century, and latterly of the world-wide consulting organisation FIDIC (Fédération Internationale des Ingénieurs Conseils) derive directly from it, and depend upon it today.'

- **Cut-and-fill calculations:** The ambitious scale of earthworks carried out on the canal in the Nominated Site was made practical by detailed analysis of the quantities of spoil and how they could be moved economically. Telford developed the co-ordinated interchange of fill between neighbouring engineering works such as Chirk Tunnel and Froncysyllte Embankment. This was a precursor of modern engineering practice and vital to the construction of later transport routes. Bryan Morgan wrote in *Civil Engineering: Railways* (1971) 'Between any canal built by Brindley at the start of this period and any built by Telford towards its end there is an obvious advance in boldness of conception and (generally) in assurance of execution: the main technical improvement was, of course, Telford's own introduction of 'cut-and-fill' calculations.'

- **Cognisance of safety:** Only one workman lost his life in building Pontcysyllte Aqueduct. Jessop and Telford both commented explicitly on safety for workers on the canal and widened the piers, gave them hollow upper parts and used construction decks to increase protection for the masons. Consideration of health and safety issues is now a prime responsibility of engineers and is widely regulated.

2.b.7 The operation and use of the canal

Near this aqueduct, ascending the left bank of the Dee, there are several basins to receive the boats that come to take in their cargoes, which chiefly consist of coal and iron…. Boats heavily laden, and the horses which tow them, securely pass over this road, hanging over an abyss, and carrying to Ellesmere the coal, the lime, and iron furnished by the mines, the quarries and forges of the vale of Llangollen.

Charles Dupin,
The Commercial Power of Great Britain:
Exhibiting a Complete View of the Public Works
of the Country, translated from the French (1825)

The completion of the canal opened up opportunities for the cheap carriage of goods throughout a large economic region and into more distant markets. Many new

Part of the Aqueduct that crosses Langothlin vale.

An early popular print of Pontcysyllte Aqueduct, after J. Baker.

enterprises to export iron, coal, lime and slate from the areas around Chirk, Trevor and Llangollen were set in motion. These used wharves on the canal or communicated with it via Telford's Ruabon Brook horse-worked railway from Trevor. Hazledine's Plas Kynaston iron foundry was among the businesses that flourished, enabled by water transport to make large castings for engineering projects throughout Britain. Hazledine was one of many who also invested in local businesses in lime and coal.

Coal exported from the areas around Chirk and Trevor was the single most important traffic. One immediate effect

The last days of the boating families on the Ellesmere Canal, 1910. A narrow boat is waiting at a wharf near the entrance to the Black Park Collieries railway dock at Chirk.

168   Llangollen.   Canal Walk.

Horse-drawn pleasure boats operated regularly from 1884: a card postmarked 1903.

of the canal was that the costs of fuel fell across a wide area, aiding a range of small industries and allowing lime to be burned for agricultural improvement. Within two years of opening, the main line was carrying large cargoes of lime, timber, building stone, roofing slates, iron, brick and grain, and the volume of traffic doubled in the next decade. The carriage of general goods also became easier. A trade directory of 1828 showed regular canal services to Chester, Manchester, Liverpool, Birmingham, Bristol, south Wales and London.

Financially, the canal was not so spectacularly successful for its investors as some earlier routes, owing to the high cost of pushing a canal through the uplands and the financial difficulties experienced in Britain at the time it was constructed. However, toll income increased and the company had no remaining debts within five years of the canal's completion. It was able to pay its shareholders dividends regularly from 1815 onwards.

In 1835, Telford's Birmingham and Liverpool Junction Canal was completed, joining the Ellesmere Canal and providing a much more direct route to the West Midlands and the south. When the travel diarist George Borrow was in Llangollen around 1850 he met a boatman who regularly carried slates from there to London, and the carriage of limestone for flux in iron furnaces in the West Midlands became one of the canal's principal traffics. Trade continued to grow. In 1838, 22,000 tons/22,350 tonnes of iron were carried from north Wales to Liverpool and Manchester. However, pressure from the new locomotive railways began to be felt from the late 1840s when the Shrewsbury and Chester Railway was completed through the coalfield. The Ellesmere Canal Company absorbed the Birmingham and Liverpool Junction in 1845 to form the Shropshire Union and considered both building railways and laying others on its canal formations.

The continuing activity of the canal within the Nominated Site after the region was thoroughly served by locomotive railways is illustrated by the census of 1881: there were fourteen narrow boats with crews living on board in and around Trevor Basin and twelve in the vicinity of Llangollen. Most of the crews had been born at places on the Ellesmere Canal but the birthplaces of their children are evidence of voyages to places across the English Midlands.

However, these were the last days of commercial traffic and, with increasing railway competition and the decline of local heavy industries, it was negligible by 1905.

Regular horse-drawn pleasure boats have operated on the canal from Llangollen since 1884. These proved increasingly successful with the growth of railway-based tourism in the Vale. In 1905 passenger boats ran regularly in the summer from Llangollen all the way to Chirk. By 1925 they offered daily trips for visitors from Llangollen to Horseshoe Falls and a twice-weekly service to Chirk. The International Musical Eisteddfod at Llangollen has been a regular source of visitors to the canal since 1947 - the poet Dylan Thomas noted in 1953 how it 'spills colourfully, multilingually and confraternally into the streets of Llangollen and the surrounding countryside'.

With the ceasing of commercial traffic almost the whole of the former Ellesmere Canal was officially abandoned under an Act of Parliament of 1944. The canal within the Nominated Site was saved from closure by the need for water supply to north-west England. After the nationalisation of the British canal network by the government in 1947 a formal agreement was drawn up between British Waterways and the Mid and South East Cheshire Water Board that served to keep the canal open for both water supply and pleasure use. The retained portion of the Ellesmere Canal was named the Llangollen Canal. By this time, the canal eastwards from Llangollen was in poor condition. However, campaigns to keep it open and the growth of pleasure cruising in residential boats on British canals during the 1960s provided a rationale for maintenance to navigational standards.

In the last fifty years, the canal has been maintained in working order by British Waterways, which now has statutory duties toward its conservation, navigation, general amenity and biodiversity. Traffic in pleasure boats has continued to grow, from large hire stations in the Nominated Site and elsewhere, and the canal has become one of the most popular waterways in the United Kingdom for visitors by boat and on foot.

2.b.8 History of conservation

...undoubtedly one of the outstanding industrial monuments in the world.

R.A. Buchanan, *Industrial Archaeology in Britain* (1972)

Pontcysyllte Aqueduct and Canal helped to inspire the development in the United Kingdom of an appreciation of the industrial heritage, leading to the formation of national and international conservation organisations. In the period after 1850 Britain was commonly called 'the workshop of the world' owing to its success in industry, but in the same period there was a tendency to disparage industry and to see the nation's history in terms of medieval churches and great mansions. The history of mining and manufacturing was largely neglected. This was not so in other countries. In Sweden, for example, ironworks of the seventeenth and eighteenth centuries were seen in the same context as stave churches or prehistoric tumuli.

In the 1930s concern began to grow for industrial heritage in the United

Pleasure boating at Froncysyllte Lift Bridge, 1936.

Two photographs of pleasure boats on the canal in 1936.

Kingdom, and in the years after 1945 increasing interest was shown in what came to be called 'industrial archaeology'. This discipline was not a British invention - a Portuguese scholar had used the term in 1896, and a Belgian in 1950 had referred to 'l'archeologie industrielle' - but the publication in Britain in 1955 of an article by Michael Rix entitled 'Industrial Archaeology' was the beginning of a process that stimulated new thinking in many countries. In his article, Rix referred to 'the two loveliest industrial monuments in the country – those soaring bridges at Chirk and Pontcysyllte'.

Pontcysyllte Aqueduct was an iconic structure for the early industrial heritage conservation movement. One of the leading figures in this movement was L.T.C. Rolt: in 1939 he planned to cross Pontcysyllte Aqueduct in his boat, *Cressy*, which had been built at Trevor Basin, but his voyage was cut short by the outbreak of war. When *Cressy* finally made its way across the aqueduct, on 26 June 1949, it was probably the first full-length narrow boat to do so for ten years. In the meantime, Rolt's highly influential book *Narrow Boat* (1944) had begun to create new interest in the canals and he had co-founded the Inland Waterways Association, a pressure group for the retention of the canal system. Popular interest in the canals had been stimulated by the pioneering documentary drama film, *Painted Boats* (1945), released in the United States of America as *The Girl of the*

Canal, which included dramatic shots of Pontcysyllte.

In 1952 the Inland Waterways Association held a rally at Llangollen and in 1953 it formed a committee to campaign for the canal's revival. The decision the next year by the British Waterways Board to keep it open was one of the first acknowledgements that canals with no remaining industrial traffic might have a public value, to carry water, enhance townscapes or provide routes for holiday cruising. In 1958, Pontcysyllte Aqueduct was among the first industrial monuments in the United Kingdom to be designated a Scheduled Ancient Monument of National Importance, according it the same level of recognition and protection as great abbeys, castles and megaliths.

The canal was recognised in many of the pioneering works of industrial archaeology. The eminent photographer Eric de Maré included it in his influential book *Bridges of Britain* in 1954. The pioneering landscape historian W.G. Hoskins, wrote about both Chirk and Pontcysyllte in *The Making of the English Landscape* (1955), as did J.M. Richards, in *The Functional Tradition in Early Industrial Buildings* (1958), calling them 'among the masterpieces of that great age of engineering'. Kenneth Hudson, in the first book about Industrial Archaeology as a discipline, published in 1963, called Pontcysyllte the most notable of all British canal aqueducts, and in his overview of the subject in 1973, Neil Cossons called Pontcysyllte 'one of the great engineering achievements of all time… perhaps the greatest single engineering epic of the canal age.' D. Morgan Rees, in *Industrial Archaeology of Wales* (1975), identified the importance of the whole length of canal between Chirk Bank and Pontcysyllte and Anthony Burton wrote in 1983, 'For if ever a canal could be said to show virtually every aspect of the engineer's craft, then the Llangollen is that canal.' In 1992, Pontcysyllte was accorded a separate entry in *The Blackwell Encyclopedia of Industrial Archaeology*, the first international review of the discipline, as 'The most spectacular achievement of waterway engineering in Britain and a pioneer of cast iron construction.'

Pontcysyllte was visited during the first ever international congress on the conservation of industrial monuments, in 1973. Delegates from Canada, the German Democratic Republic, the German Federal Republic, Ireland, the Netherlands, Sweden, the United Kingdom and the United States of America travelled along Telford's Holyhead Road, crossed the aqueduct on foot and explored Trevor Basin. This congress led in 1978 to the formal foundation in Sweden of TICCIH (The International Committee for the Conservation of the Industrial Heritage), which advises ICOMOS and UNESCO. When the eleventh congress was held in the United Kingdom in 2000, a party again visited Pontcysyllte.

The management of the canal since 1954 has reflected the decision to maintain it for boating and amenity as well as water supply. The importance of continuous water supply resulted in urgent attention to risks of breaches and lining works on much of the canal, while the need to ensure safety for visitors prevented its conversion to a pipeline and made regular maintenance of structures imperative. Conservation of the historic fabric for much of this time was judged less important than the fitness of the canal for its new purposes. Just as throughout the British canal system, modern techniques were sometimes used in masonry repair, such as re-pointing with cement, spraying concrete

under arches and patching with brick. The two timber lift-bridges were renewed in steel with hydraulic operation for safety reasons and to prevent damage from increased use, and the decks of two footbridges were replaced. Red Bridge (number 24) and Quinta Bridge (20) were removed, having fallen out of use. Localised improvements to provide new footbridges, road crossings and moorings were not always carried out in full sympathy with the historic environment. Re-lining of sections of the canal bed with bitumen or concrete was carried out from the 1960s onwards where breaches had occurred or there was considered to be a high risk of leakage and future breaching. Bank protection at water level was installed extensively as the clay banks were not designed for the faster flow for water supply or the turbulence caused by propeller-driven craft, and they were eroding.

Awareness of conservation imperatives has risen rapidly in recent years, through both national programmes and policies and increasing emphasis on the Outstanding Universal Value of the Nominated Site. Appropriate conservation methods are now applied consistently. Details of the current conservation policies and regimes are given in Sections 4 and 5. Repairs are carried out by trained staff using carefully matched mortars and stone and the removal of even minor historic features no longer takes place. Past re-lining has protected 45 per cent of the canal in the Nominated Site, encompassing all the high-risk areas, and no further treatment of this kind is anticipated. Alternatives have been developed to methods of bank protection that are now considered to be visually intrusive. As and when sections of the existing protection come to the end of their design life they will be replaced according to improved specifications, for example using geo-textiles or stone facings.

Pontcysyllte Aqueduct was subject to an exemplary programme of major conservation in 2003-4 to protect it from corrosion, replace selected bolts in wrought-iron, refurbish the towing-path and handrail, repair masonry and reduce leakage. This

This page: The award-winning major conservation project at Pontcysyllte Aqueduct prior to its bicentenary.

Opposite page: A detail of 'Chirk Church, Aqueduct and Castle' by John Ingleby, c.1805. Jessop's ambition had been fulfilled to build an aqueduct that 'instead of an obstruction will be a romantic feature in the view'. Chirk Castle, in its parkland, commands the hill above.

was informed by prior trial works, testing of materials and documentary research into the historic treatment of the structure. It was subject to detailed recording before, during and after the works and approval of all details by the Welsh Assembly Government through the statutory process of Scheduled Monument Consent. The achievement was marked by awards from the Waterways Trust, the British Urban Regeneration Association and the Institution of Civil Engineers.

Pontcysyllte Aqueduct and the section of the Ellesmere Canal within the Nominated Site were rated highly in the ICOMOS thematic study for the World Heritage Convention, *The International Canal Monuments List* (1996), which called the aqueduct, 'One of the heroic monuments that symbolises the world's first Industrial Revolution and its transformation of technology'. The Site was included in the United Kingdom tentative list of future nominations as World Heritage Sites in 1999. Arrangements were subsequently put in place for the nomination, culminating in the formal establishment of the partnership to manage the Site in 2007.

So vast a combination of inland navigation, by procuring outlets for the territorial produce of the counties of Flint, Denbigh, Montgomery, Shropshire, and Cheshire, is an immense advantage to the numerous valleys, whose agricultural produce and manufactures it conveys. To these must be added the produce of the mines of salt, iron, and zinc, and of the quarries of slate, lime, marle, &c., with which the counties just named abound. We shall then have an idea of the riches which, thanks to the communications opened by the Ellesmere canal, are conveyed, according to the speculations of the merchants; first, by the Mersey, to Liverpool, Ireland, Manchester, and the north of England. Second, by the Severn, to Bristol and to the south. Third, and last, by various canals to London and all the eastern part of Great Britain.

Charles Dupin
The Commercial Power of Great Britain: Exhibiting a Complete View of the Public Works of the Country, translated from the French
(1825)

JUSTIFICATION FOR INSCRIPTION

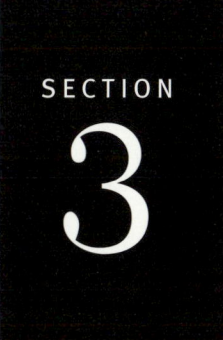

The Aqueduct bridge is a work… entitled to be regarded as one of the wonders of the age.

Benjamin Stillman,
A Visit to Europe in 1851 by Prof. Benjamin Stillman of Yale College (New York, 1854)

3.a Criteria under which inscription is proposed and justification

It is probably the most spectacular piece of engineering of the early Industrial Revolution.

Kenneth O. Morgan,
The Oxford Illustrated History of Britain (1984)

Pontcysyllte Aqueduct and Canal: **i)** is the masterpiece of two of the exceptional figures in the heroic phase of civil engineering in the late eighteenth and early nineteenth centuries; **ii)** exhibits important international interchanges of values in inland navigation, civil engineering and the application of iron to structural design; and **iv)** is an outstanding example of transport improvements in the Industrial Revolution, which initiated the process of industrialisation that spread to Europe, North America and the entire globe.

Pontcysyllte Aqueduct recorded by John Ingleby soon after completion.

The following analysis sets out why the Nominated Site is of Outstanding Universal Value in relation to criteria i, ii and iv of the World Heritage Convention. It draws upon and summarises the detailed evidence in Section 2 and Section 3.c.

The nomination of Pontcysyllte Aqueduct and Canal is consistent with the need identified by the International Council on Monuments and Sites (ICOMOS) to balance the World Heritage list with regard to technological sites of the period from 1793 to 1914. ICOMOS and The International Committee for the Conservation of the Industrial Heritage (TICCIH), as international scientific committees that act as advisors to UNESCO, have examined the Nominated Site and concluded that it is of international significance in two Thematic Studies: *The International Canal Monuments List* (1996) and *Context for World Heritage Bridges* (1997). This evaluation has been endorsed by a series of expert papers and detailed studies and by an international conference in June 2007, the findings of which are incorporated throughout this Nomination Document.

Guidelines for the inscription of heritage canals are given in Annex 3 of the *Operational Guidelines for the*

Implementation of the World Heritage Convention. These state that canals may be significant on technological, economic, social and landscape grounds. They recognise the importance of canals in economic development as the first man-made routes for the effective carriage of bulk cargoes and identify significant areas of technology, including 'the engineering structures of the line with reference to comparative structural features in other areas of architecture and technology; the development of the sophistication of construction methods; and the transfer of technologies'.

The conference about the international significance of Pontcysyllte Aqueduct, June 2007. Subjects discussed included the Canal du Midi World Heritage Site.

3.a.1 Criterion i: 'represent a masterpiece of human creative genius'

The most impressive work of art I have ever seen.

Sir Walter Scott (1825)

Thomas Telford was an innovative and prolific design genius whose influence on civil engineering was manifold and permanent: his work in the Nominated Site was his first substantial engineering project and his first opportunity to show the innovatory powers of design and project leadership that were to make him world famous. Pontcysyllte Aqueduct became his earliest internationally-recognised achievement and the major work with which he chose to be depicted in his portrait as first President of the Institution of Civil Engineers. William Jessop was a more modest man who left no account of his achievements, but he was revered by his contemporaries and was the most productive engineer of the Canal Age:

Pontcysyllte Aqueduct was seen as his greatest monument.

Pontcysyllte has been acknowledged by numerous authorities from the nineteenth century to the present day as a masterpiece of the 'heroic' phase of ambitious and imaginative civil engineering at the end of the eighteenth century and a monument that epitomises the courage and conviction of the Enlightenment era. It was recognised by contemporaries as among the world's outstanding structures. Its virtuosity was understood by engineers and architects from many countries, and its extraordinary grace and daring were appreciated by artists, poets and other visitors. Among the words most often used to describe it were 'supreme', 'magnificent', 'beautiful', 'wonderful' and 'stupendous'. Promoters of the project and independent witnesses ranked it with the architectural masterpieces of antiquity: the German landscape architect Prince Hermann von Pückler-Muskau described it as 'a work which would have done honour to Rome'.

The portrait of Thomas Telford, his masterpiece behind him, at the Institution of Civil Engineers: by Samuel Lane, 1822.

Left and far left:
The aqueduct 'light as a cloud'.

Pontcysyllte Aqueduct represents a daringly creative application of new ideas combined with supreme skills in the handling of materials. Within its eighteenth-century context the aqueduct's size alone is remarkable, but its confident early application of cast iron is breathtaking. Its designers investigated and tested the new technology of structural cast iron, drew together expert craftsmen and made successive innovations during the project's conception and development. They created a canal structure of unprecedented lightness and elegance and achieved a crossing of a height and length that would have been impossible by existing methods. It remained the tallest navigable aqueduct in the world for two centuries.

The French art historian Pierre Francastel wrote that Telford was among 'the real initiators of an intellectual revolution that led to the idea of functionalism, and started the whole complicated evolution of modern architecture.' Pontcysyllte and Chirk aqueducts may be seen as among the prominent early models of functional aesthetics. New materials and methods released them from previous restrictions of proportion and produced new structural expressions. Their designers believed that form should follow function and spurned architectural embellishment while expressly intending to create serene and noble structures, and both aqueducts were admired by commentators as objects of beauty. The French mathematician and engineer Charles Dupin called Pontcysyllte Aqueduct 'a supreme work of architecture, elegant and unadorned'.

Below: Crossing Pontcysyllte in the treetops far above the tumbling River Dee has thrilled visitors for two centuries: 'so little separates water from air. Weight becomes weightless.'

Opposite: Even the shadow of Pontcysyllte is a spectacle.

The canal as a whole was recognised as having combined rigorous engineering with sensitivity to a valued landscape. A contemporary commentator declared that 'the Canal Works between the north bank of the River Dee and the south bank of the Ceiriog, consisting of two large Aqueducts, two Tunnels and a great extent of deep cutting, will gratify those who enjoy the effects of works of art, when executed on a large scale'. Another wrote after Telford's death, 'Mr Telford executed the difficult task so as not only to avoid injuring the natural charms of the spots he touched upon, but absolutely to enhance their attractions in a high degree.' The canal's extraordinary grace as a sensitive addition to the landscape was perceived by contemporaries and continues to be appreciated by visitors today.

3.a.2 Criterion ii: 'exhibit an important interchange of human values, over a span of time or within a cultural area of the world, on developments in architecture or technology, monumental arts, town-planning or landscape design'

As France had been in the seventeenth century, so Britain was in the later eighteenth and early nineteenth centuries the leader in canal engineering, until her place was taken first by the United States, then by France, then by Germany.

Charles Hadfield, *World Canals* (1986)

Below: Chirk Aqueduct was among the features of the canal seen by early nineteenth-century artists as noble objects in a valued landscape: an engraving from a drawing by George Pickering.

Bottom: The functionalist simplicity of Chirk Aqueduct.

The Nominated Site bears testimony to an international interchange with regard to the technology and promotion of canals. The Ellesmere Canal and others of the Industrial Revolution in Britain drew on the engineering achievements of France in the seventeenth century; but they marked a new beginning in the promotion of increasingly sophisticated inland waterways for economic development, especially in coalfield areas. This model was subsequently pursued in other industrialising regions in Europe and North America. The continuing interchanges of values took place by several mechanisms: British canals were visited and studied by statesmen, promoters and engineers from other countries, accounts of the canals were widely published and circulated, British engineers advised on projects overseas, ideas were passed through successive generations of protégés and assistants, and professional engineering

institutions promoted good practice. The important works within the Nominated Site figured strongly in such interchanges.

The Nominated Site exemplifies in particular the transition between transport routes that followed the landscape and ones that commanded it to serve more efficiently the needs of industrial economies – a principle taken forward in later canals, railways and roads throughout the world. It was the greatest of a number of waterways built in the 1790s that were significantly more ambitious in design and investment than those of the previous decades. Telford wrote in 1805, 'This division of the canal is composed of works more difficult of execution, than can perhaps anywhere be found within an equal distance upon Canal Navigation.' It is understood as the first canal of the 'heroic' rather than the 'pioneering' phase of canal engineering, and the unprecedentedly ambitious crossing of the Dee Valley by embankment and aqueduct symbolises supremely the rigour and confidence of the new approach.

Pontcysyllte and Chirk Aqueducts proved emphatically, for a world-wide audience, the potential of iron in construction. They were conceived as a result of an international exchange of thinking with regard to the applications of iron in the 1790s, and their builders saw them as part of a conscious interchange of technology leading from 'Mr Darby who erected the first Iron Bridge' through the ideas of contemporary British, French and American designers and ironmasters to the next generation of iron structures around the world. The international fame of Pontcysyllte Aqueduct as a daring demonstration of what could be achieved with iron promoted ongoing development of iron construction in bridges and buildings. Telford himself went on to be recognised as one of the greatest exponents of the iron road bridge. Metal aqueducts continued to be built in many countries. Iron, steel and then steel-reinforced concrete became the materials of choice for major structures worldwide.

The Nominated Site was a testing ground for many new practices developed through

Left and below: cuttings, tunnels and embankments provided the canal with a direct route through challenging terrain.

Bottom: A loaded narrowboat, low in the water, is drawn by horse through Chirk Tunnel, about 1910.

The interlocking iron plates and ribs making up the spans of Pontcysyllte Aqueduct.

the creative dialogue between its two engineers that were carried forward into subsequent engineering and management internationally. In addition to intensively-engineered routes and iron construction, discussed above, the following were among the most important.

- Telford established the professional ethos of the engineer and principles of contract management that are still in use internationally.

- Telford and Jessop established clear lines of responsibility between specialists that permitted major projects to be achieved: this is evident in the Nominated Site in the houses for resident engineers.

- Telford developed cut-and-fill calculations, making possible the ambitious scale of earthworks on the canal by ensuring the efficient movement of spoil. This proved critical for railway-building world-wide and is still used in modern engineering practice.

- The large-scale use of construction railways to move spoil and deliver materials was fundamental to the major works in the Nominated Site. Such techniques were further developed internationally.

Telford and Jessop were directly concerned with interchanges that influenced engineering in other countries. They undertook or advised on projects in Sweden, India, Russia, Ireland, the United States of America and Canada. They mentored and influenced younger engineers who worked in all parts of the world: for example Telford's surveyor Thomas Brassey went on to use project management methods learned from him in India, Canada, Australia, South America, Turkey, France, Spain, Italy, and Denmark. The work of Telford and Jessop was studied by engineers and commentators from many countries. Telford was recognised as one of the outstanding figures in the rise of civil engineering as a profession and his principles were

incorporated into international practice. His work was extensively published and known internationally. The Institution of Civil Engineers, of which he was the first President, now has 80,000 members in 150 nations.

Pontcysyllte Aqueduct also exhibits an interchange of human values in conservation. It was recognised in the pioneering works of industrial archaeology and was one of the iconic structures of the early industrial heritage movement. In the 1940s it helped to inspire the formation of one of the earliest industrial conservation organisations, the Inland Waterways Association, which campaigned to save it from closure. It was among the earliest industrial structures to be designated a Scheduled Ancient Monument of National Importance, in 1958. In 1973 it was visited by the first ever international conference on the conservation of the industrial heritage.

The extraordinary daring of Pontcysyllte had a world-wide influence in promoting the use of iron in construction: an engraving after a drawing by George Yates, c.1805.

3.a.3 Criterion iv: 'be an outstanding example of a type of building or architectural or technological ensemble or landscape which illustrates a significant stage in human history'

One of the heroic monuments that symbolises the world's first Industrial Revolution and its transformation of technology.

ICOMOS / TICCIH, *The International Canal Monuments List* (Paris, 1996)

The Nominated Site is an outstanding material representation of the improvements in transport that stimulated and enabled the Industrial Revolution, one of the fundamental turning points of human history.

The process of industrialisation that began in Britain and spread to the rest of Europe, North America and the entire globe altered the economic and social basis of life. Pontcysyllte Aqueduct and Canal bears witness to many of the prime changes embodied by the Industrial Revolution.

Pontcysyllte Aqueduct strides across the Dee Valley to the wharves at Trevor.

- Improved means of transport are illustrated by the canal as a construction through a landscape not previously served by bulk transport.

- New technologies are illustrated by the successive technical solutions developed by Jessop and Telford during the course of the project.

- The development of new economic structures is exemplified by the construction of the canal by a joint stock company. British canals were among the first enterprises to raise capital through mass shareholding.

- Increasing capitalisation is illustrated by the canal as a technological ensemble designed to replace labour with capital through the creation of more efficient means of carriage. The canal at Pontcysyllte, with its sequence of challenging engineering works, was more highly capitalised per mile than any that preceded it.

- Increased inter-regional trade is illustrated by the physical connection made by the canal to external and world markets and by the installations for incoming and outgoing trade that grew up on its banks.

- Accelerating growth in output is reflected in the scale of waterway planned by the canal's promoters, based on their expectations of rapidly increasing trade, and the evidence for the canal's subsequent use.

- The shift to fossil fuels is illustrated by the effort expended to carry the canal across the Dee Valley to the northern part of the coalfield. Coal was the major traffic on the canal throughout its working life.

Inland waterways were the prime mode of industrial transport throughout the course of the British Industrial Revolution. They were vital in opening up the coalfields to economic exploitation and increased the efficiency of the whole economy. England and Wales were eventually served by some 5,340 miles / 8,600 kilometres of navigable inland waterways, an industrial transport system that was not surpassed until the expansion of locomotive railways after 1830. The Nominated Site is an outstanding example of a technological ensemble that illustrates these changes.

The national waterway network built in the British Canal Age was crucial to the Industrial Revolution. Goods from Pontcysyllte were carried all over the country, including to London.

The wharf at Llangollen with its warehouse and crane and a horse-drawn passenger boat.

3.b Proposed statement of Outstanding Universal Value

one of the great engineering achievements of all time… perhaps the greatest single engineering epic of the canal age.

Neil Cossons (1973)

Pontcysyllte Aqueduct and Canal in North Wales, built between 1795 and 1808, is a masterpiece of historic transport design and the greatest work of two outstanding figures in the history of civil engineering: Thomas Telford and William Jessop. Pontcysyllte Aqueduct crossed the Dee Valley by nineteen spans at a height of 126 feet / 38.4 metres. Its application of the new technology of cast iron to create the tallest and longest navigable aqueduct in the world was a daring and spectacular achievement. The associated 11 mile / 18 kilometre section of navigable waterway is an outstanding example of advances in canal building in the Industrial Revolution, one of the fundamental turning points of human history. The Site exhibits important international interchanges of values in inland navigation, civil engineering and the application of iron to structural design.

Pontcysyllte Aqueduct was begun in 1795 to carry a navigable canal across the Dee Valley in North Wales. It remained for two centuries the tallest navigable aqueduct in the world. The 11-mile / 18-kilometre section of canal centred upon it utilised a concentrated series

Pontcysyllte Aqueduct today.

of great engineering features to negotiate a challenging upland landscape.

The Site exhibits the following qualities that demonstrate Outstanding Universal Value:

- it is a spectacular example of canal engineering in the late eighteenth and early nineteenth centuries;
- it is an architectural masterpiece enhancing its dramatic landscape setting;
- it exemplifies improvements in transport that facilitated the Industrial Revolution; and
- it exhibits important international interchanges of values in inland navigation, civil engineering, project management and the application of iron to structural design.

At the time of its completion this length of canal was described as 'composed of works more difficult of execution than can perhaps be found anywhere within an equal distance of canal navigation'. The engineers intervened in the landscape with a new scale and intensity, challenged by the need to cut a waterway across the grain of the Welsh upland topography. All of the features that were to become characteristic of highly-engineered transport routes can be seen in the Nominated Site, including tunnels, cuttings, aqueducts and embankments, many of them technically innovative or of monumental scale, together with bridges, culverts, weirs and associated features. The whole Site has remained in use continuously for two hundred years. It is widely valued for its historical importance, beautiful landscape and breathtaking structures.

The Nominated Site is the masterpiece of two of the exceptional figures in the heroic phase of civil engineering in the late eighteenth and early nineteenth centuries. Thomas Telford (1757-1834) was an innovative and prolific design genius who had a permanent influence on civil engineering: Pontcysyllte Aqueduct was his earliest internationally-recognised achievement and the major work with which he chose to be depicted in his portrait as first President of the Institution of Civil Engineers. William

Jessop (1745-1814) was the most productive engineer of the Canal Age: Pontcysyllte Aqueduct was his greatest monument.

Pontcysyllte Aqueduct has been acknowledged by numerous authorities from the nineteenth century to the present day as a masterpiece that epitomises the courage and conviction of the Enlightenment era. It was recognised by contemporaries as among the world's outstanding structures. Its virtuosity was understood by engineers and architects from many countries, and its extraordinary grace and daring were appreciated by artists, poets and other visitors. It represents a daringly creative application of new ideas combined with supreme skills in the handling of materials. Within its eighteenth-century context the aqueduct's size alone is remarkable, but the confident application of a novel material is breathtaking. It was a canal structure of unprecedented lightness and elegance and achieved a crossing of a height and length that would have been impossible by existing methods. Both Pontcysyllte and Chirk aqueducts may be seen as architectural masterpieces that were among the prominent early models of functional aesthetics. The canal as a whole has been recognised for its successful combination of rigorous engineering with sensitivity to a dramatic and highly-valued landscape.

The Nominated Site exhibits important international interchanges of values in inland navigation, civil engineering and the application of iron to structural design. The canals of the Industrial Revolution in Britain drew on the engineering achievements of France in the seventeenth century but represented a new phase in the history of inland navigation. The pivotal role of canal networks in British economic development was recognised and followed in early industrialising regions in Europe and North America. The Nominated Site exemplifies in particular the transition between transport routes that followed the landscape and ones that commanded it to serve more efficiently the needs of industrial economies. It was the greatest of a number of waterways built in the 1790s that were significantly more ambitious in design and investment than those of the previous decades. This principle was taken forward in later canals, railways and roads throughout the world.

Britain in the late eighteenth and early nineteenth centuries was the leading centre of innovation in the manufacture and application of iron and pioneered

Pontcysyllte Aqueduct, the 'stream in the sky': an engraving after a drawing by E. Pugh in 1814.

A boat crossing Pontcysyllte Aqueduct.

Above: Thomas Telford's crescentic weir at Horseshoe Falls to feed the canal system with water.

Right: Chirk Aqueduct crossing the Ceiriog Valley.

The Nominated Site is an outstanding example of transport improvements in the Industrial Revolution, which initiated the process of industrialisation that spread to Europe, North America and the entire globe. It bears witness to many of the defining characteristics of the Industrial Revolution, including improved means of transport, new technologies, the development of economic structures, increasing capitalisation, increased inter-regional trade, accelerating growth in output and the shift to fossil fuels. Inland waterways were the prime mode of industrial transport throughout the course of the British Industrial Revolution. They were vital in opening up the coalfields to economic exploitation and increased the efficiency of the whole economy. England and Wales were eventually served by some 5,340 miles / 8,600 kilometres of navigable inland waterways, over 1,180 miles / 1,900 kilometres of which were built in just two decades, from 1790 to 1810.

The Nominated Site has a high degree of integrity and authenticity. The whole of the intensively-engineered section of the waterway is within the Site boundary and no major features have been lost or damaged. Changes made to the formation of the waterway and its engineering features during its continuing working life as a navigation have been largely superficial. Its central structure, Pontcysyllte Aqueduct, has been protected as a Scheduled Ancient Monument of National Importance since 1958 and was recently the subject of an exemplary conservation programme. The Nominated Site and its extensive Buffer Zone are protected and managed by multiple designations and planning controls. The canal is in state ownership through the medium of British Waterways. A robust World Heritage Site Management Plan has been prepared by the local authorities, British Waterways and national heritage bodies, who have come together in a strategic partnership for the purposes of its identification, protection, conservation, presentation and transmission to future generations.

new uses of the material in construction. Pontcysyllte Aqueduct was part of a sequence of innovations that led to the general acceptance of cast iron and then steel as construction materials and enabled ever-greater engineering achievements around the world. The Nominated Site was also a testing ground for many new practices that were carried forward into subsequent engineering and management practice internationally, including principles of contract management, the division of responsibility between specialists, cut-and-fill calculations to enable the efficient movement of spoil and the use of construction railways. Telford and Jessop participated directly in interchanges that influenced engineering in other countries, through their own work and its publication, protégés who worked overseas, and their key roles in the creation of early professional institutions. Pontcysyllte Aqueduct also exhibits an interchange of human values in conservation, as an iconic structure recognised in the pioneering works of industrial archaeology and the early industrial heritage movement.

3.c Comparative analysis

For it is not only the greatest monument of the canal age in England; it is also one of the finest examples of civil engineering in the world.

　　　　L.T.C. Rolt, *Navigable Waterways* (1969)

This Section makes national and international comparisons to judge the outstanding value of Pontcysyllte Aqueduct and Canal. It outlines the similarities between the Nominated Site and other properties as well as the features that distinguish it from them. It complements the discussion of the Site in its historical context in Section 2.b.

The Nominated Site has Outstanding Universal Value because it is the masterpiece of two of the exceptional figures of civil engineering in the late eighteenth and early nineteenth centuries, exhibits important international exchanges of values in inland navigation, civil engineering and the application of iron to structural design, and is an outstanding example of the transport improvements which underpinned and made possible the process of industrialisation that spread to continental Europe, North America and then to the whole world. It is of greatest importance when considered among other heritage canals, iron structures, intensively-engineered transport lines and illustrations of changes during the Industrial Revolution. These are the points on which the following comparisons are made.

3.c.1 Heritage Canals

The Ellesmere Canal… passes over a country so uneven as to require the construction of works which, from their magnitude, surpass those of Brindley nearly as much as the latter had surpassed all previous achievements in civil engineering in this country. In the valleys of the Ceriog, or Chirk, and of the Dee, especially, aqueducts were erected in the construction of which all existing precedent was boldly departed from.

　　　　George L. Craik and Charles Macfarlane,
　　　　***The Pictorial History of England
　　　　during the Reign of George III*** (1843)

A definition for heritage canals is given in the *Operational Guidelines for the Implementation of the World Heritage Convention* (Annex 3): 'A canal is a human-engineered waterway. It may be of Outstanding Universal Value from the point of view of history or technology, either intrinsically or as an exceptional example representative of this type of cultural property. The canal may be a monumental work, the defining feature of a linear cultural landscape, or an integral component of a complex cultural landscape.' In 1996 *The International Canal Monuments List*, a report on waterways throughout the world, was published by ICOMOS and The International Committee on the Conservation of the Industrial Heritage (TICCIH) as a thematic study in the global strategy for identifying sites and monuments in categories under-represented on the World Heritage List. This study, based on a consensus of expert opinion developed in a series of international meetings, has informed the historical discussion of canals throughout this document.

The *International Canal Monuments List* recognises both Pontcysyllte Aqueduct and the associated length of canal as among the landmarks in the world history of waterways when scored by the criteria for World Heritage Sites. It notes that the Ellesmere Canal developed new types of canal structure, spurred on by the fusion of lowland English technology with the challenges of an upland Welsh landscape and identifies it as among the most technologically important canal lines in the world. It singles out the importance of the canal's use of iron in two aqueducts

One of the expert meetings for the preparation of *The International Canal Monuments List*, in Canada.

and three composite over-bridges, the unprecedented height of the crossings of two valleys and the major earthworks and tunnels used. It judges it to be of outstanding international importance as a masterpiece of human creative genius, for having exerted great influence on developments of technical importance, and for illustrating a significant stage in human history. *The International Canal Monuments List* also judged Pontcysyllte Aqueduct as an individual structure to be among the four most important navigable aqueducts in the world. It stated it to be, 'one of the heroic monuments that symbolises the world's first Industrial Revolution and its transformation of technology'.

By the end of 2007, three canals on the *List* had been inscribed: the **Canal du Midi** in France (inscribed 1996), a 4 mile / 7 kilometre section of the **Canal du Centre** in Belgium (1998), and the **Rideau Canal** in Canada (2007).

Several canals identified in the study date from ancient times: in Sri Lanka, Greece, Egypt and China. Among these, the **Grand Canal** of China was evaluated particularly highly. Built in stages from the fourth century BC and still largely in operation, at 1,114 miles / 1,795 kilometres it is the longest canal in the world. Re-buildings and extensions of AD 605-610, when many sections of waterway were joined together, included the first ever summit-level canal. Its form generally reflects lowland canal technology and there were no aqueducts.

Canals of importance survive from pre-industrial Europe. The **Stecknitz Canal** at Lübeck in Germany and the **Naviglio Grande** at Milan in Italy are remarkable as surviving canals dating from the late Middle Ages. The **Canal du Midi** (built 1666-81) was the first summit canal of the modern period. It strongly influenced canal building in the rest of Europe, and Telford's copies of books about it show his personal annotations. There were several aqueducts, and a short tunnel, exceptional in having a towing-path, was built at Malpas. Even though the canal's builders drew on this experience none of these early canals shows the range of engineering techniques, the adaptation of new materials and the virtuosity in their use represented by Pontcysyllte Aqueduct and Canal.

The Grand Canal of China.

Right: Boat lifts on the Canal du Centre, Belgium.

Bottom left: The Rideau Canal, Canada.

Bottom right: Malpas Tunnel on the Canal du Midi, France.

The International Canal Monuments List points out in its introduction that the development of 'waterways in Europe was a significant feature of the Industrial Revolution.' The exceptional influence of the canals developed in Britain from the 1760s to the 1830s is discussed in Sections 2.b.1 and 2.b.6 of this Nomination. The **Duke of Bridgwater's Canal** established a new model for industrial transport from the 1760s by linking coal mines directly to their markets and demonstrating the consequent reductions in costs. A nomination in future of the industrial conurbation of Manchester would include the canal. However, although it was designed by the pioneer canal engineer James Brindley, its features were modest apart from the three-span masonry aqueduct over the River Irwell, considered a marvel of the age but demolished in the 1890s. As the quotation at the head of this Section indicates, contemporaries in the nineteenth century fully appreciated the radical departure from the engineering of Brindley's generation that was represented by the Ellesmere Canal. The only other canals of the Industrial Revolution to feature in the *International Canal Monuments List* are the **Birmingham and Liverpool Junction Canal**, built by Telford in the 1830s, and the **Birmingham Canal Navigations**, a dense system of waterways in the heart of the West Midlands industrial area which was redeveloped by Telford in its last phase. Telford's work on both these canals follows the approaches developed on the Ellesmere Canal and takes them to their logical conclusions, but they do not represent turning points in design in the same way and they date from a period when the leadership of British canals internationally was beginning to be eclipsed by canals in America and continental Europe. Other short sections of canals in Britain's 5,340 mile / 8,600 kilometre network pass through World Heritage Sites (discussed in Section 3.c.4 below). Although a suggestion was made that this whole system might be nominated when the United Kingdom *Tentative List* was being prepared in 1998-9, its industrial use is represented effectively

The Birmingham Canal Navigations: Telford's straight, highly-engineered route is in contrast to the older line it superseded.

by the Nominated Site together with short sections in other nominated properties of the Industrial Revolution.

The internationally important achievements of waterway engineering in Britain are represented with unique power by the Nominated Site, which was described by Telford as 'composed of works more difficult of execution, than can perhaps any where be found within an equal distance upon Canal Navigation.' Several new approaches were brought together in the Nominated Site – for example the structural use of iron, the use of construction railways, and the organisation of responsibilities and contracts – and it was unprecedentedly ambitious in commanding the landscape rather than following it. As a result it can be interpreted as the first canal of the 'heroic' age of waterway building, which led on to the achievements of great canals of later ages. This quality is not demonstrated by other canals on the World Heritage List or identified in *The International Canal Monuments List*. Its features became famous, were regularly visited and widely published, and influenced the next generation of waterways internationally. Every authoritative study of canals or of industrial archaeology in Britain has acknowledged the outstanding importance of Pontcysyllte. Brian Bracegirdle, in *The Archaeology of Canals* (1979) called it 'the greatest monument of the canal era.' Anthony Burton wrote in 1989, 'If any one structure can be said to exemplify the technical brilliance and innovation that marked the work of the greatest canal engineers, this is it.'

Some outstanding canals post-date the turning point marked by the British canal system in the Industrial Revolution. The 300 mile / 483 kilometre main line of the **Erie Canal** in the United States of America, built from 1817 to 1825, was highly rated in *The International Canal Monuments List*. It was consciously conceived as following British 'heroic' canal engineering and induced the North American 'canal fever' of the 1820s. The **Rideau Canal** (1826-32) in Canada was identified as one of the most technologically significant surviving canal lines, and was inscribed in 2007 as 'the best preserved canal in North America from the great canal-building era of the early nineteenth century to remain operational along its original line with most of its original structures intact'. It is an example of a 'slackwater navigation' created by flooding virgin territory by dams and embankments rather than a waterway cutting through upland terrain with great engineering features. The **Ganges Canal** in India is a vast system of irrigation works used also for navigation, developed between 1817 and 1901. The **Suez Canal**, completed in 1869 to connect the Red Sea and the Mediterranean, is one of the most strategically important canals in the world but it is an isthmian ship canal without the major structures to be found in the Nominated Site.

The applications of iron developed in the Nominated Site allowed a new scale of navigable aqueducts and permitted designs and forms of construction fundamentally different from those that came before, which all derived ultimately from Roman engineering. Two of the four aqueducts identified as of greatest importance in the *International Canal Monuments List* are of this traditional form. The **Répudre Aqueduct** of 1676 is now inscribed as the only original aqueduct surviving on the Canal du Midi. This follows methods of construction used by the Romans as a bulky structure sealed with hydraulic lime. The **Molgora Aqueduct** is a three-arched structure of 1462-70 at Milan in Italy. The final aqueduct of international importance

in the *List* is the **Delaware Suspension Aqueduct** of 1849 in Pennsylvania, United States of America. Designed by John Roebling, this showed a completely different form of construction in which wrought-iron suspension wires support a timber trough. This model was not copied for aqueducts elsewhere, but it is the oldest surviving suspension bridge in the United States, now in use for road traffic. By contrast the aqueducts developed in the Nominated Site were widely copied and developed upon, as described in the next Section.

3.c.2 Iron structures

I ponti di Telford e di Paine, però, si scostano nettamente dall'idea di Wilkinson; essi infatti ripropongono la soluzione a « conci » tipica dei ponti in pietra, ottenendo risultati più ragguardevoli per larghezza e peso solo grazie alla maggior portenza del materiale. In questo filone il risultato più valido si raggiunge con il ponte-canale per acquedotto sopra la valle del Dee, progettato da Telford e costruito tra il 1795 e il 1803. Qui la parte metallica è perfettamente risolta nelle arcate e nel canale, sono completamente scomparsi i riferimenti stilistici, gli appoggi sono realizzati con altissimi piloni in pietra (120 piedi) di assoluto rigore tecnico e formale. Telford progetta poi, nel 1801, un ponte sul Tamigi con una sola arcata di ghisa lunga 600 piedi….

[The bridges of Telford and Paine, however, are far removed from Wilkinson's ideas; indeed they revive the solution of voussoirs typical of masonry bridges, achieving notable breadth and load due solely to the greater strength of the material. In this vein the most impressive results are to be seen in the canal aqueduct above the valley of the River Dee, designed by Telford and built between 1795 and 1803. Here the function is perfectly resolved in the arches and the channel, which are completely free of stylistic references, and the supports are high stone piers (120 feet) of absolute technical and formal rigour. Telford then planned, in 1801, a bridge over the Thames with a single cast-iron span 600 feet long….]

Petrignani Achille, *Industrializzazione dell'edilizia* (Bari, 1980)

The wider influence of Pontcysyllte Aqueduct in promoting the use of iron in structural engineering was identified in another ICOMOS/TICCIH expert international report, the *Context for World Heritage Bridges* of 1997. This study recommended Pontcysyllte as a potential world heritage bridge for its 'extraordinarily innovative arrangements in which the cast iron had real structural value'. As discussed in Sections 2.b.4 and 2.b.6, Chirk and Pontcysyllte Aqueducts were part of an international interchange concerning the use of iron in construction that extended from the first iron bridges to iron aqueducts and to subsequent structures using iron, steel and steel-reinforced concrete.

The first widely-known iron bridge, in what is now the **Ironbridge Gorge** World Heritage Site, demonstrated the constructional possibilities of cast iron when it was built in 1789 and was followed by a succession of cast-iron arches in Europe. Four years later, an iron aqueduct was built to carry a water supply trough and a horse-worked railway: **Pontcafnau** at Merthyr Tydfil in Wales. This and **Longdon-on-Tern Aqueduct**, built by Telford in 1796 while he was developing solutions to the great valley crossings of the Ellesmere Canal, are of importance as experimental structures. The contemporary Holmes Aqueduct by Jessop and Outram does not survive.

Chirk and Pontcysyllte were produced through a process of investigation and development culminating in what was to be the ultimate expression of iron aqueduct design for many decades to come. Pontcysyllte demonstrated bravura and confidence that are breathtaking even today, applying the new methods on a scale that was to be unsurpassed for two centuries. Both Chirk and Pontcysyllte were also, for the first time, aqueducts that possessed a beauty and simplicity derived from their use of iron and proved beyond doubt the architectural possibilities of the medium.

Chirk and Pontcysyllte aqueducts and the techniques used to achieve them can be contrasted with the heights of achievement in masonry aqueducts, represented by earlier structures for water supply. **Pont du Gard** in France, inscribed on the World Heritage List in 1985, is a Roman structure of about 20 BC. It is similar in height and length to Pontcysyllte but this was achieved by three tiers of arches and the channel is of insufficient width for boats. The builders

The Iron Bridge, United Kingdom.

Detail of Telford's Longdon Aqueduct, United Kingdom.

of the Ellesmere Canal saw their aqueduct at Pontcysyllte as part of the same tradition of monumental building, but by using iron they achieved a water-channel almost three times as wide. Other water-supply aqueducts of masonry construction already on the World Heritage List include the Roman **Vallens Aqueduct** in Turkey and **Segovia Aqueduct** in Spain and the **Carolino Aqueduct**, built to supply the Caserta Royal Palace fountains in Italy in 1769. These aqueducts were impressively high but were only able to support small channels.

Pont du Gard, France.

None of the masonry aqueducts built on navigable canals approached these structures in scale. As engineering ambitions advanced in the eighteenth century, increasing problems were experienced in the deflection of large aqueducts, especially in Britain, where waterproofing was carried out with massed puddled-clay and heavy masonry walls. These methods are illustrated by two smaller aqueducts in the Nominated Site. Some British masonry aqueducts were substantial and impressive structures, for example the **Ribble Aqueduct** and **Avon Aqueduct** by John Rennie, which took traditional masonry construction to its technical limits.

The achievements in the Nominated Site were part of a sequence of innovations and developments that led to the general acceptance of iron and then steel as ubiquitous construction materials. The use of iron and, consequently, of light-weight masonry piers at Pontcysyllte allowed Telford and Jessop to achieve a channel of navigable width at unprecedented height without the deflection found in traditional masonry aqueducts. This opened the way for efficient transport systems in landscapes hitherto inaccessible.

In their authoritative study of iron bridges, Neil Cossons and Barrie Trinder refer to Pontcysyllte as 'one of the most extraordinary creations of the Industrial Revolution'. Pontcysyllte promoted ongoing development in iron bridges and iron-framed buildings in many countries. Successful iron bridges were built from around this time in many parts of the world, and Telford became one of their leading exponents. His great iron suspension bridges at **Conwy** and **Menai** benefited from the management techniques applied in the building of the Chirk and Pontcysyllte aqueducts as well as the confidence gained in the application of new materials.

The prodigious achievement and fame of Chirk and Pontcysyllte inspired further aqueducts using the new technology, but not surpassing Pontcysyllte in scale or innovatory power. Over forty were built in Britain, most of which survive. Those on the **Stratford-upon-Avon Canal** of 1813 and the **Edinburgh and Glasgow Union Canal** of 1817-22 were the most impressive and followed on directly from the innovations on the Ellesmere Canal. The former used an exposed iron trough like Pontcysyllte and the latter matched almost exactly the appearance of Chirk Aqueduct, with an iron trough set in masonry. Telford's aqueducts on the Birmingham and Liverpool Junction Canal, opened in 1835, were typical of smaller iron aqueducts that became standard practice. Such aqueducts emphasise the influence of the structures at Chirk and Pontcysyllte but none matches their importance.

Metal aqueducts continued to evolve in the late nineteenth century with wrought iron and steel. The steel-riveted **Haverud Aqueduct** on the Dalsland Canal in Sweden, built in 1868, is still in use. Metal aqueducts became essential as approach structures to vertical boat lifts after the construction of the **Anderton Boat Lift** in the United Kingdom in 1875 and Edwin Clark, its designer, was involved with the **Les Fontinettes Lift** on the Neufosse Canal in France: both have wrought-iron approach aqueducts. From 1885 the use of metal canal lifts and aqueducts spread to Belgium where the four lifts on the **Canal du Centre** are now inscribed as a World Heritage Site. In 1896 the 2,172 feet / 662 metres long steel-trough

Briare Aqueduct on the Canal latéral à la Loire in France surpassed Pontcysyllte in length. Iron aqueducts and lifts also spread at this time to the **Trent-Severn Waterway**, between the Great Lakes in Canada, and in the first half of the twentieth century were erected in the United States of America to replace timber-trough aqueducts, for example at **Au Sable Creek** and on the **Illinois and Michigan Canal**.

Railway engineers used iron for many bridges of scale and ambition, such as Robert Stephenson's **Tyne Bridge** at Newcastle. High wrought-iron viaducts such as Gustave Eiffel's **Garabit Viaduct** of 1885 were crucial to railway-building around the world. The **Forth Railway Bridge** in Scotland of 1890, currently on the United Kingdom *Tentative List*, was the first structure on such a scale to be built in steel and had an influence on subsequent civil engineering that paralleled that of Pontcysyllte Aqueduct almost a century earlier.

Structural use of steel beams and steel-reinforced concrete is now commonplace in bridges and large buildings. The **River Dee Road Viaduct**, from which there are distant views of Pontcysyllte Aqueduct, was built using reinforced-concrete box-

Cosgrove Aqueduct on the Grand Junction Canal in the United Kingdom, built to replace a failed masonry structure in 1811.

Anderton Boat Lift, 1875.

The Forth Bridge, Scotland, under construction in 1889, the first great construction project in steel.

girders in the 1990s, with piers hollow, as in Pontcysyllte Aqueduct, the tallest being 179 feet/55 metres. It demonstrates standard bridge technology in a genealogy connected to its much older neighbour.

Magnificent transport structures continue to develop. The 1.5 miles/2.4 kilometres long **Millau Viaduct** in France completed in 2004, taller than the **Eiffel Tower**, is a composite construction of reinforced concrete piers supporting a steel deck with steel cables. In Belgium the lifts in the Canal du Centre World Heritage Site have been by-passed by the **Strepy-Thieu Canal Lift** with two steel trough aqueducts on reinforced-concrete piers at a height of 240 feet/73 metres: coming into use in 2002 these finally surpassed the height of Pontcysyllte Aqueduct after two centuries. In China, the **Three Gorges Dam** on the Yangtze River has a 371 feet/113 metre lift for 3,000 ton/3,048 tonne craft, due to open in 2008, with an approach aqueduct that reaches even greater heights.

3.c.3 Intensively-engineered transport routes

Nous allons suivre les progrès de l'art de l'ingénieur civil dans l'histoire de la vie de Thomas Telford, cet homme éminent qui tour à tour a conduit de grands travaux d'architecture civile, édifié des ponts, percé des routes, ouvert des canaux, desséché des marais, creusé des docks, amélioré nos ports…

[We will trace the progress of the art of civil engineering through the story of Thomas Telford's life, this eminent man who by turn created great works of architecture, who constructed bridges, projected roads, opened canals, drained marshes, excavated docks, improved our ports....]

'La vie et les travaux de Thomas Telford, ingénieur civil', *Revue Britannique XXIV* (1839)

The development of highly-engineered transport routes, involving large cuttings, tunnels, embankments and crossings, was significantly advanced by British canals of the early nineteenth century, of which the canal at Pontcysyllte is outstanding. It was among the earliest transport routes to emphasise the intensive use of engineering features to create a level and direct route, with a concomitant increase in construction

cost and effort. With other heroic-era canals, it set new standards fundamental to railways and later roads. The project was exceptional for the large number of innovations that it passed on to later engineering practice. Among those initiated or developed by Telford and his colleagues were principles of contract management, the division of responsibility between specialists, cut-and-fill calculations, the use of construction railways and the constructional applications of iron. The exceptional influence of Jessop and Telford through protégés, professional institutions and publications is discussed in Section 2.b.6 above. The resultant ordered system of management was vital to later large-scale civil-engineering schemes.

Telford's **London to Holyhead Road** (1815-c.1830) was created to cement Britain and Ireland after the Act of Union. It included the great causeway linking Anglesey to Holyhead Island, miles of retaining-wall holding the road on mountainsides, and the Menai Suspension Bridge. It was one of the most advanced roads at the time anywhere in the world. Telford was also engineer for the Glasgow to Carlisle Road in Scotland and to the Commissioners for Highland Roads and Bridges from 1803. His international reputation in transport design was such that he was asked to advise the Russian government on the 100 mile/161 kilometre **Warsaw-Brzesc Road** completed in 1825 on the route to Moscow. He also advised on the construction of a causeway at Bombay (Salsotte) in India.

The ICOMOS study of *Railways as World Heritage Sites* published in 1999 lists eight railways of international note. In the first two decades of the nineteenth century Jessop and Telford both built railways designed for horse-drawn vehicles. Telford's largest railway project, for a line from Glasgow to Berwick, in Scotland, would have been by far the longest railway of its time and the most heavily engineered. Another line named in the study is the **Liverpool and Manchester Railway**, opened in 1830, which is generally accepted as the first 'main line' railway. The intensive use of cuttings, embankments and bridges was essential to this line and others that followed. Within little more than two decades 6,000 route miles / 9,656 kilometres of similar railway had been built in Britain, and were being constructed in continental Europe and North America. In the second half of the nineteenth century the railway was perceived as the stimulus to economic development in all parts of the world. Several of the first generation of railway engineers and contractors had worked closely with Telford. The bold engineering and efficient management systems that were features of Jessop's and Telford's work on the Ellesmere Canal profoundly influenced the ways in which railways were constructed. The **Great Western Railway**, which became known as 'the finest work in England' is included in the United Kingdom *Tentative List*.

The **Semmering Railway** in Austria, inscribed on the World Heritage List in 1998 as one of the greatest feats of engineering from the pioneering phase of railway building, was completed in 1854 in truly mountainous territory by Karl Ritter von Ghega. It used intensive engineering with tunnels and viaducts to press through terrain that would otherwise have been impassable, on an even gradient and with the most direct route possible. While such efficient, highly-capitalised design became the preferred approach to building railways, cost constraints sometimes produced less intensively engineered routes. The **Darjeeling Himalayan Railway** of 1881, inscribed as part of the Mountain Railways of India, employed a steeply-graded route with loops and zigzags. However, this type of engineering is the exception to railway design as it has developed since the age of the canals. High-speeds have made straight and level routes even more important. The **Shinkansen** high-speed railway of Japan, opened fully in 1966 and recognised in the ICOMOS railways study, achieved this by building on a raised concrete base with 3,000 bridges and sixty-seven tunnels. The approach of intensive engineering to create efficient routes is now fundamental to the design of motorways and railways across the world.

3.c.4 Representations of the Industrial Revolution

What mattered was that the coal got to the consumers at reasonable prices, that the iron-foundries and potteries could reduce costs, that the factory worker could warm his family in winter and still have some money left over to buy the products of British industry and that the bread-and-cheese-eating labourers of Southern England could have cooked meals occasionally. In these terms the Canal Age made a massive contribution to the first industrial revolution.

Phyllis Deane, *The First Industrial Revolution* (1979)

Comparatively few sites of industrial importance are currently inscribed on the World Heritage List. Early industrial sites have been inscribed in several countries, such as the **Mines of Rammelsberg** in Germany, which includes underground canals, **Engelsberg Ironworks** in Sweden and **Wieliczka Salt Mine** in Poland, developed from the thirteenth century onwards. The economic changes begun in Britain in the eighteenth century that historians have called the Industrial Revolution included significant improvements in transport, amongst which canals were pre-eminent. The unique importance of Britain in the early process of industrialisation is undoubted. Some monuments to the later development of industry have been inscribed in Germany, for example **Völklingen Ironworks** and **Zollverein Coal Mine**, but the United Kingdom *Tentative List* identifies industrialisation as 'one of Britain's major contributions to the world' and seeks to nominate '...outstanding sites representative of the industrialisation of processing and manufacture, developments in inland transport, prowess in generating and using power, and virtuosity in civil engineering, all fundamental to the development of modern society'. Sites have now been inscribed that illustrate manufacturing and mining, but Pontcysyllte Aqueduct and Canal is the first to be nominated that is representative of developments in inland transport or virtuosity in civil engineering.

Cheap transport was essential to industrialisation so it is not surprising that six of the seven industrial World Heritage Sites that have been inscribed in the United Kingdom include sections of canal. Only the Scottish textile community of **New Lanark** was without canal transport. The outstanding monuments to the early iron industry in the **Ironbridge Gorge** include a section of the Shropshire Canal built in 1788-92, with an inclined plane by which small boats were lifted up and down the side of the valley. The **Derwent Valley Mills** World Heritage Site, inscribed for its pre-eminent importance in the early cotton industry, includes part of the Cromford Canal, built in 1789-94. Sir Titus Salt's model industrial community at **Saltaire**, inscribed in 2001, was built alongside the Leeds and Liverpool Canal, the opposite end of which also forms part of the **Liverpool Maritime Mercantile City** World Heritage Site, inscribed in 2004. While canals were not an important part of the mining economy of Cornwall, a four-mile section of the Tavistock Canal is included in the **Cornwall and West Devon Mining Landscape**, inscribed in 2006 for its significance in the world history of metal mining. Canals contributed substantially to the development of the iron and coal industry in south Wales, and a short section of the Brecknock and Abergavenny Canal crosses the edge of the **Blaenavon Industrial Landscape** World Heritage Site.

The presence of canals in these World Heritage Sites attests powerfully to their significance in the Industrial Revolution. However, no other site has a canal as its central theme and none illustrates the scale or importance of great engineering works or the international interchange that arose from the work of the great canal engineers. Pontcysyllte Aqueduct and Canal is of Outstanding Universal Value in demonstrating the methods and techniques by which the cheap transport necessary to industrialisation could be provided in any region.

3.c.5 Overview of comparisons

…among the boldest efforts of human invention in recent times.

J. Phillips, *A General History of Inland Navigation, Foreign and Domestic* (1803)

The Nominated Site has been identified as having Outstanding Universal Value according to the criteria for World Heritage Sites in two expert studies contributing to the global strategy for identifying sites and monuments in categories under-represented on the World Heritage List.

Comparative study shows that canals were not new at the time of the construction of the waterways in the Nominated Site. However, the canals of the Industrial Revolution in Britain, of which the Site is an outstanding example, represented a new beginning in the creation of a network of water communication for industrial traffic that increased the efficiency of the economy and promoted the whole process of industrialization. What makes the Nominated Site distinctive from its precursors and of sufficient significance to be included on the World Heritage List is the application of a combination of new and existing engineering techniques and approaches to the problem of projecting an efficient and highly capitalised route through difficult terrain. No previous canal had used these techniques with such intensity or assurance as was achieved by Telford and Jessop. The achievement with regard to high aqueducts utilising iron, in particular, was uniquely influential and produced masterpieces of innovative design and architectural accomplishment. What makes the Nominated Site different from later canals is that it was the progenitor of a combination of engineering approaches that influenced later transport development world-wide.

A short section of canal lies within the Blaenavon Industrial Landscape World Heritage Site, Wales.

3.d Authenticity and integrity

3.d.1 Statement of authenticity

[We] think it but justice due to Mr Telford to state that the works have been planned with great skill and science, and executed with much economy and stability, doing him, as well as those employed by him, infinite credit.

Ellesmere Canal Company Report (1805)

The Nominated Site is an operating canal that retains its original elements as an advanced engineering line. This can be attributed to the outstanding design and execution of the original structures and the ownership of the canal by a succession of adequately-funded organisations, culminating in the government corporation British Waterways. The *Operational Guidelines* (Annex 3, paragraph 18) advise that changes undergone by Heritage Canals during their working lives may themselves constitute a heritage element. Some such changes have been made over many years in the Nominated Site to maintain the safety and effectiveness of navigation and water supply. The conditions of authenticity set out in the Guidelines that are relevant to Pontcysyllte Aqueduct and Canal are discussed with respect to the following attributes:

- form and design;
- materials and substance;
- use and function;
- traditions, techniques and management systems; and
- location and setting.

Form and design

The route of the canal in the Nominated Site has remained intact and complete. No major original features have been removed. The earthwork formation, composed of the channel, towing-path, hedges and land for embankments and cuttings, maintains the same form as when built, though the materials of the lining and edging have been changed extensively, as

detailed below. The canal width and depth, towing-path, earthworks and boundaries are all unchanged.

The aqueducts retain their original forms and dimensions. The only alterations to their design were those carried out in the nineteenth century as part of their continued industrial use. At Pontcysyllte, Telford recommended in 1813 that the trough should be painted, as this had not been done originally. The timber supports to the towing-path, used initially in order to save costs, had begun to decay by 1818 and were replaced with iron in Telford's lifetime. Sections of cast-iron trough were set into the abutments at each end as a form of waterproofing to seal leaks in 1866-8. Chirk Aqueduct retains its original masonry throughout, but the trough detail was altered in 1869 with the addition of iron side plates over the original waterproofing of hydraulic mortar and hard-fired bricks.

Horseshoe Falls Weir is unchanged. Chirk and Whitehouses Tunnels retain their original form and design with towing-paths, brick linings covered in clay and sweeping façades. Whitehouses Tunnel has its original iron handrails, but at Chirk cast-iron supports to the timber handrails were installed in 1822. The single ventilation

The canal formation is essentially unchanged. Embankments and cuttings were planted with trees at the time of construction: the scientist Michael Faraday walked through Canal Wood Cutting in 1819 and wrote, 'After the tunnel the canal became very pretty indeed. It was sunk considerably beneath the level of the ground about it but the sides were thickly planted with trees forming a very handsome grove'.

shaft at Chirk remains open, while a second blocked shaft was for construction purposes and was filled at the time of completion. The cuttings and embankments survive in their original form, though Telford was a pioneer in large-scale planting of major earthworks to stabilise their slopes and many are now densely covered by vegetation: the southern approach embankment at Pontcysyllte is obscured by trees and Canal Wood Cutting at Chirk is in a zone of planting that extends some 98 feet/30 metres beyond it. The integrity of the embankments has been threatened over their two hundred year life by gradual compaction. Several breaches have taken place, the most serious in 1945, 1960, 1982 and 1985, after which the damaged sections were reinstated in their previous form. The long-term viability of these important structures has been ensured by the relining of the water-channel.

The character of the canal is enhanced by many original over-bridges that survive in their entirety, but Red Bridge (number 24) and Quinta Bridge (20) were removed in the twentieth century, having fallen out of use, and one footbridge is now without a deck. The removal of even minor historic features of the canal no longer takes place. Warehouses remain at Llangollen and Trevor Basin. The form of wharves is preserved in flat areas beside the canal which may contain below-ground archaeological remains, though other characteristics of their operational life were ephemeral in nature. Houses for resident engineers and nineteenth-century canal workers survive in their original forms and groupings.

Materials and substance

Pontcysyllte Aqueduct has seen slight changes of materials. In 1879, the original timber planking under the towing-path was replaced with iron buckle plates. (Some of these were in turn replaced with steel sheet in 1975, but buckle plates were re-introduced in the 2004 conservation programme.) Four ribs of the southernmost span that had cracked due to settlement of the abutment were repaired with splints in 1866 and then replaced in steel in 1975. The 2003-4 programme of major works followed an exemplary conservation methodology. Replacements for the most corroded of the original bolts holding the trough plates were hand-made using recycled wrought iron. Where seals were damaged they were refilled in the traditional materials of oakum, wire wool and hot bitumen. The original curved ends of the railings, which had been removed to store in 1975, were reinstated and four uprights and fifteen lengths of rail were re-cast from original patterns. All the cast iron was wire-brushed and repainted with three layers of bitumastic paint of the type used traditionally. Spalled masonry at the base of the south abutment and fractured corbels were repaired with stone obtained from the original quarry at Rhos-y-medre. The only alien materials introduced consisted of stainless-steel tie-rods used to stabilise moving masonry in the southern abutment and prevent further deflection.

Inappropriate modern techniques of masonry repair were sometimes employed in the late twentieth century on bridges, culverts, minor aqueducts, overflows and

Below left: One of the many original bridges that survive intact.

Below right: Corroded fixings in the trough of Pontcysyllte Aqueduct were selectively replaced in 2003-4 with nuts and bolts in recycled wrought iron hand-made to the original design.

walls, such as re-pointing with cement, spraying concrete under arches and patching with brick. Appropriate conservation methods are now applied consistently and repairs are carried out by trained staff using carefully matched mortars and stone. The two timber lift-bridges were renewed in steel with hydraulic operation for safety reasons and to prevent damage from increased use, and the decks of two footbridges were replaced. British Waterways' *Heritage Policy and Principles* (2005) now require 'an approach based on minimum physical intervention involving minimum loss of existing fabric.'

The most visually-apparent change in materials and substance in the Nominated Site concerns the channel of the watercourse. The re-lining of sections of the canal bed with bitumen or concrete since the 1960s has affected 45 per cent of the canal where breaches occurred or there was a high risk of breaching. It is not anticipated that further treatment of this kind will be needed. Protection of clay banks at water level in steel or concrete has been installed to cope with current traffic and water flows. Such work is a necessary conservation measure, but more visually sympathetic alternative treatments, for instance incorporating stone or timber, will be introduced as sections are renewed.

Use and function

The canal still carries boats, as it was originally intended to do. Inevitably, changes in operation have been seen during two

centuries of working life. The canal no longer transports commercial cargoes, but the use of the canal by pleasure boats follows a tradition that extends back to the early nineteenth century. Boats are propeller-driven rather than horse-drawn, but propeller-driven craft were widely used on British canals by the 1880s and became typical after the introduction from Sweden of the Bolinder engine to narrow boats in 1912. A horse-drawn boat for visitors still operates in the Nominated Site. The Site's role in inspiring interchanges in the early industrial conservation movement arose partly from its popularity for pleasure boating over a long period.

The canal's use as a water supply conduit, which was crucial in ensuring its survival in 1954 and later, has resulted in a higher rate of flow than that for which the canal was designed. However, the Llangollen Branch to Horseshoe Falls was built explicitly as a water-feeder as well as a navigation. The experience of heritage canals in the United Kingdom and the United States of America has been that without continued functions in both boating and water-supply after the end of commercial traffic, canals were more likely to fall out of use and be destroyed. The current uses of the Nominated Site are consistent with its historical functions and are fundamental to its sustainable future.

Traditions, techniques and management systems

The section of canal in the Nominated Site has been maintained as an operating

Above left: Visually-sympathetic bank protection works have been used in the masonry quay walls at Trevor Basin.

Above right: One of the major historic breaches in the canal embankments, now prevented by lining works in all high-risk areas.

A British Waterways training event promoting traditional lime mortars for masonry repairs.

Protective re-lining to prevent embankment breaches near Cross Street Aqueduct.

waterway by a succession of large transport undertakings which have provided continuity of management from the Ellesmere Canal Company through the Shropshire Union Canal Company and the British Transport Commission to British Waterways. While management methods have evolved over time, there has been considerable continuity in operational maintenance, expressed through established members of staff and traditional skills passed on. The job of the canal 'lengthsman', responsible for daily maintenance of a section of canal, continued through the nineteenth century and most of the twentieth, and the present maintenance teams continue to exercise their responsibilities in the traditions and techniques of their predecessors.

Experimentation with new materials was always a characteristic of canal maintenance, from Telford's time onwards, and this has sometimes resulted in techniques of repair unsympathetic to historic structures. However, the property is now managed in accordance with agreed conservation principles that have been introduced across the British Waterways network and the techniques used in maintenance, repair and conservation respect the qualities and integrity of original workmanship.

Boating activity on the canal helps to foster aspects of the traditions of the waterway. Vessels of dimensions similar to the original narrow boats ply the canal, and with some 15,000 movements each year are seen in similar numbers. While the wharves are no longer stacked with coal or slate,

Residential narrow boats maintain a sense of activity on the canal.

there is a quality of activity and bustle and families stay overnight where the narrow boats were traditionally moored, albeit that they are passing through on holidays not commercial voyages.

Location and setting

The course followed by the canal throughout the Nominated Site has never changed. While elements of the environs have been altered by the historical processes of economic development that the canal was intended to promote, the canal's striking relationship with the landscape remains. The western half of the Buffer Zone in particular has maintained a rural aspect similar to that of the area when the canal was built and this has been recognised in its inclusion in the *Register of Landscapes of Special Historic Interest in Wales*. The canal was devised to stimulate industrial development in the coalfield. The eastern part of the waterway passes settlements that have arisen since it was built and continuing industry and population growth have created new forms in some nearby places, but owing to the wooded character of much of the canal and the lie of the land these seldom intrude on the experience of visitors to the Nominated Site.

Trees have grown up that have obscured some of the views of and from the waterway that were appreciated when it was built. These mature sylvan surroundings are now strongly valued in their own right and provide valuable screening. Nevertheless, programmes of work to maintain and enhance views are being developed as a result of the Landscape Assessment carried out in 2007.

Summary

Overall the canal retains a high degree of authenticity in all its significant attributes. Changes to the setting of the canal in some places reflect the success of its original objectives. The changes in materials used in it are generally the minimum necessary to maintain the canal's use and function as a working navigation and water supply.

3.d.2 Statement of Integrity

...it is the most interesting of all on account of its beautiful works: in this short space, it presents the stone aqueduct erected at Chirk to cross the Ceriog, then two tunnels, afterwards an aqueduct of iron to cross the Dee at Pont-y-Cyssyltan. Beyond this aqueduct, the canal is parallel to the river, and hollowed in the rock, for a great portion of its length, as far as Llandesilio, above Llangollen.

Charles Dupin, *The Commercial Power of Great Britain: Exhibiting a Complete View of the Public Works of the Country translated from the French* (1825)

The *Operational Guidelines* require that the physical fabric and significant features of cultural World Heritage Sites should be in good condition and the impact of deterioration should be under control. They also require the inclusion within the nominated area of a significant proportion of the elements necessary to convey the totality of the property's value. Relationships and dynamic functions present in cultural landscapes, historic towns or other living properties should also be maintained (*Operational Guidelines*, paragraph 89). The integrity of the Nominated Site is considered below according to the conditions set out in the *Operational*

Guidelines, which require assessment of the extent to which the property:

- includes all elements necessary to express its Outstanding Universal Value;

- is of adequate size to ensure the complete representation of the features and processes which convey the property's significance; and

- suffers from adverse effects of development and/or neglect.

Does it include all elements necessary to express its Outstanding Universal Value?

The Site includes all the elements necessary to express its Outstanding Universal Value as a spectacular example of canal engineering, an architectural masterpiece, an example of improvements in transport during the Industrial Revolution and an illustration of interchanges of values in inland navigation, civil engineering and the application of iron to structural design.

The Site includes the whole of the engineering works that comprise each section of the canal. It is based on the property boundaries of the canal company, which reflect the extent of land used in construction, for example reaching to the toes of embankments and the rims of

The Nominated Site includes the whole of the canal from Gledrid Bridge, bottom left, to Horseshoe Falls. The immediate visual surrounding of Chirk Aqueduct, centre, lies within the Nominated Site, and the Buffer Zone has been drawn to recognise the full landscape setting.

cuttings. Assets of direct relevance to the construction of the canal that lie outside current British Waterways property have been included within the Site, such as the construction platforms for Chirk and Pontcysyllte Aqueducts, land above the two tunnels and the houses built to accommodate resident engineers and maintenance workers. The nomination of the whole of the intensively-engineered line from Gledrid Bridge to Horseshoe Falls ensures that all the features and processes that convey the Outstanding Universal Value of the Site are represented.

The improvement of transport in the Industrial Revolution is represented by the canal itself and by the remains of trade installations along its course in the form of wharves, basins and warehouses. Consideration was given in preparing this Nomination to related transport developments, settlements and industrial enterprises that grew up in the generations after the canal was built. A detailed study was made of the industrial archaeology of the area served by the canal. This found that many of the associated transport and industrial developments, such as horse-worked railways, mines and quarries, post-dated the engineering works of the Site by a considerable time, were ephemeral and had left only disparate remains. Including surviving elements of these would not contribute coherently to the Site's

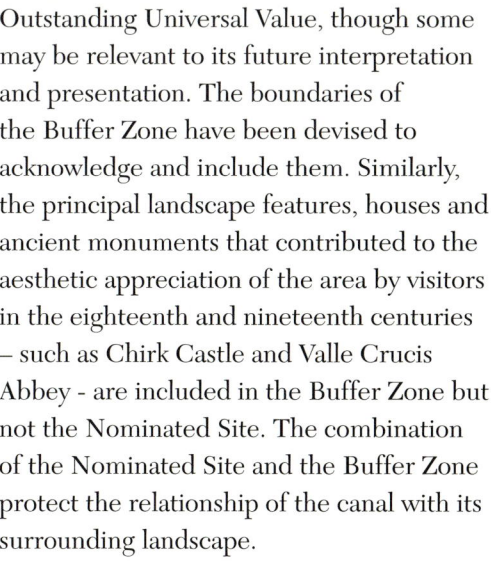

Outstanding Universal Value, though some may be relevant to its future interpretation and presentation. The boundaries of the Buffer Zone have been devised to acknowledge and include them. Similarly, the principal landscape features, houses and ancient monuments that contributed to the aesthetic appreciation of the area by visitors in the eighteenth and nineteenth centuries – such as Chirk Castle and Valle Crucis Abbey - are included in the Buffer Zone but not the Nominated Site. The combination of the Nominated Site and the Buffer Zone protect the relationship of the canal with its surrounding landscape.

Is it of adequate size to ensure the complete representation of the features and processes which convey the property's significance?

Detailed consideration has been given to determining the size of the Nominated Site and Buffer Zone. Both the aqueduct and the longer section of the Ellesmere Canal were identified separately as of significance in the ICOMOS/TICCIH *International Canal Monuments List* (1996) and it was decided to nominate the whole of the engineering works rather than define the Site exclusively by its most famous feature, Pontcysyllte Aqueduct. While the boundary could be extended further along the canal from Gledrid Bridge, the remainder of the canal is less intensively engineered and contains no features of importance that are not already represented adequately. The site of a short branch canal that existed at Plas Kynaston and was destroyed in later development is excluded - this was a private canal not built by the Ellesmere Canal Company or its engineers, and it did not come into existence until some twenty-five years after the completion of the main line.

The visual relationship of the most aesthetically significant canal monuments with their surroundings has been considered carefully. From the time of their construction Pontcysyllte Aqueduct, Chirk Aqueduct and Horseshoe Falls Weir were viewed and appreciated as masterpieces and depicted by artists in their settings. For this reason the boundary of the Site has been extended beyond the canal works themselves to give due importance to the immediate visual surroundings of the three monuments. The broader landscape setting is further protected by the Buffer Zone.

Does it suffer from adverse effects of development and/or neglect?

The Nominated Site benefits from a rigorous regime of maintenance and control, derived from extensive statutory protection and state ownership. British Waterways has in place an effective system of monitoring all its assets and their condition, as set out in Section 5, and this informs on-going programmes of maintenance, without which deterioration would occur. The legal duties placed upon British Waterways to ensure that the canal remains open as a functioning navigation and water-supply conduit provide additional assurances against neglect. Oversight by government heritage bodies, local authority conservation officers and the Pontcysyllte Aqueduct and Canal Steering Group further underline this. The physical fabric of the Nominated Site is in good condition and the processes of deterioration are well under control.

The Site is protected from adverse effects of development through statutory designation, state ownership and the planning control system, set out in Section 5. During the two hundred year working life of the waterway, operational improvements have introduced individual features such as new footbridges, road crossings and moorings in some places, but these have a minor and localised impact and do not affect the integrity of the canal. British Waterways' policies now dictate that, 'All major projects and general works should demonstrate a respect for waterway heritage,' and this is guaranteed by the need for Scheduled Monument Consent and Planning Consent for any future development. The setting of the Site includes many areas recognised for their conservation value and is generally free of adverse development. Numerous designations and strong planning policies ensure that the setting of the canal is among the most thoroughly protected landscapes in the United Kingdom.

Summary

The Nominated Site is inclusive of all of the features that reflect its Outstanding Universal Value and is large enough for the context of these to be properly appreciated and understood. Strong ownership and management measures ensure the maintenance of the Site and will continue to protect it and its wider setting from adverse development.

Regular maintenance has been carried out on the canal throughout its existence under a succession of transport undertakings, culminating in British Waterways: cleaning of the iron trough at Chirk Aqueduct in the 1950s.

Opposite: Pontcysyllte Aqueduct's superbly crafted masonry piers tower above the meadows of the Dee Valley.

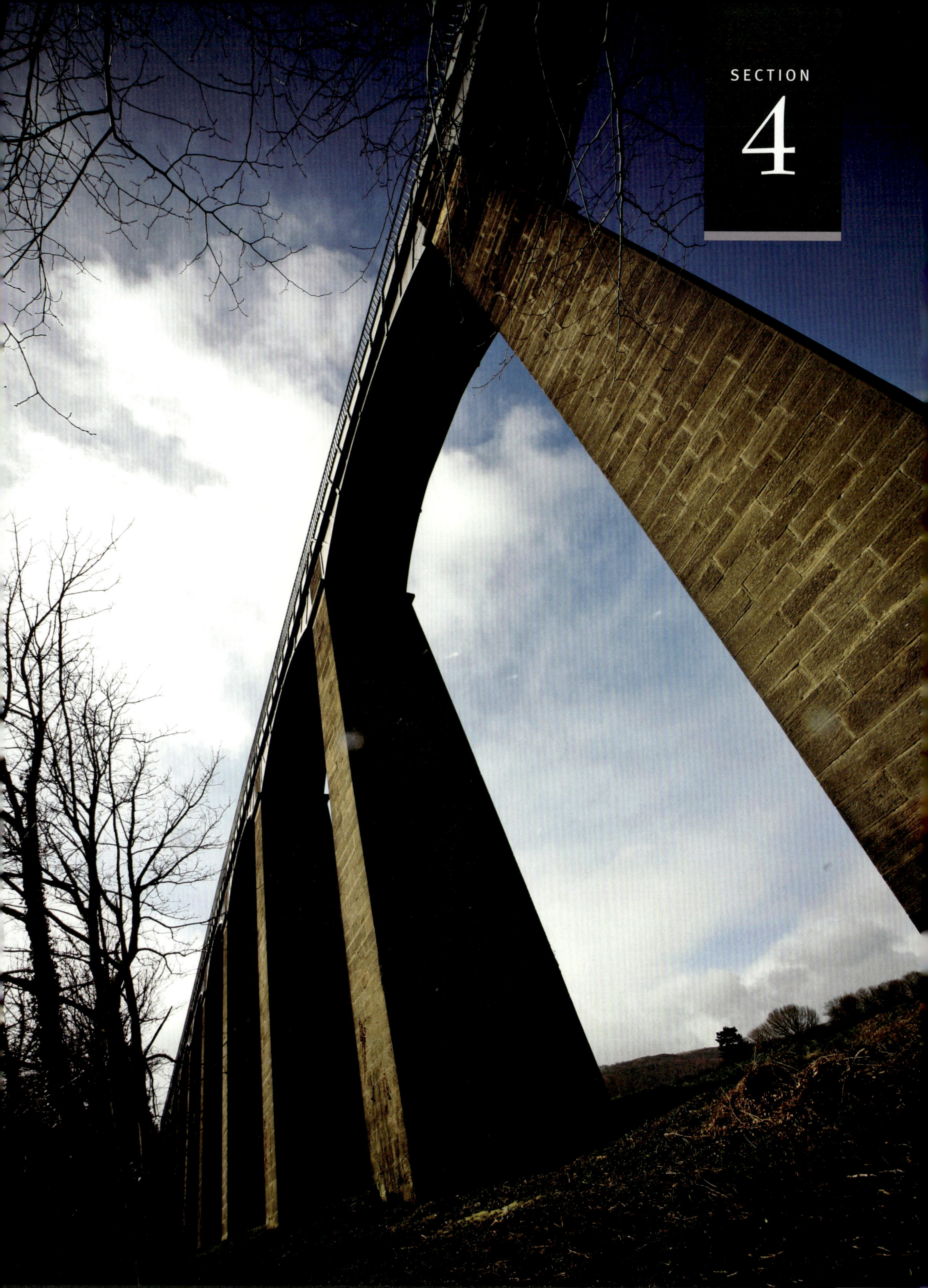

SECTION 4

On some parts of this navigation some astonishing works have been constructed, but the limits to which our work is prescribed, precludes the possibility of enumerating them; however we must not omit to notice the well known aqueduct over the Dee at Ponty-Cysylte. This stupendous work is carried over the river, at an elevation of 125 feet above its bed… and it is entirely composed of cast iron plates. There is also another very large aqueduct over the River Ceiriog, which is built of stone; it is two hundred yards in length, and is supported on ten arches, at an elevation of 65 feet above the river. This navigation, from the immediate connection it has with the Rivers Mersey and Dee, and with the Montgomeryshire Canal, and the communication it has, by means of collateral cuts and the Ruabon Branch Railway, with the mineral districts to which they severally extend, and the fertile agricultural parts of North Salop and the county palatine of Chester, through which it winds its way, is of first rate importance.

Joseph Priestly
Historical Account of the Navigable Rivers, Canals and Railways of Great Britain
(1831)

STATE OF CONSERVATION AND FACTORS AFFECTING THE PROPERTY

A great preservation scheme ensuring that this revolutionary structure will be safe with minimum of attention for the next fifty years.

Citation for the Institution of Civil Engineers Historic Bridge and Infrastructure Award (2004)

4.a Present state of conservation

This Section provides the base-line data to monitor the state of conservation of the Nominated Site. It reviews the physical condition of the property, threats and conservation measures. The benchmarks used are identified in Section 6.

4.a.1 Current physical condition

The Nominated Site contains 11 miles/ 18 kilometres of canal. It includes the two major aqueducts at Pontcysyllte and Chirk, two smaller aqueducts, two tunnels, thirty-one bridges, fifteen embankments, sixteen cuttings, seven sluices, Horseshoe Falls and two floodweirs, eighteen culverts, and associated buildings at Chirk Bank, Froncysyllte, Pontcysyllte, Trevor, Llangollen and Llantysilio. All of the canal and its key structures are in state ownership under British Waterways. Some bridges crossing the canal are publicly owned by the relevant highways authorities or are in private ownership. The Buffer Zone, which is in multiple ownerships, is an extensive area devised to protect the landscape setting of the Nominated Site and features of interest associated with past use of the waterway.

British Waterways' Asset Inspection Programme

British Waterways employs a robust system of routine inspection and engineering assessment - its Asset Inspection Programme. The purpose of this programme is to identify and manage any risks associated with waterway assets and ensure that remedial works are identified and prioritised. The inspections are carried out in accordance with a formal timetable to identify any faults that might undermine the business of British Waterways or represent a threat to the health and safety of customers, neighbours, staff or the general public. Reports on each asset give a clear and accurate description of its condition and identify any defects. The findings of successive reports are compared to enable the rate and nature of deterioration or improvement in the asset to be assessed. This provides sound data on which to identify and prioritise remedial works in a systematic manner to minimise any risks of failure.

British Waterways has identified twenty-five structures within the Nominated Site the failure of which would lead to major operational disruption or have serious consequences for properties downslope (for instance the aqueducts, tunnels, major cuttings and embankments). These are termed "Principal Assets" within the Asset Inspection Programme. Loss or damage to these would also severely affect the proposed Outstanding Universal Value of the Nominated Site. Principal Assets are subject to the following inspections

- **Length Inspections:** walkovers of a section of waterway to a monthly or quarterly schedule;
- **Intermediate Inspections:** visual inspections of individual assets every one or five years;
- **Principal Inspections:** full, detailed inspection, involving draining a section of canal or access to elevated and internal areas every ten or twenty years, or as required.

In addition, British Waterways carries out an annual *Customer Service Inspection* of the whole waterway to ensure that it is in a satisfactory condition for the use of customers.

Training for British Waterways staff in conservation techniques.

As well as identifying priority works, inspections grade the condition of structures on a scale of 'fitness for purpose', from excellent condition (A) through adequate (C) to poor (D) or bad, with significant repairs required in the short term (E). Where structures are D or E the works required are prioritised. British Waterways' maintenance programme is aimed at keeping the majority of structures at grade C or better, but a proportion of structures at any given time will be in categories D and E. At the end of 2006, British Waterways' inspections classified 70 per cent of the 'principal assets' in the Nominated Site as category A to C. Of the remaining 30

per cent, improvements are required for operational purposes, but this does not always indicate a need for works to improve the state of conservation, as discussed below.

State of Conservation Report 2007

Pontcysyllte Aqueduct is now in an excellent state of conservation, following the completion of an award-winning major refurbishment in 2005, for which details are given in Section 4.a.3 below. An assessment of the historic fabric of the whole Nominated Site was commissioned in 2007 to establish a base line of the state of conservation of all features. The State of Conservation Report (see Supporting Information) extended the British Waterways 'fitness for purpose' classification described above to all the structures and features of the Nominated Site. More importantly, it added grading of authenticity and integrity of the heritage fabric to give a 'State of Conservation' grade of Good, Fair, Fair* or Poor.

Good – the authenticity and integrity of the asset are intact and as close to its original state as is reasonable (allows for replacement on 'like for like' basis or historical changes).

Fair – the authenticity and integrity is largely intact. There may be minor alterations or inappropriate repairs but they do not significantly threaten the asset.

Fair* – for the majority of the structure overall the authenticity and integrity is largely intact but there are significant alterations, inappropriate repairs, deficiencies in maintenance or structural problems associated with limited areas that require remedial work.

Poor – the authenticity and integrity of the structure is damaged and significant conservation work is required to bring the asset to an acceptable condition.

This additional grading now allows future maintenance and conservation to be targeted at maintaining operational condition and improving the integrity of the historic fabric throughout the Nominated Site and Buffer Zone

Condition of Channel: Substantial sections of the waterway have been relined (some 45 per cent of the total length – typically with a new concrete lining installed) or had bank protection installed (sheet piling, concrete or timber walling, geotextile fabric – another 40 per cent of the total). These works have been in response to erosion of the banks, leakage and even breaches of the waterway where the original construction (typically clay-lined dish) has been compromised by ground movement, leakage and erosion from water flow or boat traffic. These repairs have been essential to maintain the waterway itself in working order and without them the Canal would have been closed or converted to a water-supply pipe.

These necessary interventions have been taken into account by the Report when considering the State of Conservation of sections of the channel (termed "Reaches" in the Report). Of the 27 reaches, 2 are assessed as Good; 19 Fair; 4 Fair*; and 2 relatively short sections Poor.

Condition of the major features:

The 'fitness for purpose' and 'State of Conservation' grading of the major features within the Nominated Site is as follows:

Above: Bank protection against erosion at Millars Bridge.

Left: Unsympathetic patching in brick to a masonry culvert, probably dating from about the 1960s; an example of repair needs identified in the State of Conservation Report.

Structure	Fitness for Purpose	State of Conservation
Horseshoe Falls	C	Fair
Pentrefelin Aqueduct	C	Fair
Llangollen Wharf buildings	C	Fair
Trevor Basin	C	Fair
Pontcysyllte Aqueduct	A	Good (following recent refurbishment detailed in Section 4.a.3; this sets the standard for future works within the Nominated Site)
Froncysyllte Embankment	A	Fair
Whitehouses Tunnel	C	Fair
Canal Wood cutting	C	Fair
Chirk Tunnel	C	Fair
Chirk Aqueduct	C	Fair* (Vegetation, previous repairs)
Chirk Bank embankment	C	Fair

Chirk Bank Bridge.

This illustrates that the major structures are generally in acceptable condition and also shows the value of the separate 'State of Conservation' grading which sometimes provides a different result to the 'fitness for purpose' assessment.

Other Structures: as indicated above, 30 per cent of the structures termed 'Principal Assets' by British Waterways within the Nominated Site are considered to be in poor condition from a 'fitness for purpose' assessment, requiring some works (this is a typical distribution for British Waterways assets). Assessment of all assets within the Nominated Site shows only 12 per cent of the total are 'Poor' from a State of Conservation view.

Structures	State of Conservation					
	Total No	Good	Fair	Fair*	Poor	Not Assessed
Weirs	3		33%	33%		33%
Aqueducts	4	25%	25%	25%	25%	
Bridges	35	11%	23%	17%	17%	32%
Houses / Cottages (some as groups)	15	20%	53%	14%	13%	
Operational buildings eg warehouses etc	9	22%	33%	11%	11%	23%
Tunnels	2		100%			
Culverts, sluices and drainage channels	30	3%	50%	7%	10%	30%
Embankments	19	10%	90%			
Cuttings	16		87%	13%		
Wharves, docks and basins	21		81%		19%	
Other associated features	27	4%	70%		15%	11%
TOTALS	181	8%	58%	9%	12%	13%

Note: 'Not Assessed' means features were either not accessible during the survey or state of conservation is not appropriate (i.e. for thoroughly modern structures).

The tall over-bridge at Irish Bridge Cutting.

Landscape assessment 2007

The whole of the landscape through which the waterway passes lies within the Nominated Site or its Buffer Zone. The landscape is important both as an expression of the physical challenges overcome by the engineers constructing the canal and as the setting for viewing and appreciating the canal today. A significant part of the landscape of the canal corridor is formed by the embankments, cuttings and visual envelopes within the boundaries of the Nominated Site and will be actively managed. The wider setting, in the Buffer Zone, will be subject to control through the land-use planning system. Both levels of management require a base-line character assessment. This was carried out by staff from Wrexham County Borough Council, British Waterways, Denbighshire County Council and Oswestry Borough Council in 2007 (see Supporting Information). The key findings were as follows :

- assessment of the landscape character and key views was carried out in accordance with the joint Institute of Environmental Management and Assessment (IEMA) / Landscape Institute (LI) standards for assessing significance of impacts on landscape;

- important views to and from the Nominated Site and landscape setting were identified, at Pontcysyllte and Chirk aqueducts, Horseshoe Falls and the wider canal network;

- the immediate visual envelopes of Pontcysyllte and Chirk aqueducts and Horseshoe Falls were recommended for inclusion within the Nominated Site to allow these large structures to be fully appreciated within the Nominated Site boundary. However, it was determined that a Buffer Zone based upon views would be intermittent and changeable over time, due to the extent of woodland within the study area;

- a Buffer Zone, adequate to support future planning decisions aimed at protecting the landscape setting of the Nominated Site and key structures, was therefore extended to the top of ridgelines defining the valleys around the canal, with variations to include areas of important historic association, identified within the Industrial Archaeology Audit; and

- outline recommendations were made for vegetation management both to open up important views and to provide appropriate screening. It was not considered desirable to reinstate every historic view, as this would reduce beneficial screening or have negative conservation impacts in some locations.

Industrial archaeology audit 2007

In 2007 a comprehensive industrial archaeology audit of the Buffer Zone was undertaken to identify and evaluate features associated with the construction of the canal and remains of industries that used the canal for transport. Industries present in the area prior to the construction of the canal included: stone quarrying, lime production, coal mining, iron ore extraction and slate quarrying. Serving these was one of the reasons for the canal crossing the River Dee in the vicinity of Pontcysyllte. Industries that developed after the construction of the canal included: iron-making, engineering, chemical production, the manufacture of bricks, tiles and terracotta and slate quarrying. The canal also stimulated the development of an extensive system of early railways. The remains of these activities generally lie outside the Nominated Site but within the Buffer Zone and are relevant to the Nominated Site's interpretation. This baseline audit informs the Management Plan for their future conservation and presentation.

The complete audit is included in the Supporting Information. It found that the archaeological and landscape survival is high for lime production but poor for coal-mining, brick-making and iron-processing.

Associated industries: limekilns at Froncysyllte.

The Llangollen Railway, representative of the next phase of transport development after the canals, lies within the Buffer Zone.

The remains of feeder transport systems, including a branch canal and a network of early railways, are moderately preserved. It confirms that the canal lies within the immediate vicinity of two analogous and well preserved historic transport systems, (Telford's road to Holyhead and the Llangollen Railway), and several industrial-period settlements. Recommendations are made in the report as to future study, conservation and interpretation of these features and the boundaries for the Buffer Zone were drawn so as to incorporate them.

4.a.2 Threats to the state of conservation

There are no substantial current threats to the state of conservation of the Nominated Site or its setting.

Lesser threats that may pertain include decay if there were to be a deficit of maintenance, wear and tear to operational features, and the impact of past instances of inappropriate repair, most notably through the use of cement pointing. These are discussed in Section 4b, and measures to deal with them are in Section 5 and the Management Plan. The main control measure is the programme of inspection and conservation work by British Waterways and other property owners.

4.a.3 Conservation measures

The Nominated Site is protected by a range of statutory designations and land-use planning controls that safeguard its integrity. These are detailed in Section 5. The Management Plan identifies actions to protect and enhance the condition of the historic fabric. Key amongst these is the development of a Conservation Management Plan (CMP) for the whole Nominated Site (action 27) building on the 2007 State of Conservation report and the existing CMP for Pontcysyllte Aqueduct and Trevor Basin that was produced during the bicentenary refurbishment in 2004-5 (see page 147).

British Waterways' heritage policy

British Waterways recognises conservation as an integral part of its function as a public body. The organisation's Heritage Policy states:

Our aim is for the heritage of the waterways to be treasured as a valued national asset. The careful protection and management of that heritage is an essential part of the ongoing work to achieve our vision.

Under its policy of Heritage Action begun in 2005, British Waterways is committed to achieving and maintaining high standards of management, maintenance and repair of the historic fabric in its care. The Policy, a copy of which is included in the Supporting Information, sets out principles for all works affecting the waterways heritage:

Our heritage principles provide the framework within which British Waterways manages the waterway heritage. The principles establish best practice in the maintenance and repair of historic structures, the management of historic man-made landscapes, the relationship with new development, the importance of archaeology and the use of interpretation and public events. We will monitor our activities and outputs through an annual State of the Waterways Heritage report.

We will promote best practice amongst our employees, contractors, suppliers, customers and partners. We will seek suppliers, contractors and partners with standards consistent with our own.

Major conservation works at Pontcysyllte Aqueduct

Pontcysyllte Aqueduct and Trevor Basin were the subject of major refurbishment works in advance of the 2005 bicentenary. The project was awarded the Waterways Renaissance Historic Environment Award and the Institution of Civil Engineers national Historic Bridge and Infrastructure Award.

These works were funded by British Waterways and the European Regional Development Fund with support from Wrexham County Borough Council and Cadw, the Welsh Assembly Government's historic environment division.

Works to the Aqueduct were necessary to repair leaks in the iron trough and address defects. The works were monitored independently by Cadw and carried out with Scheduled Monument Consent granted by the Welsh Assembly Government. A full Report on the works is provided in the supporting information to the Nomination, but the main elements were:

- comprehensive inspection and recording before, during and after the work;
- reinstatement of a bitumen-based paint to the cast ironwork following wire brushing;
- selective bolt replacements;
- refurbishment of the towing-path and handrail;
- masonry repairs to the pier tops;
- reinforcement of joint sealant with traditional tar/hemp; and
- removal of vegetation from lower slopes.

Following a trial refurbishment of a single span in 2000, when different methods of preparing the cast iron were tested, it became evident that preparation by grit blasting caused excessive damage to the historic metalwork. The approved method of surface preparation was to prepare the cast iron by mechanical wire brushing. Research into the historical painting of the aqueduct revealed that Thomas Telford had recommended painting in 1813 and that the system last applied, in 1965, was a traditional, bitumen-based type paint that had provided good protection. A similar system was therefore used in the refurbishment.

The towing-path has undergone a number of changes during the aqueduct's lifetime. The condition of the towing-path was poor, with longitudinal mild-steel angles along the edge severely corroded. The cast-iron supports generally were in good condition, but five were replaced in cast iron using the pattern retained in British Waterways' Ellesmere Yard, where a significant store of original patterns are retained for this type of replacement work. Two further supports were repaired using low voltage welding techniques. The

The major conservation works in progress at Pontcysyllte Aqueduct in 2003-4.

majority of the cast-iron towing-path cross members also remained intact but twenty-two were replaced. Steel sheet piling that had been used inappropriately during towing-path repair in 1965 was replaced with new, purpose-made plates to match the earlier form.

The masonry piers generally were in good condition. Ivy was found on six piers but the excellent-quality original mortar joints had not suffered significant damage and re-pointing was not necessary. A poor drainage detail at the top of the piers had led to some deterioration of the stonework. Where necessary, new pieces of masonry were cut from a local quarry – the same stone as used in the original construction - and fixed with stainless-steel dowels and lime mortar.

The original cast-iron railing remained intact but many of the ballusters had become loose and several top rails had cracked because of poor past maintenance of expansion joints. The ineffective joints

Repair work to damaged corbels at Pontcysyllte Aqueduct.

were replaced, loose ballusters were secured using metal shim packing pieces to the bottom connection detail and caulking of the top fixing with wire wool. Four ballusters and fifteen sections of handrail were re-cast from patterns stored at British Waterways' Ellesmere Yard. The curved braces at the northern end of the aqueduct, which had been removed in 1987, were recovered from storage and repositioned.

A visual and hand inspection of every bolt assembly showed that some were no longer sound after two hundred years. Five hundred complete assemblies (bolt, nut and washer) and 750 nuts and washers were replaced like-for-like with components hand-made from reclaimed wrought iron. Areas of defective jointing material (some original and some recent) were refurbished using oakum (hemp impregnated with bitumen). Narrower joints, up to 8 millimetres, were refurbished with wire wool and caulked. All of the joints were re-sealed with hot bitumen.

Aspects of best practice that were commended by Cadw and in the awards received included:

- the research into the likely original joint-sealing and paint materials to ensure a high level of authenticity, avoiding modern materials;

- tests on methods of work such as paint removal to minimise impact on the fabric;

- accurate matching of stone, sourced from the original quarry;

- replacement bolts through bespoke fabrication in wrought-iron;

- replacement of railings using an historical pattern and re-instatement of missing curved sections; and

- replacement of inappropriate earlier repairs to the towing-path.

The refurbishment of Trevor Basin was supported by the former Wales Tourist Board (now Visit Wales) and Wrexham County Borough Council. The works included rebuilding the north wharf wall, clearance of the two eastern arms to bring them back into use, landscape and access improvements, community art and interpretation with extensive consultation and public involvement and refurbishment of an operational building as an interpretation centre.

Forthcoming works

British Waterways maintains a three to four year programme of major refurbishment of significant assets in addition to its routine maintenance and minor repairs. This programme currently contains the following works within the Nominated Site:

- repairs in the vicinity of Pentrefelin to address leakage from the canal channel, with advance tree management in winter 2007 and channel works in winter 2008;

- repairs to the retaining wall at Llangollen; and

- improvements to the water intake structures at Llantysilio.

There are no other significant works planned (as of 2007) by other property owners / Steering Group members within the Nominated Site.

This list will be reviewed and expanded in the light of the development of the Management Plan for the Nominated Site.

4.b Factors affecting the Property

The Steering Group have reviewed all issues potentially affecting the Nominated Site under the following categories:

- conservation and maintenance;

- development;

- presentation - visitor management, community and education;

- environmental pressures; and

- disasters and risk preparedness.

4.b.1 Conservation and maintenance

Wear and tear – man-made structures require maintenance and repair to keep pace with natural decay. Routine maintenance arrests minor defects before they threaten the integrity of the asset and the Outstanding Universal Value of the Nominated Site. This may include renewal of pointing, vegetation management, painting, replacement of small areas of failed material, infilling of potholes in the towing-path or bridge decks and repair of small water leaks. The number of assets makes it likely that there will always be some waterway assets in 'poor' condition and awaiting repair.

Inappropriate past repairs – there have been examples of inappropriate repair in the past that have damaged the historic fabric, for instance the use of engineering brick to replace damaged stonework (Chirk Aqueduct), cement pointing on some structures instead of lime mortar and the replacement of buckle plates with sheet piles in the towing-path of Pontcysyllte Aqueduct (replaced during the recent refurbishment). Some replacement with new materials has been necessary, however, notably re-lining and bank protection to the canal channel to reduce the risk of breaches, persistent leakage, slope instability and erosion. Consideration is being given to determining preferred methods of protection for the canal channel where this is needed in future.

Left: British Waterways' training in the use of lime mortars.

Inappropriate repair is being actively combated by research, changes in working practices to favour lime mortar, stone and wrought iron over cement, machined bricks, concrete and steel, and re-introduction of traditional skills. (See British Waterways' Heritage Policy in the Supporting Information). There can be conflict between historic designs and modern building regulations or visitor safety standards, but this is reduced when those carrying out works are properly informed, trained and supplied and those designing solutions are aware of the need to safeguard the heritage value of the asset.

Sufficient resources for maintenance - in the past there have been times when competing demands have reduced the resources available to maintain the Site. In recent years external funding has been secured for a number of initiatives, notably the bicentenary refurbishment of Pontcysyllte Aqueduct and Trevor Basin. The raised awareness of the Outstanding Universal Value of the Nominated Site will help to ensure that such support continues where required. The operational use of the waterway creates a clear need for maintenance of critical structures and British Waterways has a public commitment in its heritage policy to ensure its conservation (see Supporting Information).

Vegetation management – vegetation requires careful management in the vicinity of built structures. However, the embankments and cuttings were planted originally to produce timber and to stabilise slopes. The Landscape Study has identified that the wooded nature of the waterway corridor is one of its defining features and helps to screen modern development, but that some areas need to be cut back to open up significant views. It is therefore essential that vegetation is managed against clear objectives for protection and presentation of the Nominated Site.

Co-ordination of owners and partners - it is important to ensure consistency of approach and efficient allocation of resources within all parts of the Nominated Site. This function is being performed by the Steering Group, which will continue to develop its processes to ensure the effectiveness of implementation.

4.b.2 Development pressures

As a linear site, the canal and its setting is subject to potential pressures from development or changes in land use over a large area, defined by the Nominated Site and its Buffer Zone.

Inappropriate alterations or additions to properties could affect the presentation of the Nominated Site. The pressure for these changes can come from a number of sources, such as changing safety regulations and standards, improvement, extension and renewal of residential properties and the conversion of former industrial properties to new uses. Most of these changes are controlled within the planning system, and for designated properties by Listed Building Consent or Scheduled Monument Consent.

Economic activities have potential for significant impacts. Some are an essential part of public engagement with and enjoyment of the property and provide income for reinvestment in maintenance. However, it is recognised that popular sites may become commercialised to the detriment of their value. British Waterways is currently developing a 'Destination Management Plan' for the waterway as one of the top waterway destinations in the UK, and this will identify how the provision of facilities and development of economic opportunities will be carried out in ways sympathetic to the significance of the Nominated Site.

Wrexham County Borough Council and Denbighshire County Council are likely to be required to plan for growth in urban areas within the Buffer Zone over the next five years, for example Cefn Mawr, Chirk and Llangollen. Properly designed and located development need not detract from the Nominated Site or its

setting and existing development control policies identify design and landscape as issues that must be addressed (see Section 5.d). Emerging policies, which may have to permit expansion of development boundaries will include arrangements for protection of the Nominated Site and its setting and the local authorities are working together to ensure consistency across the Nominated Site. The Steering Group is committed to ensuring that policies relating to development will protect the integrity of the Nominated Site.

Changes to land use within the Buffer Zone could affect the setting of the Nominated Site, for example large-scale forestry operations, major developments or cumulative small impacts. As detailed in Section 5.d, development control designations and policies cover the proposed Buffer Zone and the setting of Listed or Scheduled structures.

Historic changes that have adversely affected the setting also need to be addressed to enhance the Nominated Site (see Section 5e).

Loss of associated features to land-use change. There are many features identified by the industrial archaeology audit as being associated with the Nominated Site but not part of its Outstanding Universal Value within the Buffer Zone. As most of them relate to long redundant activities they may be vulnerable to proposals for development

or change of use. This is controlled by existing planning policies (see 5.d) for protection of archaeological resources and these features are also being considered within the review of heritage protection being undertaken for the Nominated Site by Cadw and English Heritage

4.b.3 Presentation - visitor management, community and education

Presentation of the Outstanding Universal Value is part of the purpose of a World Heritage Site. Many bodies on the Steering Group are already engaged in activities associated with promotion, visitor management, community participation and education, both using the waterway and in the wider area. The Management Plan addresses opportunities to strengthen this work and to deliver it in a coordinated manner.

Landscape and Vegetation Management – the 2007 landscape study identifies the need to establish standards for vegetation management to protect and enhance views to and from the key parts of the Nominated Site. Management of the wider landscape of the Buffer Zone is also carried out through the development control processes outlined in Section 5.d.

How to get the story across – the complexity and diversity of the history of the Nominated Site and its surroundings

Left: Trevor Basin is an important focus for boating but protected from inappropriate development by its status as a Conservation Area.

Above: Crowds cross Pontcysyllte Aqueduct at the Bicentenary events of November 2005.

The Bicentenary events at Trevor Basin, November 2005.

presents a challenge in how to present such a wealth of information to diverse audiences. Work began on community interpretation at Pontcysyllte Aqueduct and Trevor Basin in 2004-5 and through the public consultation on this Nomination in 2007. Educational resources about the aqueduct have been produced as part of the joint Inland Waterways Association / British Waterways initiative Wild Over Waterways (WOW). The Management Plan recognises the need to review existing provision, refresh what has worked and introduce new initiatives to present the Nominated Site to a wider audience. This will be addressed by an Interpretation Strategy that will ensure consistency and high standards.

Community engagement – an essential part of presentation, and of wider management, is to ensure engagement of the local community. British Waterways and the local authority partners are engaged with a wide range of community-based groups in and around the Nominated Site, such as Community / Parish Councils and countryside volunteers, and with organisations focused on the waterways, such as Shropshire Union Canal Society and the Inland Waterways Association. A 'Friends of Pontcysyllte' group has already been established by the local communities to work with the Steering Group to ensure active involvement of the local communities in decision making and management.

The annual Community Fun Day at Trevor Basin.

Recent events at Pontcysyllte have attracted up to 5,000 people a day.

Sustainable access – avoiding unacceptable damage to the Nominated Site from use is essential. As in many World Heritage Sites, the large numbers of visitors present can create erosion, wear and tear and failure of operating structures, while changing health and safety standards may raise questions about alterations to historic fabric. The Nominated Site and Buffer Zone already attract large numbers of visitors, especially to Pontcysyllte Aqueduct (approximately 200,000 a year) and Llangollen town (also approximately 200,000 a year). Recent community events at the aqueduct have attracted up to 5,000 people in a day. The canal is subject to 15,000 boat movements a year, making it one of the busiest in the UK. Visitor numbers are likely to continue to increase, but many measures can be used to offset potential impacts.

Provided these are implemented, there is no reason to believe that the Nominated Site will exceed a sustainable capacity.

Sustainable access may be improved by physical access enhancements to encourage visitors to spread out across the Nominated Site, and providing a greater capacity through group boat trips, 'remote tours' and other innovations.

There is a need to improve physical access and the visitor experience at some parts of the Nominated Site. Most of the towing-path has been upgraded in recent years with grants directed through local authority partners, but the section between Llangollen and Trevor is difficult in the winter. There is a need to improve access to some of the key viewpoints for Pontcysyllte and Chirk aqueducts and other major structures. British Waterways has completed a Welsh Assembly Government funded survey of all its waterways in Wales for their physical accessibility to people with disabilities. Recommendations for reducing restrictions will be incorporated into future management proposals.

Managing litter and graffiti is important for presentation of the Nominated Site. Measures should not detract from the setting or harm the fabric, but will focus on maintenance standards in litter picking and cleaning to address problems within an acceptable timescale and using appropriate methods.

4.b.4 Environmental pressures

The environmental pressure of greatest concern currently is Climate Change. For North Wales and Western England, the general predictions of climate change models are for drier, hotter summers, generally wetter winters and an increase in high intensity rainfall events. The timescale for significant changes is in tens of years, but the scientific consensus is that some impacts are now inevitable. The challenges that will arise from this include:

1. Pressure on the water-supply for the canal in the summer, which is critical to maintaining the waterway during its period of highest use. British Waterways

Litter and graffiti have to be managed and deterred.

is engaged in a national programme to improve monitoring of water usage and supplies, reduce losses and investigate options for optimising the use of water.

2. Increased likelihood of flooding of the canal, river and hillsides. (See Section 4.b.5)

3. Potential for increased weather-related damage to structures. Increased maintenance requirements will be managed through the existing routine programmes of inspection and maintenance, although additional resources may be required. Given the timescales for change, there is sufficient time to plan preventative measures and to increase resources for routine repairs if necessary.

Natural environment conservation issues – The Rivers Dee and Ceiriog are part of a Special Area for Conservation (SAC), a European nature conservation designation. The Nominated Site overlaps with the SAC designation at Horseshoe Falls, Pontcysyllte and Chirk Aqueduct and is close to it for much of its length. Maintenance and improvement may affect the SAC and need to be carefully considered in the light of the positive management required by the designation. Environmental interests are specifically represented on the Steering Group by the Countryside Council for Wales, which is the regulator for Special Areas of Conservation in Wales. Works potentially affecting the sites in England (at Chirk) will require consultation with Natural England.

In addition, the Nominated Site and Buffer Zone contain many statutorily protected plant and animal species as well as habitats of local and regional importance. These need to be taken into account in management of the Nominated Site and Buffer Zone to ensure they are protected and enhanced where practicable. Many member bodies on the Steering Group are involved in local Biodiversity Action Plans (BAPs) or have their own corporate BAPs and have internal procedures for ensuring wildlife issues are addressed in any works undertaken.

4.b.5 *Natural disasters and risk preparedness*

British Waterways maintains standing instructions for dealing with a range of foreseeable emergency incidents on the waterways, the British Waterways Emergency Procedures Manual (included in the Supporting Information). This provides guidance on pollution, incidents in tunnels, flooding or breach, major structural damage or failure, fire or explosion and trip boat emergency.

In addition, the local authorities have Civil Emergency duties to plan for and help manage large-scale incidents involving the public. For instance there are two site specific plans for dealing with potentially serious incidents from industrial plants at Trevor (Flexsys) and Chirk (Kronospan).

The Steering Group will coordinate efforts to ensure these plans and procedures are kept up to date as use of the Nominated Site develops.

The Nominated Site is not in a region subject to earthquakes, hurricanes, eruptions, landslides or other major natural disasters. The principal active risks to the Nominated Site are dealt with below.

Breaches in the canal are failures of an embankment causing a sudden release of water. The entire Nominated Site is part of a single 'pound' without locks to hold back water, stretching over 12 miles / 19 kilometres from Horseshoe Falls to New Marton Lock (outside the Nominated Site) and containing some 200,000 m³ / 44 million gallons of water. The impact of a breach could, therefore, be significant. Breaches generally occur from one of three causes :-

i) water flooding over the embankment and eroding it;

ii) leakage through the bed of the canal creating a 'pipe'; and

iii) failure of a culvert under the canal causing a collapse.

There have been historic breaches of all three types within the Nominated Site, at Bryn Howel, Sun Trevor and Chirk Bank. These sections and others deemed

Stop-planks are kept at slots under bridges and in other places to dam the canal for maintenance of the banks or in the event of a breach.

vulnerable have subsequently been re-lined in concrete to protect the waterway. Other existing control measures include flood prevention measures (detailed below), regular inspection for leaks as part of routine maintenance programmes, and installation of 'stop-plank grooves' to allow the installation of emergency dams to isolate sections of the canal and minimise water loss overall. Given the level of awareness and the re-lining of the vulnerable parts of the waterway, the risk of a significant breach in the future is considered to be small.

Major structural failure must be a concern in any site with such a large number of engineering structures. The risk is managed to acceptable levels through the routine inspections detailed in Section 4a above. The Steering Group will coordinate implementation of appropriate inspection and maintenance procedures by all structure owners throughout the Nominated Site.

Flooding within the canal is controlled by a daily water management regime implemented by British Waterways. The canal is fed from the Horseshoe Falls by a gravity inlet, which can be restricted in times of heavy flows and rainfall, but it also receives water from the slopes above it along much of its length. Two flood-weirs are passive controls on the water level (excess water flows over the weirs to the River Dee)

and seven sluices can be manually operated to release excess water. The daily water management routine checks the flow from the River Dee, notes water levels at critical points and checks that the weirs are clear. In times of heavy rainfall, staff are available day or night, 365 days a year, to carry out checks and if necessary shut off the feed, clear weirs of debris or open sluices.

Flooding in the River Dee has the potential to affect Horseshoe Falls weir and Pontcysyllte Aqueduct. Flows in the river are regulated by the Environment Agency Wales (a member of the Steering Group) through headwater reservoirs. The most recent engineering inspections of the weir and the footings of the aqueduct found no significant defects. These will continue to be inspected on a regular basis. The Environment Agency is currently developing a Catchment Flood Management Plan for the River Dee, including the River Ceiriog at Chirk Aqueduct.

Major pollution events are rare in the UK due to pollution control and water quality legislation regulated primarily by the Environment Agency (a member of the Steering Group). Minor incidents occur of oil leakage from boats or failed drainage but rarely have lasting effects. The flow in the canal is sufficient to dilute and disperse most problems. However, the River Dee Special

Area of Conservation must be protected from any impact and pollution control booms are available for deployment at the flood weirs feeding the River Dee. British Waterways works closely with the Environment Agency's Oil Care Campaign, providing educational signage at boating facilities, and with the Green Blue campaign of environment awareness for waterways users.

The two major industrial sites adjacent to the Nominated Site do not pose significant threats from spillage or discharge due to their locations (Flexsys is downstream of the Nominated Site) and existing site controls regulated by the Environment Agency.

Storm damage, primarily through tree fall, is a regular occurrence within the Nominated Site because of the number of trees in the waterway corridor. Tree fall normally results only in temporary blockage of the canal and minor damage, but it has the potential for causing more significant harm. British Waterways inspects its property regularly for problem trees that need management to reduce the likelihood of wind-throw or other incident, and other landowners adjoining the canal carry out similar assessments. There are no known cases of wind-blown trees having caused breaches.

Fire / explosion - Major Industrial Sites – Kronospan (Chirk) and Flexsys (Trevor) are 'Top Tier' facilities under the UK COMAH (Control of Major Accident Hazards) regulations, i.e. they are manufacturing sites with potentially high risks in the event of a catastrophic incident and the Nominated Site is within the potential area of effect. However, both are well managed and regulated, for instance Flexsys follow the Chemical Industry's code of 'Responsible Care' and the Site holds ISO standards for Quality, Environmental and Health and Safety Management.

As required by the regulations, an Off Site Emergency Plan exists for both sites, compiled by the operator, regulators and the local authority (Wrexham County Borough Council) to provide for effective management of any major incident from the sites.

4.b.6 *Number of inhabitants within the Nominated Site and the Buffer Zone*

Population pressure is not a significant issue for the Nominated Site except as noted in 4.b.2 above.

The population within the Nominated Site itself is less than 100 as there are few residential properties. Although a significant number of boats moor within the Nominated Site, they are not residential.

The Buffer Zone is predominantly rural, although the settlements close to the Nominated Site (notably Llangollen, Pontcysyllte, Trevor, Cefn Mawr, Froncysyllte, Chirk and Chirk Bank) bring the population of the Buffer Zone to approximately 16,000, based on census data from 2001.

The structure and the landscape thus become as one, and the experience of moving slowly in a boat out from the shadows of the valley side and across the aqueduct, looking down at the Dee tumbling over rocks far below, approaches the sublime. Up there, so little separates water from air. Weight becomes weightless. Even at the time, it was acclaimed as a work of art as much as engineering.... Two centuries on, it still functions exactly as intended. It is still awe-inspiring. It was thoroughly restored for its bicentennial, but it had stoically survived decade after decade of neglect in the 20th century. Looking at it today, it is as miraculous a fusion of architecture, engineering and nature as ever. This is a work of prodigious genius.

Hugh Pearman
Wall Street Journal
(4 February 2006)

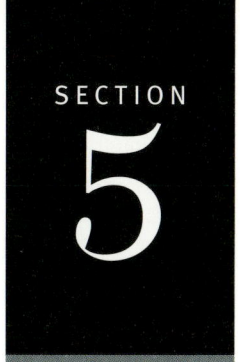

PROTECTION AND MANAGEMENT OF THE PROPERTY

…the Llangollen Canal, from Hurleston Junction on the main line to Llantysilio in Wales, is, in the view of my family, the most beautiful canal in the country. It has simply everything from fine scenery including the Vale of Llangollen… lift bridges and tunnels and even an inland port to the thrilling Chirk and Pontcysyllte aqueducts…

Frederic Doerflinger,
Slow Boat through England (1970)

5.a Ownership

The majority of the assets within the Nominated Site are owned by British Waterways, a public corporation owned by the United Kingdom Government that is responsible for the care and enhancement of over 2,000 miles of the nation's network of canals and rivers. British Waterways controls the canal channel throughout the Nominated Site and all the principal waterway structures and earthworks. The only significant parts of the Nominated Site outside the ownership of British Waterways are some over-bridges owned by the public highway authorities or private landowners and land comprising the immediate visual surroundings of Pontcysyllte and Chirk aqueducts and the Horseshoe Falls that is in mixed public and private ownership. Ownership details for the Nominated Site are shown in the Gazetteer in Section 2.

The Buffer Zone is predominantly in private ownership, but important elements of it are owned by public bodies. For instance the large area of parkland around

Chirk Castle is held in perpetuity by the National Trust, who also own land at Velvet Mountain around Llantysilio. Valle Crucis Abbey and Eliseg's Pillar are managed by Cadw. Castell Dinas Brân is owned and cared for by Denbighshire County Council and Tŷ Mawr Country Park is owned by Wrexham County Borough Council.

5.b Protective designations

5.b.1 Waterway designation
The Transport Acts 1962 and 1968 designate waterways as Commercial, Cruising or Remainder and require British Waterways to maintain them in suitable condition for their respective use and general amenity. The Llangollen Canal within the Nominated

Tŷ Mawr Country Park, an extensive area in the Dee Valley, is owned by Wrexham County Borough Council.

Site is designated as a Cruising waterway and British Waterways therefore has a duty to maintain it throughout the Nominated Site for public navigation and amenity. *The British Waterways Act 1995* places a general duty on the organisation to take account of heritage conservation and environmental issues when planning its works.

British Waterways received further instruction from the United Kingdom Government in the form of a Framework Agreement in 1999 setting out the following aims and purpose:

'Britain's inland waterways, comprising canals and navigable rivers, are an important national asset for future generations to enjoy. The UK Government is keen to see them maintained and developed in a sustainable manner so that they fulfill their full economic, social and environmental potential. British Waterways has responsibility for over 3,200 kilometres of canals and rivers, including statutory navigation and safety functions. The Government looks to British Waterways to carry out these statutory responsibilities within a wider

Dinas Brân Castle is managed by Denbighshire County Council.

context whereby, subject to economic and environmental appraisal, it aims to:

- promote and accommodate conservation and regeneration;
- maintain and enhance leisure, recreation, tourism and educational opportunities for the general public; and
- facilitate waterway transport.'

The Llangollen Canal also delivers water to Hurleston Reservoir in Cheshire for public supply under a contract between British Waterways and United Utilities, (who hold an abstraction licence from the Environment Agency for the intake at Horseshoe Falls).

5.b.2 Scheduled Ancient Monuments of National Importance

The United Kingdom has had a statutory system of legally protecting ancient monuments for over 120 years. Scheduling is the highest level of heritage designation for ancient monuments in the United Kingdom and is governed by the provisions of *The Ancient Monuments and Archaeological Areas Act 1979*. Scheduling designates the site of the monument and its component structures. English Heritage is the agency which delivers advice to the Department of Culture, Media and Sport on the inclusion of sites on the schedule and the granting of consents in England. Cadw is the Welsh Assembly Government's historic environment division and undertakes scheduling and grants consents on behalf of Welsh Ministers.

Pontcysyllte Aqueduct has been a Scheduled Ancient Monument since 1958. Cysylltau Bridge, within the Nominated Site to the west of the aqueduct, is also a Scheduled Ancient Monument.

Following recent survey work, Cadw and English Heritage are considering scheduling or other designation for the entire canal from the Horseshoe Falls to Gledrid.

A further twelve monuments in the Buffer Zone are protected by Scheduling, including Castell Dinas Brân, Offa's Dyke, and Valle Crucis Abbey.

Listed Buildings of special architectural or historic interest

Listing is the highest level of heritage designation in the United Kingdom for buildings in use. Buildings and structures of 'special or architectural or historic interest' are designated as 'Listed Buildings' under the *Planning (Listed Buildings and Conservation Areas) Act 1990* by the Department of Culture, Media and Sport in England and Cadw in Wales.

As of November 2007 there were thirty-two Listed structures within the Nominated Site and 301 in the Buffer Zone.

5.b.3 Conservation Areas

Conservation Areas are designated under the *Planning (Listed Buildings and Conservation Areas) Act 1990* to protect, 'areas of special architectural and historic interest, the character and appearance of which it is desirable to preserve or enhance'. Three Conservation Areas cover parts of the Nominated Site:

- Trevor Basin, including Pontcysyllte Aqueduct;
- Llangollen; and
- Trevor Mill / Plas yn Pentre

An extension of the Trevor Basin Conservation Area is being considered to the area around the canal at Froncysyllte. Three further Conservation Areas cover parts of the Buffer Zone in close proximity to the Nominated Site:

- Llantysilio;
- Cefn Mawr; and
- Chirk

All these heritage and planning protections are shown on Maps 10 and 11.

5.b.4 World Heritage Sites – the Heritage Protection Review

In March 2007, the United Kingdom Government announced proposals for a major reform of the protection of the heritage in England and Wales. In both countries, a new unified register of historic assets is proposed, to incorporate all

Valle Crucis Abbey is in state care under Cadw, the heritage division of the Welsh Assembly Government.

Scheduled Ancient Monuments, Listed Buildings, Historic Parks and Gardens, Battlefields and World Heritage Sites. This will give separate and enhanced statutory recognition to World Heritage Sites when legislation comes into effect, probably in 2010. In the interim, World Heritage Sites are fully protected under the terms of Planning Policy Guidance (PPG15) and Welsh Office Circular 61/96 and policies adopted in local authority development plans (see Section 5.b.3 above).

The principal changes are designed to ensure, through the regulations for call-in of planning applications for decision by Ministers, that proposals likely to have a significant impact on World Heritage Sites will be decided nationally rather than locally. Also more control may be exerted over small-scale changes that over time may have an adverse impact on the Outstanding Universal Value of a World Heritage Site. This will be achieved by including World Heritage Sites in Article 1(5) of the General Permitted Development Order (GPDO). Consideration of World Heritage Sites within the planning system will also be strengthened by the issue of a planning circular:

'which will further recognise in national policy the need to protect World Heritage Sites as sites of Outstanding Universal Value, and will make more prominent the need to create a management plan for each WHS, including, where needed, the delineation of a Buffer Zone around it'.

Over: Map 10. Heritage Designations in the Nominated Site and Buffer Zone.

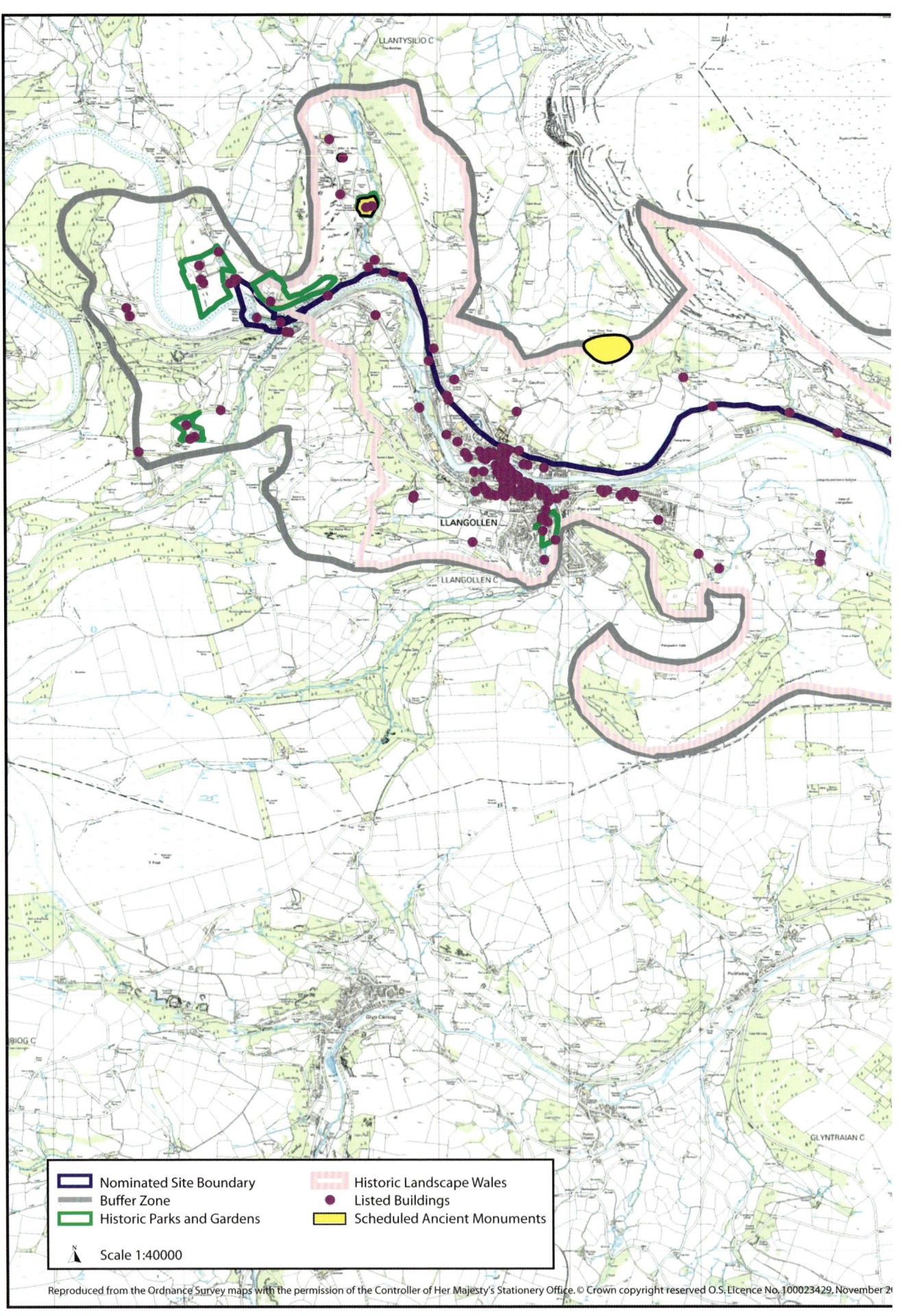

LLANTYSILIO C

LLANGOLLEN

LLANGOLLEN C

BIOG C

GLYNTRAIAN C

	Nominated Site Boundary		Historic Landscape Wales
	Buffer Zone	●	Listed Buildings
	Historic Parks and Gardens		Scheduled Ancient Monuments

N   Scale 1:40000

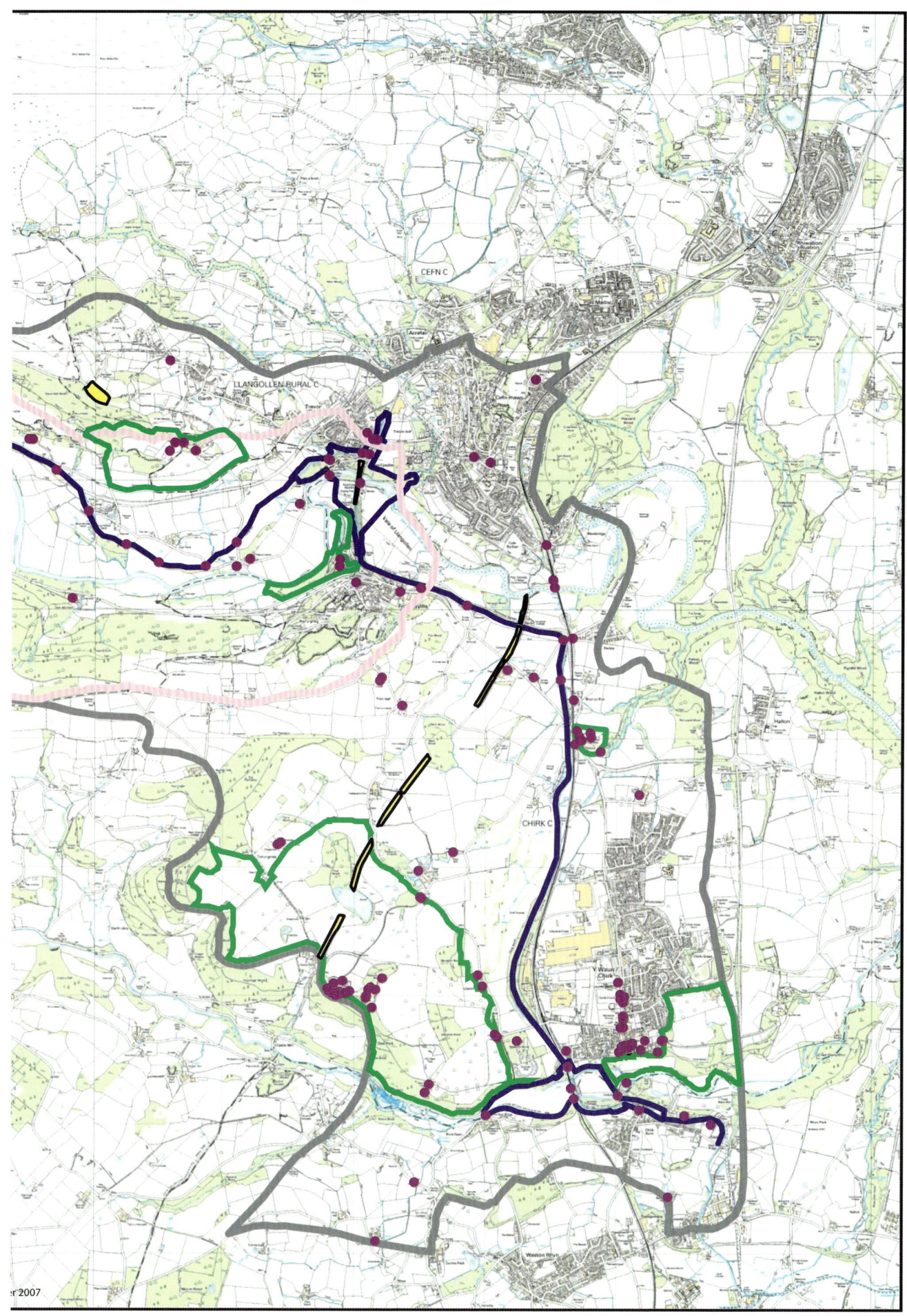

er 2007

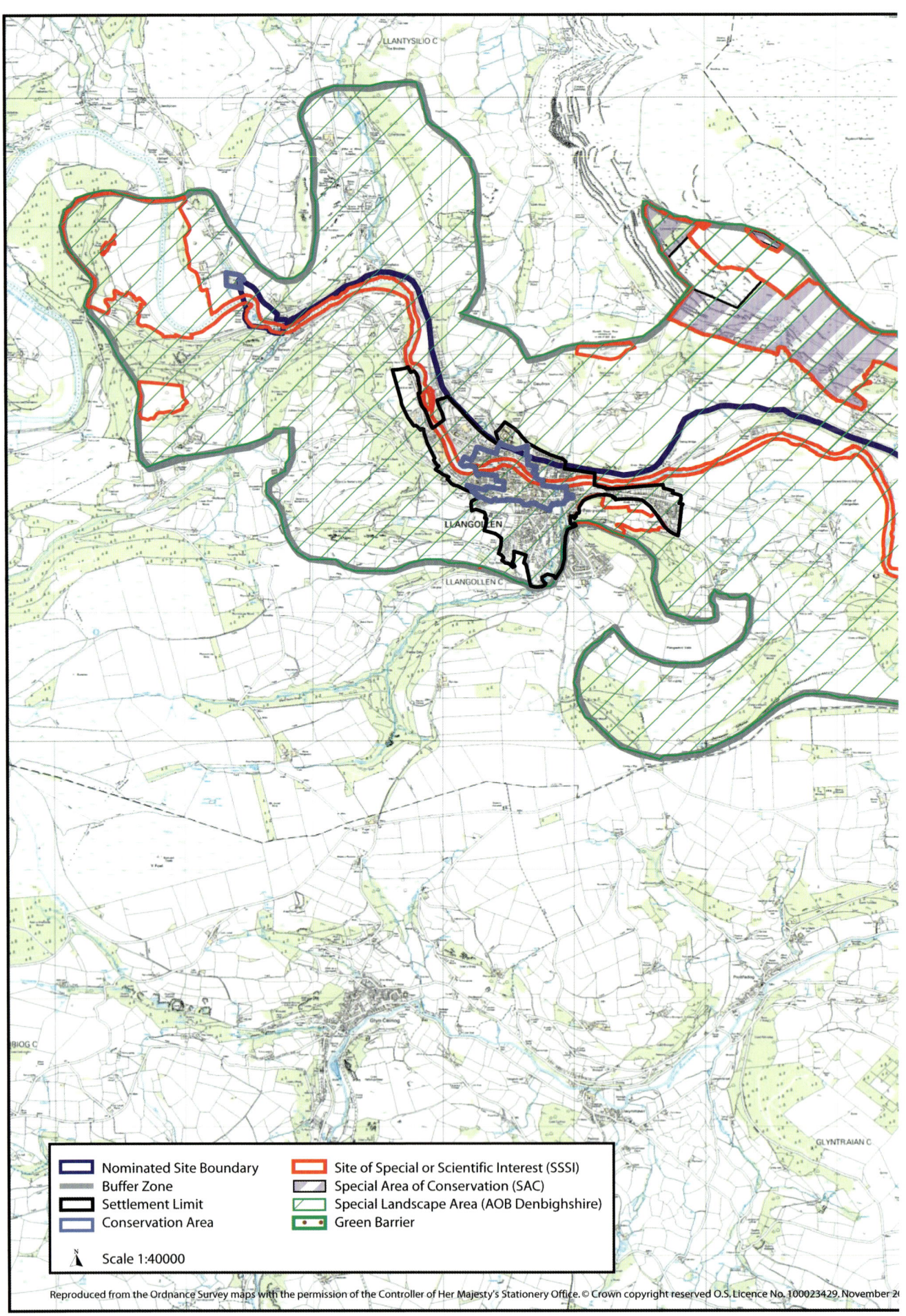

	Nominated Site Boundary		Site of Special or Scientific Interest (SSSI)
	Buffer Zone		Special Area of Conservation (SAC)
	Settlement Limit		Special Landscape Area (AOB Denbighshire)
	Conservation Area		Green Barrier

Scale 1:40000

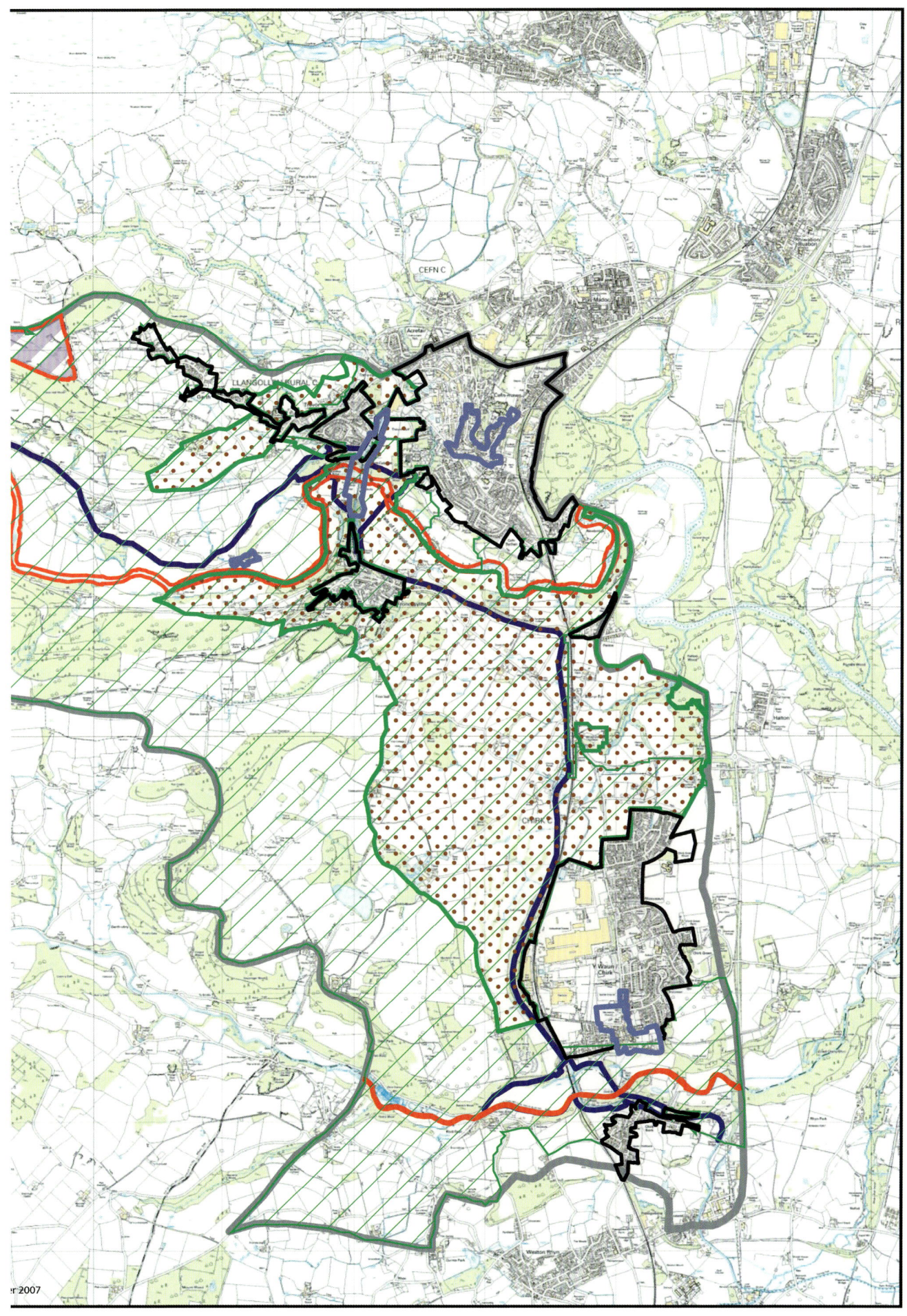

er 2007

Previous pages:
Map 11. Planning
Designations
that enhance
protection through
the development
control system
from inappropriate
development.

Below: The River Dee
at Llangollen: the centre
of the Vale of Llangollen
Historic Landscape
and a Special Area for
Conservation.

5.b.5 Planning Designations

No part of the Nominated Site or the
Buffer Zone is 'white land' (land without
some form of designation in local authority
development plans). The entire area is
therefore subject to some form of control on
development and enjoys protection under
the development control system described
in more detail in Section 5.c.3 below. Most
areas of currently undeveloped land are
subject of local designations for protection
of landscape or green space, for example
as Green Barriers or Special Landscape
Areas. Relevant designations are shown on
Map 11 and details of protective policies
are in Section 5.c.3 below. Full copies of the
local development plans are included in the
supporting information. .

5.b.6 Vale of Llangollen Historic Landscape

The Vale of Llangollen and Eglwyseg is one
of twenty-two landscapes included in the
*Register of Landscapes of Special Historic
Interest in Wales*, issued in 2001 by Cadw,
the Countryside Council for Wales and
ICOMOS UK. This covers the whole of
the western half of the Buffer Zone and
Nominated Site, including Pontcysyllte
Aqueduct and its environs. In practice, given
the topography of the Nominated Site and
the formation of the canal, it protects all
those areas where extensive views of and
from the Nominated Site are of importance.
Inclusion on the Register highlights the
area as one of the best historic landscapes in
Wales and this strengthens consideration of
landscape issues (vital for protection of the
Buffer Zone) in planning decisions.

5.b.7 Cadw Register of Parks and Gardens

Cadw has undertaken a comprehensive
survey of historic parks and gardens in
Wales. Those of national importance have
been included on the Cadw/ICOMOS UK
*Register of Parks and Gardens of Special
Historic Interest in Wales*. The Register
is non-statutory but aids the informed
conservation of historic parks and gardens

by owners, local planning authorities, developers, statutory bodies and others. The following sites, shown on Map 10, are within the Buffer Zone:

Site	National Grid reference	Evaluation	Proximity to Site (all are within Buffer Zone)
Argoed Hall	SJ 268 414	Grade II	Immediate Vicinity
Brynkinalt	SJ 304 378	Grade II*	Within area
Bryntysilio	SJ 196 435	Grade II	Immediate vicinity
Chirk Castle	SJ 268 380	Grade I	Immediate vicinity
Llantysilio Hall	SJ 192 436	Grade II	Within area
Plas Newydd	SJ 218 417	Grade II*	Within area
Trevor Hall	SJ 257 424	Grade II*	Within area
Valle Crucis	SJ 205 443	Grade II	Within area
Vivod	SJ 191 423	Grade II	Within area
Whitehurst	SJ 288 400	Grade II*	Immediate vicinity

5.b.8 River Dee and Bala Lake Special Area for Conservation (SAC) and River Dee Sites of Special Scientific Interest (SSSI)

The Nominated Site includes sections of the River Dee and Bala Lake Special Area of Conservation at Horseshoe Falls, Pontcysyllte and Chirk Aqueduct and is in close proximity to it for a significant part of its length. Special Areas of Conservation (SACs) are designated under the European Community Habitats Directive as part of a European network of high-quality sites that will make a significant contribution to conserving the 189 habitat types and 788 species most in need at a European level (excluding birds). They are protected in the UK by the *Conservation (natural habitats) Regulations 1994*. Habitats and species for which this site is designated are:

- Water courses of plain to montane levels with *Ranunculion fluitantis* and *Callitricho-Batrachion* vegetation
- Atlantic salmon *Salmo salar*
- Floating water-plantain *Luronium natans*
- Sea lamprey *Petromyzon marinus*
- Brook lamprey *Lampetra planeri*
- River lamprey *Lampetra fluviatilis*
- Bullhead *Cottus gobio*
- Otter *Lutra lutra*.

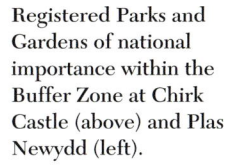

Registered Parks and Gardens of national importance within the Buffer Zone at Chirk Castle (above) and Plas Newydd (left).

Otters and salmon are among the species for which the River Dee is recognised as a Special Area of Conservation.

The Rivers Dee and Ceiriog are also covered by separate English and Welsh designations as Sites of Special Scientific Interest. This is a United Kingdom nature conservation designation under the *Wildlife and Countryside Act*, 1981. It is designated for the features above and for aquatic and shingle-dwelling invertebrates, a further three habitat types, saltmarsh transition habitats, three vascular plants and geological features.

5.b.9 Clwydian Range Area of Outstanding Natural Beauty (AONB)

This national landscape designation under the *National Parks and Access to the Countryside Act of 1949* currently covers areas to the north of the Nominated Site. An extension currently being considered would include the whole western part of the Nominated Site and the Buffer Zone as far as Pontcysyllte Aqueduct. Designation of the extension is expected in 2010.

5.b.10 Offa's Dyke National Trail

This prestigious long-distance trail utilises the canal towing-path for part of its length and crosses the River Dee by Pontcysyllte Aqueduct and Cyslltau Bridge within the Nominated Site. As an important national route it brings thousands of visitors into the Nominated Site and demonstrates the importance of linkages between the waterway and other assets. It is designated under *The National Parks and Access to the Countryside Act 1949* (amended) and also by other protective systems such as planning.

The Site and Buffer Zone are popular with walkers (above) and include a designated National Trail that crosses the Dee by Pontcysylle Aqueduct and Cysylltau Bridge (right).

5.c Means of implementing protective measures

5.c.1 Waterway management

British Waterways is required by the United Kingdom Government to operate and maintain its waterways to standards that reflect their use and prospects of use and any land drainage requirements. It has standards established for the maintenance of the structural integrity of all its assets. Target conditions for the assets have been set and are reviewed through a system of routine inspections, as described in Section 4 above.

British Waterways' *Environmental Code of Practice* ensures compliance with its statutory environmental and recreational obligations, and gives appropriate emphasis to environmental and heritage aspects in its management of the waterways. In addition, works by third parties within British Waterways' estate are subject to controls which aim to achieve the same standards as British Waterways aspire to for its own works through a works approval procedure set out in the *Code of Practice for Works Affecting British Waterways*. Boats on the canal are required to hold Licences from British Waterways and are subject to the relevant *Byelaws*. Commercial operators on the canal are managed through commercial Licences and Agreements.

5.c.2 Heritage designations

Any works that affect, damage or alter **Scheduled Ancient Monuments** require prior scheduled monument consent, a statutory procedure administered by Cadw, Welsh Assembly Government, in Wales and the Department of Culture, Media and Sport (advised by English Heritage) in England. There is a presumption against proposals which would cause damage to, significantly alter or affect the setting of monuments, and undertaking works without consent is a criminal offence. *The Ancient Monuments (Class Consents) Order 1994* grants British Waterways a class consent permitting 'works of repair or maintenance, not involving a material alteration to a scheduled monument, which are essential for the purpose of ensuring the functioning of a canal.' Any larger-scale repair or alteration requires Scheduled Monument Consent. Lesser works of general maintenance, while not requiring formal consent, will nonetheless be governed by management agreements between British Waterways and the regulators. In certain circumstances, class consent may be withdrawn by the issue of a direction, in which case consent would be required for all actions.

Any works that would alter the character of a **Listed Building** or structures in its curtilage require the prior consent of the local authority and it is a criminal offence to undertake works without consent. Denbighshire, Oswestry and Wrexham Councils all employ Conservation Officers to assist with determining these applications in accordance with published guidance. Applications are subject to public advertising and statutory consultation with expert bodies, including the Council for British Archaeology and the Royal Commission on the Ancient and Historical Monuments of Wales. The Listed Buildings and Conservation Areas Act provides for the protection and positive management of Listed Buildings. There are provisions for local authorities to require improvement where a building is at risk.

Cadw can help with the protection of **historic parks and gardens** through advice to local planning authorities on planning applications affecting registered sites. The aim is to prevent damage to significant features of the sites, such as historic layout, structure, built features and planted elements. It is not the intention to preserve everything as it is; in fact, in many cases development is both benign and beneficial. However, it is important not to let insensitive development harm the historic and visual character of historic parks and gardens and consultation on planning applications is a necessary and helpful mechanism to try to prevent this.

Existing planning and listed building controls are not affected by the *Register* *of historic parks and gardens in Wales* but statutory consultation on planning applications affecting parks and gardens on the Register is in the process of being introduced in Wales. All applications will be referred to the Garden History Society and those graded I and II* will also be referred to Cadw. In the meantime a similar but voluntary system of consultation is in place.

Recognising and raising awareness of the importance and wealth of the historic fabric of the landscape has been the central theme and message of the non-statutory, *Register of Landscapes of Historic Interest in Wales*, and designations on the Register are linked to local authority planning policies on landscape protection.

The United Kingdom **Heritage Protection Review** proposes the establishment of Heritage Partnership Agreements to enable owners of complex sites to agree types of work that can be carried out without the need for separate consent. It may be appropriate for parts of a World Heritage Site in single ownership to be the subject of a Heritage Partnership Agreement within the framework of the World Heritage Site Management Plan. It is intended to develop such an agreement for the Nominated Site when the new legislation comes into force.

Buildings in a **Conservation Area** cannot be demolished without consent from the local authority and certain types of development are restricted. Conservation Area Character Assessments have been produced for all six Conservation Areas in the World Heritage Site and its Buffer Zone to define their special architectural and historic interest and create a clear context for future development in accordance with conservation policies in the adopted local plan. Character Assessments outline the development of the area and highlight buildings, trees and views of importance to ensure its special character is protected by the Development Control process. They set out general enhancement proposals for the public and private realm. (Copies of the Character Assessments are in the Supporting Information). For the Trevor Basin Conservation Area a revised Conservation Area Character Assessment and an Enhancement Plan are being produced, and it is proposed that an Article 4(2) Direction be applied to remove permitted development rights. Where such a Direction is in place, planning permission is normally required for any alteration that would affect the appearance of a property, including changes to windows, doors, porches, chimneys, paint and materials. Article 4 (2) Directions are already in place in the Conservation Areas of Cefn Mawr and Chirk. Conservation Area designation also affects the standards of design that are acceptable for new development and building alterations, with a requirement to retain the character for which the Conservation Area was designated.

5.c.3 *Land-use Planning*

The system

England and Wales have had a system for control of development based on statute law for around sixty years. It controls development through spatial planning policies in the form of government guidance and development plans prepared by local authorities.

All local authorities are required to produce a Local Development Plan/ Framework in accordance with guidance and to review it at prescribed intervals.

Wood Bank at Trevor, believed to have been the drawing office for the construction of Pontcysyllte Aqueduct, is a Listed Building.

The plans identify areas where certain developments may be permitted and where additional constraints apply. Development control policies specify matters that must be considered when an application for planning permission is made. These may be general, or be specific to certain areas defined in the plan. Plans have statutory backing and legal status, and departure from them can lay a local authority open to judicial action.

Applications for development are subject to public advertisement and circulated to statutory consultees. Officers then produce a report assessing the proposals against published policies and national guidance and make a recommendation to Committee. Some forms of development do not require formal planning permission if covered by *The Town and Country Planning (General Permitted Development) Order 1995 (GPDO)*. Permitted development rights allow certain types of minor and uncontentious development without a planning application, but Article 4 Directions may be issued by the local planning authority to restrict this.

Policy guidance

Planning Policy Wales (2002) sets out Government land-use planning policies for Wales, guidance on the preparation and content of development plans and advice on development control decisions and appeals. Further guidance specific to the historic environment is published in Planning Policy Guidance Notes, which explain the law and set out national policy from which local authorities may depart only in exceptional circumstances. They have considerable force in directing the use of local authorities' planning powers both in dealing with individual cases and in drawing up development plans. In Wales, current guidance is set out in *Welsh Office Circulars 60/96 – Planning and Historic Environment: Archaeology, and Welsh Office Circular 61/96 – Planning and the Historic Environment: Historic Buildings and Conservation Areas.* For England, advice is given in *Planning Policy Statement 1* and *Planning Policy Guidance Notes 15* and *16,*

for *Historic Buildings and Conservation Areas and for Archaeology.*

These documents set out government policies for the identification and protection of historic buildings, conservation areas, and other elements of the historic environment, and require their treatment as a material consideration in development proposals. They establish the policy of preservation *in situ* of nationally important archaeological remains and advise on the handling of archaeological remains, including the use of planning conditions, the requirement for developers to provide adequate information on the impact of proposals on archaeological remains, and arrangements for recording and publication. There is a presumption against development that would harm the historic environment, sites, buildings and their settings. Planning permission in respect of Listed Buildings, Conservation Areas and Scheduled Ancient Monuments will not normally be granted until separate Consent had been granted.

World Heritage Sites and planning

While **World Heritage Sites** are not in themselves yet designated, they are protected under the terms of *Planning Policy Guidance 15* and *Welsh Office Circular 61/96* and resulting policies in local authority development plans. These state:

'No additional statutory controls follow from the inclusion of a site in the World Heritage list. Inclusion does, however, highlight the outstanding international importance of the Site as a key material consideration to be taken into account by local planning authorities in determining planning and listed building consent applications, and by the Secretary of State in determining cases on appeal or following call-in.

Each local authority concerned, taking account of World Heritage Site designation and other relevant statutory designations, should formulate specific planning policies for protecting these sites and include these policies in their development plans. Policies should reflect the fact that all these sites have been designated for their Outstanding Universal Value, and they should place great weight on the need to protect them for the benefit of future generations as well as our own. Development proposals affecting these sites or their setting may be compatible with this objective, but should always be carefully scrutinised for their likely effect on the Site or its setting in the longer term. Significant development proposals affecting World Heritage Sites will generally require formal environmental assessment, to ensure that their immediate impact and their implications for the longer term are fully evaluated.'

Holiday boats at Trevor Basin.

Current revisions of Local Development Plans / Frameworks

Through the current revision of local Plans and Frameworks the local authorities are working together, with support from Cadw and English Heritage, to ensure that consistent planning policies are developed and implemented for the protection of the Nominated Site and the Buffer Zone. The Steering Group is committed to co-ordinating efforts to ensure there is an effective protection system for the whole of the Nominated Site and Buffer Zone.

5.c.4 *Landscape protection*

Most landscape protection is delivered through the Planning system described above (see policies detailed in Section 5.d below).

The inclusion of the Vale of Llangollen and Eglwyseg on the non-statutory *Register of Landscapes of Special Historic Interest in Wales* creates a requirement that the effect of development on that landscape will be considered when determining planning applications. A Historic Landscape Characterisation study carried out by Clwyd-Powys Archaeological Trust defines the significance of Pontcysyllte Aqueduct, the canal and the associated industrial heritage features to the registered Historic Landscape. *The Guide to Good Practice in the Use of the Register of Special Historic Landscapes in Wales in the Planning Process*, and a complementary synoptic booklet *Caring for Historic Landscapes* published by Cadw, explain how the Register should be used in assessing the effect of developments of more than local impact.

Local authorities in Wales are also making use of the LANDMAP system developed by a partnership headed by the Countryside Council for Wales (a member of the Steering Group). LANDMAP is a unique system, allowing information about landscape to be gathered, organised and evaluated into a nationally consistent data set. This, with the incorporation of information from the Landscape Assessment for the Nominated Site and Buffer Zone detailed in Section 4 above, provides a comprehensive and integrated landscape baseline from which change can be monitored and to assist with protection of the landscape through the planning system.

5.c.5 *Nature Conservation designations*

In **Special Areas of Conservation (SACs)** and **Sites of Special Scientific Interest (SSSIs)** any owner or occupier of land must consult with the Countryside Council for Wales in Wales or Natural England in England before carrying out works or giving permission for any works that may affect the site. Activities that could affect the site's integrity have to be assessed and may require formal Consent. Any operation or activity that may affect the features for which the River Dee is designated as a Site of Special Scientific Interest requires Consent from the Countryside Council for Wales or Natural England.

Under paragraph 6(1) of Schedule 11 of the *Countryside and Rights of Way Act 2000* the Countryside Council for Wales / Natural England have notified every owner and occupier of land within a Site of Special Scientific Interest of their views about the management of the land. *The Site of Special Scientific Interest: Management Statement for the River Dee* recommends management to maintain its special interest and provides a basis for future discussions and decisions.

5.d Existing plans related to municipality and region in which the proposed Property is located

The UK employs land use planning at national, regional and local level. The Nominated Site is covered by national and regional plans produced for Wales, the West Midlands and Shropshire as well as local plans for the three local planning authorities that are represented on the Steering Group, Denbighshire County Council, Oswestry Borough Council and Wrexham County Borough Council. These contain measures to prevent inappropriate development adversely affecting the Nominated Site, as detailed below. These include policies which:

- locate development within defined settlement limits and employment areas;
- ensure that the general character of development does not materially detrimentally affect countryside, landscape or townscape character, open space, or the quality of the natural environment;
- ensure that new development should, in scale, design, layout and use of materials and landscaping, accord with the character of the Nominated Site and make a positive contribution to the appearance of the locality;
- define 'green barriers' and other zones restricting development, for instance in open space around the canal corridor;

The River Dee at Horseshoe Falls.

- prevent the loss of good quality agricultural land to development;
- presume in favour of retaining woodland not planted for forestry (such as the wooded hillsides around the canal);
- protect Special Landscape Areas throughout the Dee Valley;
- protect designated heritage sites and their settings; and
- support the proposal to extend the Clwydian Range Area of Outstanding Natural Beauty to include the Dee Valley.

Through the current revision (2007-10) of local Plans and Frameworks the local authorities are working together, with support from Cadw and English Heritage, to ensure that consistent planning policies are developed and implemented for the protection of the Nominated Site and the Buffer Zone. The Steering Group is committed to co-ordinating efforts to ensure there is an effective protection system for the whole of the Nominated Site and Buffer Zone and to facilitate the implementation of the Management Plan.

The following Sections are organised by country / region and provide summaries of policies or reproduce actual policy text.

5.d.1 England, regional and local

West Midlands Regional Spatial Strategy (RSS). Published by West Midlands Regional Assembly and adopted in 2004, the Regional Planning Guidance provides a Spatial Strategy to guide the preparation of local authority development plans and local transport plans so that they deliver a coherent framework for regional development. The Strategy includes broad policies supporting sustainable development in rural parts of the West Midlands (Rural Renaissance) and maintaining and enhancing the quality of the environment (Environmental Policies – which contain specific reference to World Heritage Sites).

The RSS is currently being reviewed on a phased basis and phase 3, looking at issues relating to rural areas and the quality of the environment, is due to be launched in Autumn 2007. Oswestry District (which contains the part of the Nominated Site in England) has been classed as a 'lagging rural district' – a District where the average income was below the lower quartile for England. GOWM (Government Office West Midlands) and regional partners responsible for the RSS are agreed that interventions should be targeted to achieve an improvement in incomes and it is anticipated that World Heritage status could bring benefits that would help to assist those interventions.

Policy RR2: The Rural Regeneration Zone

vi) maintaining and enhancing the landscape (especially the three Areas of Outstanding Natural Beauty), natural, built and historic environment and distinctive character of the zone and particular areas within it, and minimising the negative effects of any new development.

Policy QE1: Conserving and Enhancing the Environment

A. Environmental improvement is a key component of the Spatial Strategy to underpin the quality of life of all areas and support wider economic and social objectives.

B. Local authorities and other agencies in their plans, policies and proposals should:

ii) conserve and enhance those areas of the Region where exceptional qualities should be reinforced by sustainable use and management, including … the World Heritage Site;

iii) protect and where possible enhance other irreplaceable assets and those of a limited or declining quantity, which are of fundamental importance to the Region's overall environmental quality, such as specific wildlife habitats, historic landscape features and built heritage, river environments and groundwater aquifers.

Policy QE5: Protection and Enhancement of the Historic Environment

A. Development plans and other strategies should identify, protect, conserve and enhance the Region's diverse historic environment and manage change in such a way that respects local character and distinctiveness.

B. Of particular historic significance to the West Midlands are:

i) the historic rural landscapes and their settlement patterns;

iii) listed buildings, scheduled and unscheduled ancient monuments, conservation areas, historic parks and gardens, all in their settings, and battlefields;

v) the historic transport network;

vii) Ironbridge Gorge World Heritage Site.

D. In particular, strategies should explore the regeneration potential of:

vii) the canal network.

Policy QE5 is perhaps the RSS policy of most relevance to the Nominated Site. The Ironbridge Gorge World Heritage site is specifically referred to in this policy, as is the historic transport network and the canal network. The future review of this policy could easily incorporate specific reference to the Pontcysyllte Aqueduct and Canal.

Shropshire Joint Structure Plan 1996-2011. The purpose of a structure plan is to lay out a plan for local development and use of land. The plan is set in a context of sustainable development objectives. Shropshire County Council and Telford and Wrekin Council jointly prepared Shropshire's plan, which became operative on 15 November 2002.

The plan includes references to built heritage protection and to World Heritage Sites. It:

- establishes the general amount and location of new development;

- shows how development relates to transport and other services;

- indicates how a balance will be struck between development and the conservation of the countryside, wildlife and important open space;

- provides the basis for detailed local planning and co-ordination of services; and

- shows how national and regional policy will be made to work in the area.

With the introduction of Local Development Frameworks (LDFs), the County Structure Plan is being phased out. Only a small number of policies will be 'saved' and remain in force beyond September 2007 as the new LDFs come into force.

Oswestry Local Plan 1996-2006. Published by Oswestry Borough Council and adopted July 1999. The Local Plan sets out the Council's Planning Strategy for the future development of the Borough. It contains detailed planning policies which are used by the Council to form the basis for its decisions on planning applications. The Plan is now at the end of its intended lifespan. To ensure continuity in the local development plan as a basis for development control, the majority of policies in the Plan are to be 'saved' beyond September 2007, until such time as new policies come forward to replace them through the new Local Development Framework. A full copy of the Plan is included in the Supporting Information, but relevant provisions are reproduced below

Local Plan Aims:

10.3 - The main aim of the Local Plan in relation to the historic environment is: 'to preserve and enhance the architectural and historic character of the Borough.

10.4 - This will be achieved by setting out planning policies and proposals which reconcile the need for development with the interests of conservation of the historic environment.

10.5 - In particular the Borough Council will :

a) have special regard to the desirability of preserving any Listed Building or its setting, or any features of special architectural or historic interest which it possesses;

b) pay special attention to the desirability of preserving or enhancing the character or appearance of existing and future Conservation Areas;

c) protect, enhance and preserve sites of archaeological interest, and their settings;

d) protect Registered Parks and Gardens;

e) through its general planning policies for the countryside, protect the Borough's wider historic landscape.

Policy HE1: Development and the Historic Environment

The Borough Council will require that, where applicable, all new development in the Borough pays special attention to:

1. Preservation of Listed Buildings or their setting, or any features of special architectural interest which they possess, and

2. Preservation or enhancement of the character or appearance of the Borough's Conservation Areas, and

3. Protection of sites of archaeological importance, and

4. Protection of Historic Parks and Gardens, and

5. Protection of the Borough's historic landscapes.

Policy HE2 Demolition of Listed and Unlisted Buildings

Development proposals involving the demolition of Listed Buildings, and unlisted buildings in Conservation Areas, will only be approved in exceptional circumstances. In determining, applications for planning permission and related applications for Listed Building/

Conservation Area Consent, the Borough Council will have regard to the following:

1. In the case of Listed Buildings, the importance of the building in both national and local terms; the building's setting and its contribution to the local scene; the physical features of the building which justify its inclusion in the list.

2. In the case of unlisted buildings in Conservation Areas, the contribution made by the building to the character or appearance of the area.

3. In all cases, the condition of the building and the cost of repairing and maintaining it.

4. Applications will not be granted unless it can be clearly demonstrated that:

i. clear and convincing efforts have been made to retain the building, but these have failed; and or

ii. redevelopment will provide substantial planning benefits for the community which would decisively outweigh the loss resulting from demolition.

Policy HE4: Alterations to Historic Buildings

Planning permission for the alteration of Historic Buildings will be allowed provided that:

1. In the case of Listed Buildings, proposals do not adversely affect the special architectural or historic interest of the building by virtue of proposed alterations to its external appearance, internal layout or its features of historic interest;

2. In the case of unlisted buildings within Conservation Areas, proposals are compatible with the character of the individual building and do not adversely affect the contribution made by the building to the character or appearance of the Conservation Area, by virtue of any proposed alterations to its external appearance.

Policy HE13: Archaeological Remains of National Importance

There will be a presumption against development proposals which would involve significant alteration to, or which would cause damage to, nationally important archaeological remains, whether scheduled or not, or which would have a significant impact on the setting of visible remains.

Policy NE1: Areas of Special Landscape Character

The Borough Council will protect the visual quality of the countryside. Particular importance will be placed on landscape conservation within the Areas of Special Landscape Character in the North West Uplands, The Cliffe and along the River Severn as shown on the Proposals Map and Inset Maps.

5.d.2 Wales national

The Wales Spatial Plan: People, Places, Futures. Published in 2004 by the Welsh Assembly Government, the Plan investigates the interaction of different policies and practice across regional space and sets the role of places in a wider context. It goes beyond 'traditional' land-use planning and sets out a strategic framework to guide future development and policy interventions, whether or not these relate to formal land-use planning control. The Plan makes sure that decisions are taken with regard to their impact beyond the immediate sectoral or administrative boundaries; that there is co-ordination of investment and services through understanding the roles of and interactions between places; and that we place the core values of sustainable development in everything we do.

In particular, the Plan will:

- Provide a clear framework for future collaborative action (involving the Welsh Assembly Government and its agencies, local authorities, the private and voluntary sectors) to achieve the

The mayors and civic leaders representing the towns and local authorities along the course of the canal took part in the international conference to support the nomination in June 2007.

priorities it sets out nationally and regionally

- Influence the location of expenditure by the Assembly Government and its agencies

- Influence the mix and balance of public sector delivery agencies' programmes in different areas

- Set the context for local and community planning

- Provide a clear evidence base for the public, private and voluntary sectors to develop policy and action.

Local detailing of the Plan will drive future investment by the Welsh Assembly Government and the north-east Wales Section includes reference to the development and protection of Pontcysyllte Aqueduct.

5.d.3 Wrexham County Borough Council (WCBC) area

Wrexham Unitary Development Plan 1996-2011. Adopted in February 2005, this provides a framework for local decision making and the reconciliation of development and conservation interests in order that land-use changes proceed coherently and with maximum community benefit. The Strategy outlines the Council's broad intention for development in the area and provides a framework for the more specific policies and proposals.

Specific policies accompanied by reasoned justifications expand on the strategic vision for the County Borough and provide detailed guidance for the development and other use of land. The Proposals Map and Insets either define sites for development or areas within which various policies will apply. A full copy of the Plan is included in the Supporting Information.

Policy GDP1 : Development Objectives

In addition to the specific land-use or locational policies of the Plan, all development proposals must satisfy certain general requirements, the regulation of which is a key function of the planning system. All new development should:

a) Ensure that built development in its scale, design and layout, and in its use of materials and landscaping, accords with the character of the Site and makes a positive contribution to the appearance of the nearby locality.

Policy EC5 : Special Landscape Areas

Within Special Landscape Areas, priority will be given to the conservation and enhancement of the landscape. Development, other than for agriculture,

small-scale farm-based and other rural enterprises, and essential operational development by utility service providers, will be strictly controlled. Development will be required to conform to a high standard of design and landscaping, and special attention will be paid to minimising its visual impact both from nearby and distant viewpoints.

Area of Outstanding Natural Beauty

During the plan period the existing Clwydian Range Area of Outstanding Natural Beauty (AONB) may be extended to include sections of Ruabon Mountain and the Berwyn Mountain Range, which includes much of the Ceiriog Valley. The Council supports such a proposal. Such designation would recognise the national importance of that landscape and the need to protect, manage, and enhance it. Landscape conservation would be the primary consideration and development which detracts from the character and appearance of the landscape would be resisted. Any development permitted must be of the highest standard of design, and use materials appropriate to the locality.

Open country at Ruabon is being considered as an extension of the Clwydian Hills Area of Outstanding Natural Beauty.

Policy EC7 : Conservation Areas

Within, and in close proximity to, Conservation Areas, the priority will be to preserve and/ or enhance those buildings, structures, streets, trees, open spaces, archaeological remains, views, and other elements which contribute to the unique character of the area. New buildings and alterations or additions to existing buildings in Conservation Areas, whether listed as of special architectural or historic interest or not, must reflect the design and character of the area as a whole and the form, scale, detailing and materials of existing buildings.

The Council may introduce Article 4 Directions where changes resulting from permitted development rights adversely affect the character of Conservation Areas. Outline planning permission will not be granted for development in Conservation Areas; the Council will require detailed plans of proposals, including elevations, which show the proposed development in its setting. The Council will prepare and publish enhancement proposals for designated Conservation Areas.

Policy EC8 : Demolition

The demolition of any building in a Conservation Area will not be permitted unless, in exceptional circumstances:

a) the building or structure is beyond reasonable repair; or

b) demolition would be a positive benefit to the Conservation Area's enhancement; and

c) planning permission has been granted and a legal agreement entered into for the erection of an appropriate replacement building reflecting the design and character of the Conservation Area.

d) the material generated from the demolition of the building will, where appropriate, be used for the construction of the replacement building or structure.

Policy EC9 : Listed Buildings

Alterations or additions to, and development or redevelopment within the curtilage of, buildings or structures listed as of special architectural or historic interest must respect the setting and character of the Listed Buildings or structures.

Policy EC11 : Archaeology

Development which would adversely affect the site or setting of a Scheduled Ancient Monument or archaeological site of national significance will not be permitted. Development that directly affects non-scheduled sites of archaeological importance will only be permitted if an archaeological investigation has been carried out to determine the nature, extent and significance of the remains, and this investigation indicates that in-situ preservation is not justified, and a programme of excavation and recording has been agreed. Development will also be carefully controlled, where appropriate, to ensure that the settings of non-scheduled sites of archaeological importance are not harmed.

Buildings at Risk Strategy 2004. Published by Wrexham County Borough Council. Adopted in 2004 and referring to Listed 'Historic Buildings at Risk through Neglect and Decay', the key objective of the strategy is to increase the appreciation and care of the built historic environment within the Wrexham County Borough. The strategy aims to address the causes of risk to Listed Buildings and identify possible courses of action to be taken to reduce the number at risk within the County Borough. The strategy also seeks to prevent future problems arising by encouraging regular maintenance and through the establishment of an effective monitoring system. There are 115 buildings identified as being 'at risk' within the County Borough, one of which is in the Nominated Site, but has received attention and is now stable.

Local Planning Guidance Notes. The Council has approved a series of Local Planning Guidance Notes, adopted in 2006, which amplify Development Plan policy. Those most relevant to the Nominated Site are:

LPGN2 Agricultural Appraisal Housing

Development in the countryside is strictly controlled, housing for agricultural workers is allowed but it is necessary, in all cases, to establish whether the dwelling is essential for the proper functioning of the enterprise concerned.

Produced by WCBC, Adopted October 1993; updated 2000.

LPGN 3 Converting Rural Buildings

There is a varied range of buildings in the countryside which are no longer suitable for their original purposes. Many of these buildings make a positive contribution to the character and appearance of the area.

Produced by WCBC, Adopted March 2006.

LPGN4 Conservation Areas

Such an area can be designated because of its 'special architectural or historic interest, the character and appearance of which is desirable to preserve or enhance'. Produced by WCBC, Adopted September 1993; updated 2000.

LPGN7 Landscape and Development

In assessing the landscape implications of planning applications the site context, proposed layout, future uses and maintenance all need to be taken into account. Produced by WCBC, Adopted November 2003.

LPGN13 Housing in the Countryside

National and local planning policies impose strict controls on the amount of new housing development in the open countryside. These policies apply to formally designated areas including green barriers; special landscape areas; and sites of biodiversity interest; and to other land which is not specifically protected. The aim is to protect open countryside for its importance as part of the landscape heritage; as a natural habitat; and to ensure the best agricultural land is retained as a national resource for the future.

Economic Development Department Service Strategy 2007-2010. This document sets out the three-year strategy for Wrexham County Borough Council's Economic Development Department. It underpins the department's service planning, identifying the department's key priorities. Its aim is 'To provide economic opportunities for local people thereby helping to improve their quality of life'. Pontcysyllte Aqueduct and the bid for World Heritage Status is identified in the department's Service Plan as a headline project meeting the Council's core Corporate Business Priority 'Prosperous Business, a Skilled Workforce and Regenerated Communities'.

Emerging Physical Regeneration Strategy 2008-2011. This will set out a clear vision for the direction of major physical regeneration projects in the County Borough. Trevor Basin and the proposed Pontcysyllte Aqueduct World Heritage Site corridor is identified as a major asset to north-east Wales and the inscription of the aqueduct and its associated features is a major priority for the Council and its partners.

Cefn Mawr Conservation Area Management Plan Strategy identifying measures for protection and enhancement of the Cefn Mawr Conservation Area and supporting the successful Stage 2 application to the Heritage Lottery Fund Townscape Heritage Initiative, adopted in June 2005.

5.d.4 Denbighshire County Council area

Denbighshire Unitary Development Plan (UDP) 1996-2011. Adopted in July 2002, this provides the strategic and detailed policy framework within which provision will be made for development and conservation needs. It guides development for fifteen years, 1996-2011. A full copy of the Plan is included in the Supporting Information.

6.1 Denbighshire possesses an extensive and well preserved historical character much of which is recognised as being of national importance. The presence of sites, features and buildings and Conservation Areas undoubtedly adds to the quality of our lives and the physical remains of our past are to be valued and protected as a central part of our culture, heritage and sense of national identity.

6.2 Conservation must never be regarded as a negative process - nothing more than antiquarianism or a modern day version of luddism. Our responsibility to this historic environment goes beyond simply preventing its destruction essential though that is. It involves actively caring for the heritage, maintaining it in good physical condition, making it readily accessible for study, enjoyment, recreation, and tourism. Above all it means ensuring that, to the fullest possible extent, the heritage remains in active use, as an integral part of the living and working community, a material asset that makes a positive contribution to economic prosperity and overall quality of life. (Protecting Our Heritage - published by the Department of National Heritage and the Welsh Office 1996).

6.3 Positive attitudes are therefore required through the UDP towards the protection of the built environment for maintaining the architectural and historic continuity and distinctive character of each settlement. A fine balance therefore needs to be struck between conservation and enhancement on the one hand, and promoting development and growth on the other. However, conservation of the built environment and archaeological features should be viewed as an asset to be promoted and not as a constraint to be overcome. The historic environment in practice cannot remain unchanged, and the role of planning is to reconcile the needs for development against the need to conserve and protect the historic environment. To do that there is a need to identify what is special in the historic environment, define its capacity for change and to assess and control the impact of development proposals. The preservation of the County's historic, architectural and cultural heritage will play an important role in ensuring sustainability.

Policy CON 1 - The Setting of Listed Buildings

The Council will seek to preserve the setting of a listed building particularly where the setting is an essential part of the character of the building.

Policy CON 2 - Extension or Alteration to Listed Buildings

Extensions or alterations to a listed building that would detrimentally affect its character as a building of architectural or historic interest will not be permitted.

Policy CON 3 - Change of Use of Listed Buildings

The change of use of a listed building will only be permitted if any alterations associated with the change of use are not detrimental to its character as a building of architectural or historic interest.

Policy CON 4 - Indigenous Building Materials

The use of indigenous building materials for the maintenance, alteration or extension of historic buildings will be preferred.

Policy CON 5 - Development within Conservation Areas

The Council will permit applications that demonstrate that they preserve or enhance the character or appearance of conservation areas.

Policy CON 6 - Development Adjacent to Conservation Areas

The Authority will permit applications adjacent to conservation areas that do not detrimentally affect important views into and out of the conservation area.

Policy CON 7 - Demolition in Conservation Areas

Demolition within a conservation area will only be permitted where:

i) it can be demonstrated that the building / structure is beyond economic repair and that viable alternative uses cannot be found;

ii) it can be demonstrated that the building / structure makes no contribution to the character and appearance of the area;

iii) an acceptable redevelopment proposal which respects the character and appearance of the area is undertaken within an agreed time scale secured by condition;

iv) a fully detailed scheme has been submitted and approved including full details of redevelopment where appropriate.

Policy CON 8 - Advertisements in Conservation Areas

Advertisements within conservation areas will be permitted provided that:

i) the proposal preserves or enhances the character of the area;

ii) the signage is in a style appropriate to the character of the area;

iii) traditional materials and finishes are used and glossy or highly reflective materials are excluded from proposals;

iv) internally illuminated box fascia and projecting box signs are excluded from the proposals;

v) where illumination is acceptable, the intensity of illumination is kept to a minimum.

Advertisements close to conservation areas must respect and preserve the character and appearance of the area to ensure that views out of and into such areas are protected.

Policy CON 9 - Article 4 Directions (Restrictions of Permitted Development Rights)

In the interests of protecting or enhancing the essential characteristics of conservation areas, the local planning authority will seek to withdraw permitted development rights based on the following criteria:

i) where conservation area appraisals have identified important features which could be altered irreversibly by permitted development, therefore detracting from the essential character or quality of the area;

ii) where the individual or cumulative effect of changes has or is likely to lead to significant damage.

Policy CON 10 - Scheduled Ancient Monuments

Development which would cause unacceptable harm to a nationally important monument, or its setting, including those shown on the proposals map will not be permitted.

Wherever possible, planning applications which affect a scheduled ancient monument or its setting should be accompanied by the completed scheduled monument consent approval from Cadw.

Policy CON 11 - Areas of Archaeological Importance

The council will require, in line with Planning Policy Wales (2002) and Circular 60/96, that an acceptable report on the results of archaeological evaluations is submitted prior to the determination of proposals affecting sites of known or potential archaeological significance. In cases where remains are affected but preservation in situ is not merited, the Council will expect to secure excavations and/or recording in advance of construction work either by the imposition of suitable conditions attached to a planning permission, or through a formal obligation entered into with the developer.

Policy CON 12 - Historic Landscapes, Parks and Gardens

Development which would unacceptably harm the character of a historic landscape, park or garden, or its essential setting will not be permitted.

Local Planning Guidance Notes.

The Council has approved a series of Supplementary Planning Guidance Notes which amplify Development Plan policy. Those most relevant to the Nominated Site are:

SPGN2 Landscaping

The aims of these policies are to ensure that the proposed development is designed to make the best use of the topography, site features and local conditions, with appropriate siting of buildings, roads, paths, open areas, planting etc. This should result from an analysis of the natural features, views etc. A scheme should be designed which fits into the local surroundings as well as satisfying the functional requirements of the development. Buildings, particularly large structures, should where possible be positioned where they will be least intrusive in the overall landscape, and space for any large trees and necessary screen planting should be left free of obstructions and services. Produced by DCC, Adopted June 2003.

SPGN 13 Conservation Areas

Local Authorities are required to designate as a Conservation Area 'any area of Special Architectural or Historic Interest the character or appearance of which it is desirable to preserve or enhance'. Produced by DCC, Adopted Jan 2003.

SPGN 14 Listed Buildings

The guiding principle to follow whenever a listed (or listable) building is to be restored, altered or extended, is that any work carried out should not be detrimental to its essential and listed character. Produced by DCC, Adopted Jan 2003.

SPGN 15 Archaeology

Denbighshire contains an extremely rich resource of archaeological and historic features. In an area such as this there is nowhere which has been unaffected by human influence at some time. This archaeological resource is finite and vulnerable to damage and change. Recent work has identified a series of important Historic Parks and Gardens within Denbighshire and the area of the Vale of Clwyd, and the western slopes of the Clwydian Hills have been identified as an Historic Landscape. Produced by DCC, Adopted June 2003.

SPGN 16 Conversion of Rural Buildings

Rural buildings are an integral part of Denbighshire's attractive countryside and are also important to its rural heritage. However, changes in the rural economy, particularly to farming, have resulted in many of these buildings becoming economically redundant and it is vital to preserve them and find suitable new uses. Produced by DCC, Adopted June 2003.

Caring for our Countryside: A Countryside Strategy for Denbighshire.

This sets out a framework for ongoing management and enhancement of the countryside in Denbighshire. It includes proposals to extend the Clwydian Range Area of Outstanding Natural Beauty into the Dee and Ceiriog Valleys covering the western part of the Nominated Site.

Raising the Standard: The Visitor Economy Strategy for the Dee Valley.

Published by The Dee Valley Business Action Group (Rural Business Action), with financial assistance from the Welsh Development Agency and Cadwyn Clwyd. A review of the current tourism performance of the Dee Valley within Denbighshire and proposals:

> to harness the area's remarkable resources in order to deepen, broaden and add value to the experience of visiting the area by creating a recognisable and integrated product which draws on the area's many distinctive features.

Supports efforts to raise the quality and extent of interpretation, the tourism product, service and customer care, and the quality of the public realm. This will support many of the enhancements proposed for the Nominated Site within the Management Plan.

5.e Property Management Plan

The Management Plan, which accompanies this Nomination, has been developed to meet the future management needs of the Nominated Site and to coordinate the many interested bodies, groups and individuals. To be successful, management planning needs to follow an ongoing process of assessment, objective setting, consultation, monitoring and review as set out in the draft ICOMOS UK draft guidance paper *Management of the Historic Environment* 2007.

The process of developing this Plan has been led by British Waterways as the majority landowner and the public body with responsibility for the canal and its major structures. However, the process has involved all members of the Steering Group and drawn on a public consultation. It is related closely to the proposed Outstanding Universal Value and the assessment of the current condition, pressures and threats outlined elsewhere in this nomination document.

The Plan expresses a vision for management of the Nominated Site, to:

> *Manage the World Heritage Site, its Buffer Zone and wider setting in a sustainable manner to conserve, enhance and present the Outstanding Universal Value of the Nominated Site locally and internationally.*
>
> *Balance the needs of conservation, access, the interests of the local community and the achievement of sustainable economic growth.*
>
> *Consequently to engage with and deliver benefits to the local communities around the Nominated Site; to attract visitors to the area; to develop opportunities for education and learning and to generate income that adds value to the local economy or is reinvested in the day-to-day running of the Nominated Site.*

A list of opportunities for improvement and actions proposed for protection and conservation to deliver this vision were produced by the Steering Group and subject to public consultation (see Supporting Information). The Plan sets out a prioritised list of agreed action for a six year period, with lead partners for each. This action plan is subject to measurement and monitoring as set out in Section 6 of this Nomination. It will be under regular review by the Steering Group and Friends of Pontcysyllte to ensure co-ordination of effort and alteration of actions to reflect any changes in the condition or needs of the Nominated Site. Resources for implementation are identified in Sections 5.f; 5.g; and 5.j below.

5.e.1 The World Heritage Site Steering Group

A Steering Group has been formed comprising representatives from the following public bodies:

- British Waterways as the major landowner for the Nominated Site;

- the four local authorities (Wrexham County Borough Council, Denbighshire County Council, Oswestry Borough Council and Shropshire County Council) as controllers of the planning system vital for protection of the Buffer Zone, and for their existing contributions to management of the property directly; and

- relevant Welsh and English national bodies (Cadw, English Heritage, the Environment Agency Wales, the Royal Commission on Ancient and Historical Monuments of Wales, the Countryside Council for Wales) covering remits in heritage, environmental protection, landscape and wildlife.

The Steering Group meets regularly, with a secretariat provided by Wrexham County Borough Council, and has overseen the production of the Nomination and Management Plan. It will continue to coordinate actions for the implementation of the Management Plan and the agreed Vision. A concordat to this effect was signed in June 2007:

We, the representatives of the Welsh Ministers, British Waterways, Wrexham County Borough, Denbighshire County, Oswestry Borough and Shropshire County Councils, and the Royal Commission for the Ancient and Historical Monuments of Wales, state our support for the nomination of the Pontcysyllte Aqueduct and its canal as a World Heritage Site. We confirm that all parties are committed to working together to achieve recognition of the appropriate place for the Pontcysyllte Aqueduct and its canal in the cultural heritage of Wales and its wider international context. Further, all parties confirm that they will work together to improve the protection, management, presentation and interpretation of the Pontcysyllte Aqueduct and its canal to deliver sustainable development for the economic and social benefit of the communities that live alongside it.

Membership of the Steering Group remains open and other bodies and landowners with interests within the Nominated Site or Buffer Zone will be encouraged to join. A community-based Friends of Pontcysyllte group has been formed to work with the Steering Group and ensure community

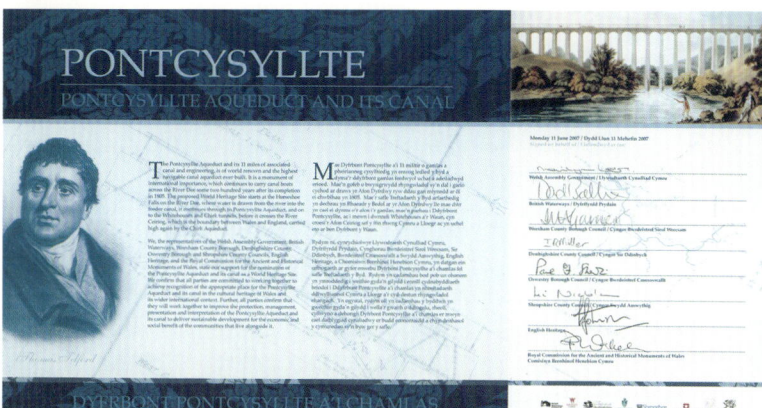

engagement in the management of the Site (see 5.e.3 below for more details).

5.e.2 The Management Plan

The Management Plan is intended as a living document, separate from the Nomination itself. It therefore contains the relevant information from the Nomination document to support future reviews of the Plan, comprising:

- the Site description, extent, details of ownership and baseline condition;

- the Statement of Significance and details of existing heritage protection, land-use planning, statutory duties of main bodies and other existing management arrangements;

- summary of the pressures on / threats to the Nominated Site and opportunities for change or improvements;

- means of implementation of the Plan; and

- measures by which it will be monitored.

Representatives of the partner bodies in the World Heritage Site Steering Group sign the concordat committing their support to Pontcysyllte Aqueduct and Canal, June 2007.

Most importantly, the Management Plan contains a six-year action plan. As part of the process of development for the Management Plan, several key Management Principles were derived from the Outstanding Universal Value, the current condition of the Nominated Site, the threats and pressures identified in Section 4 above and the aspirations of the agreed vision for future management. The action plan is arranged around these Principles, as follows:

Identification
- to undertake research and surveys to identify the features of the Nominated Site and associated remains in the Buffer Zone.

Protection
- to review the protection afforded to the Site and Buffer Zone; and
- to use existing controls and to develop a consistent framework for future control to ensure the adequate protection of the Outstanding Universal Value of the Nominated Site and the landscape and associated archaeological features of the Buffer Zone.

Conservation
- to implement a common system of assessment and monitoring of the state of conservation of the Nominated Site and Buffer Zone;
- to prioritise and carry out maintenance works to ensure an appropriate state of conservation of the Site, securing additional resources where necessary; and
- to develop and implement effective management measures for all identified environmental pressures, disasters and risks to the Nominated Site.

Presentation
- to implement sustainable visitor management to improve the attractiveness of the Nominated Site and features of the Buffer Zone to visitors without detriment to its Outstanding Universal Value; and
- to carry out research and interpretation to develop understanding of the Site and present its values to a range of audiences.

Transmission to future generations;
- to engage the local communities in the understanding of the Nominated Site, decision making and management action to protect it for future generations.

The most urgent actions are separated out into the Year One Plan, with details of the lead partner responsible for taking each forward. As a minimum, the Steering Group will review the Plan every year to update the six-year action plan and agree priorities for the new Year One Plan.

Some key actions in the current Year One Plan are:

Identification
- to carry out further surveys and assessments as identified / recommended by the 2007 State of Conservation Report; Landscape Assessment and Industrial Archaeology Assessment.

Protection
- to review designation – update Listing and Scheduling of the whole Nominated Site; and
- with support from the Local Authority World Heritage Forum, to develop new planning policies for protection and presentation of the Nominated Site, consistent across all authorities, as an exemplar for UK sites and taking advantage of expected changes under Heritage Protection Reform.

Conservation
- to agree standards of maintenance in the Steering Group and implement them through property owners;
- to develop a site-wide Conservation Management Plan (building on the existing model for Pontcysyllte Aqueduct) to identify works required to improve the state of conservation of structures and standards for all future repairs and maintenance within the Nominated Site; and
- to develop a Training Plan based on works within the Nominated Site to ensure partners, contractors and

volunteers develop and maintain the appropriate skills for maintenance into the future.

Presentation

- to develop a site-wide Audience Development Plan, identifying who we are not reaching and how we can present the Nominated Site;
- to widen existing educational support to cover the whole Nominated Site's Outstanding Universal Value and historical development.
- to develop a programme of education opportunities to increase access; and
- to reduce the impact of the Dŵr Cymru sewage works and to work towards its removal during 2010 to 2015.

Transmission to future generations

- to bring together existing community groups within the Nominated Site and Buffer Zone under the umbrella of the Friends of Pontcysyllte and to develop with them an ongoing programme of activity and events.

5.e.3 Community Involvement

A Friends of Pontcysyllte World Heritage Site group has been established by the local communities to work with the Steering Group to ensure their active involvement in decision-making and management. This follows naturally from existing community involvement in Pontcysyllte Aqueduct's bicentenary celebrations, the strong local sense of ownership of the Nominated Site and high levels of support demonstrated by the recent public consultation.

The Consultation Process for the Nomination

The process of developing the World Heritage Site nomination has included a comprehensive twelve-week public consultation exercise to provide an opportunity for local residents, local businesses, organisations, visitors and others to comment on the nomination and management proposals for Pontcysyllte Aqueduct and Canal. Every household within the Site and Buffer Zone (over 5,000 households) received a mailshot informing them of the consultation exercise and how to make views known.

A public consultation document was produced which contained a summary of the proposals for nomination and management of the Site, highlighting the key issues, including potential benefits, threats, opportunities and restrictions. A consultation questionnaire accompanied the document, and both were made available in Welsh and English throughout the twelve-week period at ten public venues across the area. The consultation commenced on Monday 2 July 2007 and ended on Friday 14 September. The documents were also made available on the website www.wrexham.gov.uk/aqueduct.

In addition, seven drop-in sessions were arranged thought July and August 2007 to enable the public to speak to officers about the proposals. These sessions were attended by 153 members of the public. The overall response to the public consultation process totalled 200 completed questionnaires, of which 94 per cent were supportive on the nomination. The details of the exercise and the responses received are provided as supporting documents.

For public bodies and organisations, including Government Departments, a six-week consultation exercise was undertaken from Monday 16 July 2007 to Friday 31 August. This generated twenty-nine responses. Full details are included in the supporting documentation. The Nomination Document and Management Plan have been revised in the light of comments made.

Communities within the Site and Buffer Zone and beyond have been consulted through their respective Community Councils. Officers made presentations to Llangollen Rural Community Council, Llangollen Town Council, Llantysilio Community Council, Chirk Town Council, Cefn Mawr Community Council, Glyn Traian Community Council, Glyn Ceiriog Community Council and Ceiriog Uchaf Community Council. All have given their support.

Examples of activities of note by the local community include:

- Froncysyllte Community Council cream teas at the Community Centre;

- Pontcysyllte featured strongly in the recent Visioning day exercise at Trevor Community centre run by Northern Marches Cymru;

- August family fun day run by Wrexham County Borough Council and the local Community Councils, attracting 5,000 visitors;

- Llangollen Tidy Town team – some 20 individuals regularly carry out litter sweeps in the town and along the Canal; and

- Chirk Community Forum proposals for volunteer action at Chirk Aqueduct to support vegetation management, access improvements and interpretation.

British Waterways and Wrexham County Borough Council are already working to secure resources for a full-time Community Development project officer post.

5.f Sources and Levels of Finance

The current level of revenue funding and recent capital investments in the Nominated Site are outlined below. Levels of revenue funding are adequate for the on-going management and maintenance of the Nominated Site and it is envisaged that additional revenue will be available as a result of increased income as improvements mature. Many key features of the Nominated Site and within the Buffer Zone are in an excellent state of conservation owing to substantial recent investments. Additional capital investment will be sought for projects defined in the Management Plan. This funding cannot be guaranteed, but previous successes (see 5.f.2) and the inclusion of the Nominated Site in the Wales Spatial Plan and other key strategies significantly increase the

likelihood of successful outcomes. This will need augmenting to give positive signals/ commitment on how the property is to be taken forward.

5.f.1 British Waterways' Business Plan 2007-10

British Waterways' Wales and Border Counties unit, which has responsibility for the day-to-day management of the waterway asset within the proposed World Heritage Site produced a confidential four-year Business Plan in 2006-07 covering financial years 2007-08 to 2010-11. This Plan includes a number of commitments / objectives of relevance to the management of the Nominated Site.

Priorities in the Plan include:
- delivering Customer Service Transformation;

- investment in destination sites (includes Pontcysyllte);

- asset management;

- managing heritage assets through improved skills, awareness and understanding of our heritage assets, dedicated Heritage Advisor;

- Welsh strategic development; and

- input of waterways into the Wales Spatial Plan process which will be used to prioritise and direct funding in Wales.

The Plan also provides for investment planned in the Nominated Site area on leak stopping works at Llantysilio, ongoing maintenance provision for the waterway and the commitment of staff resources to developing schemes for external funding support to enhancements at the Nominated Site, covering improvements to heritage assets, access and interpretation.

5.f.2 Revenue Funding

British Waterways' routine maintenance and management expenditure for this length of canal and its component features within the Nominated Site amounted to approximately £150,000 in 2007 with an additional £10,000 allocated purely to heritage improvement works within the Nominated Site. The British Waterways major works budget is allocated across the whole of its waterways based on national priorities, so it is not possible to provide an annual figure for expenditure on this specific length. However, current planned works are detailed in 5.f.3 below.

Denbighshire County Council maintains the public road bridges in its area that cross the canal and river and form part of the Nominated Site; many are statutorily protected. The Council also maintains the public toilets at Llantysilio Green at a cost of £4,200 per annum to the Countryside Service. The site (picnic and parking) is adjacent to Horseshoe Falls, the uppermost feature within the Nominated Site.

Wrexham County Borough Council maintains the public toilets and car park at Trevor Basin and public road bridges in its district. It has also allocated £10,000 per annum to a joint marketing programme for the Nominated Site, including an annual event at Pontcysyllte, website development and literature.

The Countryside Council for Wales provides grant aid in support of the development, management and maintenance of the Offa's Dyke National Trail.

Shropshire County Council maintains the public road bridges at Chirk Bank.

5.f.3 Recent Investments

- Pontcysyllte Bicentenary marketing and events led by Wrexham County Borough Council, LEADER+ European funding and British Waterways - £71,000.
- Refurbishment of Pontcysyllte Aqueduct and Trevor Basin, as detailed in Section 4.- £2 million from British Waterways, Wrexham County Borough Council and external funders (European Regional Development Fund).
- Creation of a new mooring basin and

improvement to linear moorings at Llangollen - £1.6million by British Waterways, Denbighshire County Council and European Union Objective 1 funding.
- Cefn Mawr Regeneration and Townscape Heritage Initiative - currently £3.06million over five years.
- Investment in communities through work undertaken by the Dee Valley Community Partnership in Cefn Mawr and Wrexham County Borough Council and the rural partnership Northern Marches Cymru in community engagement in Trevor, Froncysyllte, Chirk and the Ceiriog Valley.

5.f.4 Planned investments

The following investments in development of the Nominated Site are in advanced stages of planning at the time of writing the Nomination Document:

British Waterways' major works currently planned for 2007-08 to 2010-11:
- Leak repairs on Pentrefelin section of feeder - £400,000
- Repairs to retaining wall at Llangollen - £50,000
- Improvements to Llantysilio feeder intakes - £40,000.

British Waterways' Buildings at Risk improvement programme targets expenditure to Listed structures in its ownership which have been identified as at risk. British Waterways aims to address all of those designated as such at the start of the programme in 2005. The only structure identified as at risk within the Site is:

- Bridge 46, Pen-y-Ddol, estimate of works £13,000 programmed 2009-10.

British Waterways Destination Management investment – targeted at improving audience experience - as yet uncosted.

With the Heritage Lottery Fund:
- £50,000 committed to carrying out a full

Conservation Management Plan and Audience Development Plan to develop a £1million scheme for improvements to the Nominated Site.

Rural Development bid to Welsh Assembly Government for Community Engagement – as yet uncosted.

Bid to Big Lottery People and Places fund for a Community Development Officer – as yet uncosted.

Interpretation and signage strategy for the Nominated Site (drawing on existing budgets of Steering Group members).

5.g Sources of expertise and training in conservation and management techniques

British Waterways is one of the largest owners of historic structures in the United Kingdom. Each local business unit employs a specialist Heritage Advisor to ensure compliance with legislation and use of sympathetic methods and materials for repairs and maintenance to historic structures. They are supported by a budget for 'live site' training and specialist advice delivered by local and national craftsmen and consultants. Key British Waterways staff associated with the Nominated Site (the Heritage and Environment Manager, Heritage Advisor, local supervisors and operational teams) are engaged in an ongoing programme of heritage awareness and skills development.

Cadw is the historic environment division of the Welsh Assembly Government. **English Heritage** is the non-departmental public body in England that advises Government on the historic environment. Both have a wide range and high degree of professional skills in the conservation field, including archaeology, architecture and engineering. English Heritage is the United Kingdom Government's advisor on World Heritage matters.

Countryside Council for Wales is the statutory adviser to government on sustaining natural beauty, wildlife and the opportunity for outdoor enjoyment throughout Wales and its inshore waters. Conservation and Countryside Officers provide advice and guidance in relation to protection and enhancement of the designated wildlife sites within the Nominated Site, together with promoting conservation of the wider landscape and the provision of facilities for access and enjoyment of the local countryside.

Denbighshire County Council has a number of officers with expertise who contribute to the conservation and management of the Nominated Site. In particular, the Council has a County Archaeologist, County Ecologist, Biodiversity Officer, Woodlands Specialist, Conservation Officer, Landscape Architect and Officers who work in Interpretation and Sites Management.

Officers in the Highways Section cover issues relating to access and footpaths/bridleways etc, bridges and the highway itself. Officers in the Planning Department, particularly those in the Planning Policy Section develop and monitor suitable protective policies for the Nominated Site.

Environment Agency Wales provides expertise in biodiversity, nature conservation, fisheries, water resources and water quality management.

The Institution of Civil Engineers has assisted with events associated with the 250th anniversary of the birth of Thomas Telford and provides expertise through the Panel for Historical Engineering Works to identify, record and promote knowledge of works illustrative of the history and development of civil engineering and to encourage excellence in the conservation of significant examples.

Oswestry Borough Council and **Shropshire County Council** have a number of Officers with relevant expertise and remits, in particular the Borough Conservation Officer and the County Archaeologist advise on heritage conservation matters. The Borough Economic Development team and County Sustainability Group also contribute to the management of the Nominated Site. County Engineers in the Highways Section deal with issues relating to access and footpaths/ bridleways etc, bridges and the highway itself and Borough Officers in the Planning Department, develop and monitor suitable protective policies for the Nominated Site and implement Development Control.

The Royal Commission on the Ancient and Historical Monuments of Wales is the Welsh Assembly Government sponsored body of record for the historic environment in Wales. It has a large survey section responsible for recording sites and monuments in Wales and several staff with a high level of expertise in industrial archaeology and the history of civil engineering. This team has contributed considerable resources to the understanding and recording of the special features of the Nominated Site and this work will be ongoing.

Wrexham County Borough Council has a wealth of expertise and experience through its professional officers/managers. This includes specialists in heritage and culture; tourism development and marketing; conservation; events management; planning (policy, development control, built conservation, landscape, cartography); environment and countryside; public realm and infrastructure; transport and highways; community development/regeneration; education and curriculum. These specialists help implement the Management Plan and ensure that the integrity of the Nominated Site is maintained and safeguarded. This team has contributed considerable resources in bringing forward the Nomination and has led the community consultation process. This work will be on-going. In addition, the Council's Conservation Team comprises the Senior Conservation Officer

and the Conservation Officer. The prime responsibility of the team is to secure a high quality built environment, protecting and enhancing assets of special architectural and historic value. The Cefn Mawr Townscape Heritage Initiative is staffed by a Manager and a Grants Officer. It has a built-in training element, which allows for traditional building skills training events for the repair of historic buildings. This is delivered in partnership with the Northern Marches Cymru and Cadwyn Clwyd Leader+ groups, as well as with Denbighshire County Council and Flintshire County Council. This initiative allows local companies to benefit from training in traditional building and repair techniques, and helps support local conservation initiatives, by helping to revive traditional techniques locally.

5.h Visitor facilities and statistics

As well as providing statistics of visitor numbers and patterns over several years, this Section describes the facilities available for visitors, including interpretation overnight accommodation, restaurant or refreshment facilities, shops, car parking, lavatories and search and rescue.

The canal is one of the busiest inland leisure waterways in the United Kingdom with some 15,000 boat movements per year. Within the Nominated Site there are many areas for short-term mooring (14 days at most areas is permitted within British Waterways' standard Licences) and also a marina for some 300 berths, at Chirk, providing permanent moorings and a hire boat base. Existing permanent moorings on the Froncysyllte side of the Pontcysyllte Aqueduct will be included in proposed water-space management revisions which will also include Trevor Basin, where there is another hire boat base, trip boat and restaurant boat. British Waterways operate short-term moorings at the popular Llangollen wharf, where there are further trip boat services and boats for disabled users. There are at least eight waterside pubs and other facilities.

Tourism in this part of north-east Wales is significant, lying as it does between the two significant visitor attractions of Chester and Llangollen and on a major route to Snowdonia. In 2006, tourism contributed £70.1 million to the local economy in Wrexham County Borough, with day visitors contributing the most (£29.6 million spent by some 1.1 million visitors). In Rural Denbighshire tourism contributed £91.4 million to the local economy, with day visitors generating £41.4 million from 1.583 million visitors. Whilst day visitors are undoubtedly the main sector, the area has a good accommodation base offering a range of accommodation in country house hotels, bed and breakfast and self-catering establishments, touring and static caravan sites, and canal boats. Visitors are provided for by Tourist Information Centres at Llangollen (100,000 visitors per annum), Wrexham (49,500) and Oswestry Mile End (84,300) in addition to Tourist Information points in Chirk and Oswestry.

In addition to the canal and its key features there are a number of major tourist attractions, activities and events within the Buffer Zone.

Horseshoe Falls are served by a public car park and toilets operated by Denbighshire County Council with access to the towing-path and land alongside the weir. There is all-ability level access from Chain Bridge Hotel car park and further facilities are available within the hotel.

Llangollen Wharf is accessible from Llangollen or the canal. It has a trip-boat operator, a café with information and British Waterways seasonal Customer Service staff at the moorings. Llangollen provides public toilets, shops and a wide range of facilities.

Llangollen Railway carries 83,000 visitors each year, who can alight at various stations along the Dee Valley. In particular the section from Llangollen to Berwyn provides a view of the Site and enables visitors to access Horseshoe Falls and walk back along the towing-path or take a return train ride.

Pontcysyllte Aqueduct and Trevor Basin has a car park and toilets managed by Wrexham County Borough Council, a café, refreshments and a canal-side pub. British Waterways Customer Service staff maintain a seasonal Interpretation Centre. Information and interpretation panels were

Hire craft at Trevor Basin.

recently installed as part of a community art programme. The site attracts up to 200,000 visitors per year and recent events have drawn approximately 5,000 visitors per day. The visitor to the aqueduct can experience it in a number of ways - by trip boat, restaurant boat, self-drive boat or foot.

Cefn Mawr and District Urban Trail was developed by the Cefn Heritage Group and offers a walk around the industrial landscape of Cefn Mawr and Pontcysyllte Aqueduct. Leaflets are available to follow the trail, and interpretation boards are displayed in prominent locations, including the aqueduct.

Tŷ Mawr Country Park, located downstream of Pontcysyllte Aqueduct, offers a country experience for all and works closely with local schools. It has over 65,000 visitors a year and operates a circular walk to Pontcysyllte Aqueduct.

Walking routes have been developed in the area of the canal. The Offa's Dyke Path is a National Trail along the foot of the Eglwyseg Scarp, through Llangollen and across the River Dee using the road bridge

Top: The Llangollen Railway offers important facilities for visitors.

Above: Horse-drawn passenger boats operate at Llangollen.

or Pontcysyllte Aqueduct and the towing-path. The Dee Valley Way, a regional route, runs from Llangollen to Corwen and uses the towing-path between Llangollen and Horseshoe Falls. It links with the recently-opened route south of the Dee, the North Berwyn Way. There is also a signed History trail from Llangollen which takes in Valle Crucis Abbey and Dinas Brân castle.

Chirk Aqueduct and moorings are five minutes walk from Chirk, which provides public toilets, shops and a wide range of facilities. The National Trust property Chirk Castle attracts over 95,000 visitors a year.

Major Events held in the Buffer Zone provide further reasons for visits to the area and Nominated Site. The annual Llangollen International Musical Eisteddfod attracts visitors from across the world to its venue next to the canal.

Public transport connects Chirk and Trevor to Llangollen, Wrexham and Oswestry by bus, with train services operating from Ruabon and Chirk stations.

Outdoor activities are strongly supported. The attractive landscape of the Nominated Site and Buffer Zone, especially the Vale of Llangollen and the Ceiriog Valley, make it popular with walkers, anglers, cyclists, horse riders and boaters, including canoeists. The Llangollen Canal Boat Trust provides facilities for disabled visitors and the towing-path is easily accessible for walkers of all abilities.

Top: The permanent venue for the International Musical Eisteddfod at Llangollen, established in 1947, is on the banks of the canal.

Above: Outdoor activities are promoted by wheelchair access at Trevor Basin.

Right: Public artwork at Trevor Basin.

5.i Policies and programmes related to the presentation and promotion of the Property

The Outstanding Universal Value of the Nominated Site forms part of the promotion of the area by Wrexham and Denbighshire Councils. Pontcysyllte Aqueduct and other features of the Site have long featured in guidebooks, television programmes and media articles . They are the focus of one of the Wild over Waterways educational packages (see Supporting Information).

A step change in the promotion of the Nominated Site occurred in 2005, the two hundredth anniversary of the opening of Pontcysyllte Aqueduct. Celebrations and activities continued throughout the year and focused primarily on supporting the local communities around the aqueduct in learning more about their special landmark. For example, there was an oral history project which resulted in a series of story-telling events and a published book.

A Pontcysyllte Aqueduct newsletter provides updates on progress and events related to the aqueduct and canal and is made widely available. A touring exhibition

The history of the canal was promoted effectively at the Bicentenary events in 2005.

has been displayed in libraries, museums and other public places to make local residents aware of the work underway and giving them an opportunity to signal their support. Since 2006, there have been web pages devoted to the aqueduct at www. wrexham.gov.uk/aqueduct. A 2007 calendar promotes both the aqueduct and the 250th Anniversary of the birth of Thomas Telford. A great deal of press coverage has been generated by the nomination work and the Froncysyllte Male Voice Choir. In June 2007 an International Canal Conference

Fron Male Voice Choir has developed an international profile.

was held to raise the profile of the proposed World Heritage Site. A community day now takes place at Trevor Basin each year at which local organisations have fundraising stalls alongside activities for children, boat rides and other events. It is community-led but with funding from Wrexham County Borough Council and support from British Waterways.

A number of investigations have been undertaken and research papers prepared concerning the Nominated Site since 2005, as listed in the bibliography. An authoritative study of the Nominated Site will be published drawing this material together.

Future promotion will build on these successes on a number of fronts – community engagement, tourism development, education strategy, interpretation, signage and site style and economic development. These proposals are developed in more detail in the Management Plan.

Key elements are:

- to develop a site-wide Audience Development Plan addressing who it is not reaching, how the Nominated Site can be presented and the need to spread visitor numbers and infrastructure to improve capacity;

- to develop a site-wide signage and interpretation strategy to ensure consistency across the Nominated Site and prevent signage 'overload', including the introduction of mobile interpretation;

- to develop off-site marketing and pre-visit information through existing and potential new routes;

- to bring together community groups within the Nominated Site and Buffer Zone under the Friends of Pontcysyllte and develop an ongoing programme of activities and events;

- to widen existing educational support to cover the whole Nominated Site's Outstanding Universal Values and historical development.

- to develop a programme of education opportunities to increase access;

- to implement a landscape and vegetation management programme of works based on the 2007 Landscape Assessment;

- to develop a site-wide programme of improvements to boundaries, signage and facilities; and

- to agree standards of maintenance through the Steering Group and implement them through property owners.

Visitor facilities at Trevor Basin include the visitor centre (above), interpretation panels and public artworks.

5.j Staffing levels (professional, technical, maintenance)

5.j.1 World Heritage Site Steering Group

The Steering Group established to develop the Nomination has continued as a forum for communication and cooperation between the Steering Group and is overseeing implementation of the Management Plan. The majority of staff resources available will come from members of the Steering Group:

British Waterways Wales and Border Counties supports the Nominated Site with their existing Heritage and Environment Manager and Heritage Advisor who also call upon British Waterways' national Head of Heritage. The Third Party Funding team assists in securing external resources for development projects. A team of some two dozen maintenance staff cover the operational area which includes the Nominated Site. Five seasonal staff operate a rota covering Pontcysyllte Aqueduct and Llangollen moorings during the spring and summer peak season. In addition a wide range of specialist staff can be called upon to deal with specific management needs.

Cadw and English Heritage, because of the trans-boundary nature of the Nominated Site, collaborate to provide specialist advice as required and within available resources. The relevant English Heritage personnel are within its West Midlands Regional Team, based in Birmingham, and its Policy Team based in London, while the relevant Cadw staff are at the headquarters in Nantgarw and specialist works unit in Caernarfon. Relevant staff include Field Monument Wardens, Conservation Architects and Inspectors of Ancient Monuments. The Inspectorate scrutinises all applications for activities that could impact upon scheduled ancient monuments, provide advice that leads to the granting or refusal of consent for these activities depending upon the effect of the proposals on the monument.

Planning regulations in Wales and England (*General Development Procedure Order 1995*) requires the local planning authority (LPA) to consult Cadw or English Heritage on any development proposal that is likely to affect a scheduled ancient monument or its setting. The Inspectorate will advise the LPA on any issues that might have an adverse impact and will monitor the subsequent implementation of conditional consent.

Denbighshire Countryside Service has a Senior Warden and Warden based in Llangollen. They cover the whole of the south of Denbighshire from Ruthin southwards. Recently they have been involved in developing walking routes in the Dee Valley, Dee Valley Way and North Berwyn Way, parts of which include the canal towing-path from Llantysilio to Llangollen. Denbighshire also provide maintenance staff for the facilities under their management.

Wrexham County Borough Council has a wealth of expertise and experience through its professional officers/managers. This includes specialists in heritage and culture; tourism development and marketing; conservation; events management; planning (policy, development control, built conservation, landscape); environment and countryside; public realm and infrastructure; transport and highways; community

Members of the World Heritage Site Steering Group: from left Dr Peter Wakelin of the Royal Commission, Dr Dawn Roberts of Wrexham County Borough Council and Peter Birch of British Waterways.

development/regeneration; economic development; education and curriculum. These specialists will be available to help implement the Management Plan and ensure that the integrity of the Nominated Site is maintained and safeguarded.

Oswestry Borough Council and **Shropshire County Council** have a number of officers with relevant expertise and remits, in particular the Borough Conservation Officer and the County Archaeologist who advise on heritage conservation matters. The Borough Economic Development Team and County Sustainability Group will also contribute to the future management of the Nominated Site.

County Engineers in the Highways Section will deal with issues relating to access and footpaths/bridleways etc, bridges and the highway itself and Borough Officers in the Planning Departments, will develop suitable protective policies for the Nominated Site and implement Development Control.

Royal Commission on the Ancient and Historical Monuments of Wales
The Royal Commission has a staff of 36 based in Aberystwyth that includes specialists in the recording, analysis and interpretation of historical and archaeological sites. The Royal Commission has developed considerable expertise in the study of canals and early engineering features. Annual aerial photographic recording of all scheduled ancient monuments is systematically undertaken by the Royal Commission on behalf of Cadw so that every monument in Wales is photographed from the air every three to five years. This record commenced in 1984 and is planned to continue for the foreseeable future.

5.j.2 Additional resources available from outside the Steering Group:

Clwyd Powys Archaeological Trust. The four regional Welsh Archaeological Trusts act as the archaeological advisors for the local planning authorities in Wales and similarly advise on potential impact on monuments and their setting. This consultation forms part of planning guidance in Wales and Trust staff will monitor activity authorised by conditional planning consent to ensure strict adherence to planning conditions set to protect non-scheduled monuments. Clwyd Powys Archaeological Trust advises on developments in Denbighshire and Wrexham. The County Archaeologist in Shropshire undertakes the same function for the English section of the property.

Externally funded posts – British Waterways and Wrexham County Borough Council are currently pursuing funding for full time project officers to help manage community engagement and the delivery of the Management Plan.

Opposite:
Public artwork at
Trevor Basin.

One soon begins to realise why this canal is so famous. The approach of the Welsh mountains drives the navigation into a side cutting half way up the side of a hill. Passing Chirk Bank, one rounds a corner and suddenly finds oneself on Chirk Aqueduct – an impressive structure by any canal enthusiast's standards…. At the end of the aqueduct the canal enters a tunnel immediately…. A long wooded cutting follows, then the railway appears alongside. Another shorter tunnel at Whitehouses is negotiated before the canal meets the valley of the river Dee. Here… the canal clings to the hillside. By now the scenery is superb and the views excellent. But more is yet to come! Passing the village of Froncysyllte the canal launches out into this deep valley on a massive embankment then crosses the river Dee on the breathtaking Pontcysyllte Aqueduct.

Nicholson's Guides to the Waterways 2: North West
(c.1970)

MONITORING

In accordance with Article 29 of the World Heritage Convention, the Department for Culture, Media and Sport, on behalf of the United Kingdom Government, must produce periodic reports on the legislative and administrative provisions and state of conservation of the World Heritage Site. To assist in this process, key indicators for measuring quantitatively and qualitatively the state of conservation have been established in the Management Plan for Pontcysyllte Aqueduct and Canal. They will be undertaken within the six-year time scale of the World Heritage Convention periodic reporting exercise and guided by best practice. The results will be used to assess the implementation of the Strategic Action Plans detailed in Section 7 of the Management Plan.

6.a Key Indicators for measuring state of conservation

Indicator	Periodicity	Location of Records
State of Conservation of assets in the Nominated Site graded Good, Fair and Poor	Baseline in State of Conservation Report 2007, reviewed every six years	British Waterways
Fitness for Purpose of assets in the Nominated Site graded A (Excellent) to E (Bad)	Monthly, annual and ten-yearly Asset Inspection Programme	British Waterways
Maintenance of operation of the cruising waterway for appropriate navigation	Annual Customer Service Inspection and annual closure/maintenance records	British Waterways
Number of Listed Buildings and Scheduled Ancient Monuments in the Nominated Site	Baseline 2006, reviewed every six years	Cadw English Heritage
Number of Listed Buildings and Scheduled Ancient Monuments in the Buffer Zone	Baseline 2006, reviewed every six years	Cadw English Heritage
Condition of Scheduled Ancient Monuments in the Nominated Site and Buffer Zone	Cadw and English Heritage Field Monument Warden condition reports based on field visits and aerial monitoring	Cadw Royal Commission English Heritage
Number of buildings in the Nominated Site and Buffer Zone on the Buildings at Risk Registers	Baseline 2006, reviewed every six years	Wrexham CBC Denbighshire CC Oswestry BC
State of conservation of the Historic Landscape and Parks and Gardens in the Nominated Site and Buffer Zone	Baseline Landscape Character Assessment 2007, reviewed every six years	Wrexham CBC Denbighshire CC Oswestry BC
Enhancement or maintenance of Significant Views from and into the Nominated Site	Baseline Landscape Plan 2007 reviewed by fixed point photography every six years	British Waterways Wrexham CBC Denbighshire CC Oswestry BC

6.b Administrative arrangements for monitoring the Property

The Nominated Site and Buffer Zone are a composite landscape, in which the canal, aqueducts, tunnels, and associated industrial features and housing are the primary characteristic components. The condition of the landscape as a whole and that of its component structures, many of which are statutorily protected by Listing or Scheduling, is continuously monitored in a number of ways. The World Heritage Site Steering Group will scrutinise the records produced, review the Management Plan to ensure consistency in the standards of planned works and improvements and compile annual summaries of works undertaken and changes in condition. Annual reports by the Steering Group will draw together information from all sources and other activities of member organisations and individuals. The findings of monitoring will be reviewed holistically by the World Heritage Site Steering Group and reported upon every six years.

Contact:
World Heritage Site Steering Group; secretariat
Wrexham County Borough Council

State of Conservation of assets in the Nominated Site graded Good, Fair or Poor Fitness for Purpose of assets in the Nominated Site graded A (Excellent) to E (Bad).

The baseline *State of Conservation Report* prepared in 2007 graded all features in the Nominated Site within the categories Good, Fair, Fair* and Poor. British Waterways as owner and manager of the canal undertakes monthly asset inspections, an annual engineering inspection and a ten-yearly principal inspection which grade the Fitness for Purpose of assets from Excellent (A) to Bad (E). These two systems of reporting together serve to identify necessary works that are prioritised and executed after appropriate consultation with Cadw or English Heritage.

The State of Conservation Reports, which will be repeated regularly, will guide British Waterways inspectors on conservation issues for their routine Fitness for Purpose inspections and will update the record of State of Conservation Grades. Regular fixed point photography, organised by the Steering Group, will be used as a supplementary tool for condition monitoring.

Changes in State of Conservation Grades will be used to indicate appropriate conservation of the Nominated Site and will be reviewed formally by the World Heritage Site Steering Group every six years.

Contact:
Heritage and Environment Manager, British Waterways, Wales and Border Counties Office, Navigation Road, Northwich, Cheshire, CW8 1BH
Enquiries.Walesandbordercounties@ britishwaterways.co.uk
Telephone 44 (0)1606 723800

Maintenance of operation of the cruising waterway for appropriate navigation

The Transport Acts require British Waterways to maintain the cruising waterway in suitable condition for its use by appropriate canal boats and for general amenity. British Waterways maintains records of any temporary closures of the waterway and statistics for use are reviewed annually. It also undertakes an annual Customer Service Inspection.

Contact:
Heritage and Environment Manager, British Waterways, Wales and Border Counties Office, Navigation Road, Northwich, Cheshire, CW8 1BH
Enquiries.Walesandbordercounties@ britishwaterways.co.uk
Telephone 44 (0)1606 723800

Number of Listed Buildings and Scheduled Ancient Monuments in the Nominated Site Number of Listed Buildings and Scheduled Ancient Monuments in the Buffer Zone

The Nominated Site and Buffer Zone were surveyed by Cadw and English Heritage in 2007 to ensure that all buildings or features of national importance or special architectural or historic interest were afforded appropriate statutory protection. Consequently the entire line of the canal within the Nominated Site is in process of being scheduled, while two sites (Pontcysyllte Aqueduct and Cysyllte Bridge) are already statutorily protected. There are also twelve further Scheduled Ancient Monuments in the Buffer Zone. The removal of Listed Buildings or Scheduled Ancient Monuments from statutory protection is extremely rare, and such action would be indicative of a serious loss of architectural or historic character and/or archaeological potential. The number of Listed Buildings and Scheduled Ancient Monuments in the Nominated Site will be reviewed by Cadw and English Heritage and reported to the World Heritage Site Steering Group every six years.

Contacts:
Inspectorate Records Section, Cadw, Plas Carew, Unit 5/7 Cefn Coed, Parc Nantgarw, Cardiff, CF15 7QQ
Cadw@Wales.GSI.Gov.UK
Telephone: 44 (0)1443 336000

English Heritage,
West Midland Regional Office,
112 Colmore Row, Birmingham, B3 3AG
www.English-Heritage.org.uk
Telephone 44 (0)121 6256820

Condition of Scheduled Ancient Monuments in the Nominated Site and Buffer Zone

Field Monument Wardens employed by Cadw and English Heritage visit all ancient monuments scheduled under the *Ancient Monuments and Archaeological Areas Act 1979* in Wales on a five-year cycle, and in England according to an assessment of perceived risk. Wardens record their condition in the form of a textual description, drawings and photographs. Cadw also takes into account monitoring of Scheduled Ancient Monuments from the air, undertaken on its behalf by the Royal Commission on the Ancient and Historical Monuments of Wales since 1984. The wardens are part of the Cadw and English Heritage Inspectorates, teams of professional staff that undertake a range of duties with regard to the identification and protection of historic assets. The regional Inspectors of Ancient Monuments are responsible for dealing with any problems identified in these reports as well as monitoring all works to protected monuments, subject to the statutory consent regime. Descriptions and aerial and ground photographs of all features were produced in 2006-7 by Cadw and the Royal Commission on the Ancient and Historical Monuments of Wales as a base-line record to enable effective monitoring of future deterioration or enhancement.

Contacts:
Inspectorate Scheduling Team,
Cadw, Plas Carew, Unit 5/7 Cefn Coed,
Parc Nantgarw, Cardiff, CF15 7QQ
Cadw@Wales.GSI.Gov.UK
Telephone: 44 (0)1443 336000

English Heritage,
West Midland Regional Office,
112 Colmore Row, Birmingham, B3 3AG
www.English-Heritage.org.uk
Telephone 44 (0)121 6256820

Number of buildings in the Nominated Site and Buffer Zone on the Buildings at Risk Registers

The Nominated Site includes thirty-two statutorily protected Listed Buildings, including the canal bridges, and buildings associated with the construction and operation of the canal. The Buffer Zone includes a further 301 listed buildings. Wrexham County Borough Council, Denbighshire County Council and Oswestry Borough Council have compiled Buildings at Risk Registers, subject to periodic review, that list all historic buildings deemed to be at risk of deterioration through neglect. Their Conservation Officers seek to negotiate a secure future for such buildings, scrutinise all applications for works that may affect them or their settings and advise private owners of best conservation practice. The number of Listed Buildings on the Buildings at Risk Registers will be reported to the World Heritage Site Steering Group every six years.

Contacts:
Conservation Officer,
Wrexham County Borough Council,
The Guildhall, Wrexham, LL11 1AV
Webmaster@wrexham.gov.uk
Telephone 44 (0)1978 292000

Conservation Officer,
Denbighshire County Council, County Hall, Wynnstay Road, Ruthin, LL15 1YN
Enquiries@denbighshire.gov.uk
Telephone 44 (0)1824 706000

Conservation Officer,
Oswestry Borough Council, Castle View, Oswestry, Shropshire, SY11 1JR
Generalenquiries@Oswestrybc.gov.uk
Telephone 44 (0)1691 671111

State of conservation of the Historic Landscape and Parks and Gardens in the Nominated Site and Buffer Zone

The baseline Landscape Character Assessment for the whole of the Nominated Site and Buffer Zone was carried out in 2007 in accordance with the joint Institute of Environmental Management and Assessment/ Landscape Institute standards for assessing significance of impacts on landscape. This assessed the overall condition of the landscape and the state of important views to and from the Nominated Site. The baseline assessment was prepared by staff from Wrexham County Borough Council, British Waterways, Denbighshire County Council and Oswestry Borough Council. A reassessment will be carried out and reviewed by the World Heritage Site Steering Group every six years.

Contact:
World Heritage Site Steering Group: secretariat, Wrexham County Borough Council.

Maintenance of operation: boats at Wern Isaf Moorings.

6.c Results of previous reporting exercises

British Waterways' assessments of the State of Conservation of historic assets within the Nominated Site showed that all major structures are in Good (e.g. Pontcysyllte Aqueduct), Fair or Fair* condition. Grading all the features of the site found 8 per cent to be Good, 58 per cent Fair and 9 per cent Fair*. Only 12 per cent of all assets were considered to be in Poor condition from a State of Conservation viewpoint.

The British Waterways' Asset Inspection Programme grades features as to their Fitness for Purpose and showed 70 per cent of the twenty-five principal assets in the Nominated Site to be graded between A (Excellent) to C (Fair).

The Assessment reports are available from: British Waterways.

All Scheduled Ancient Monuments within the Nominated Site and Buffer Zone were inspected by Cadw's Field Monument Wardens between 2002 and 2007. The two Scheduled Ancient Monuments in the Nominated Site were classed as Improved; the twelve in the Buffer Zone were classed as Stable (nine), Improved (two) and Worsened (one – a section of Offa's Dyke).

The past condition reports, the scheduled monument consent reports on the major conservation exercise on the Pontcysyllte Aqueduct in 2004, and all aerial record photographs of Scheduled Ancient Monuments and Historic Landscapes are available from:

Contacts:
Inspectorate Scheduling Team,
Cadw, Plas Carew, Unit 5/7 Cefn Coed,
Parc Nantgarw, Cardiff, CF15 7QQ
Cadw@Wales.GSI.Gov.UK
Telephone: 44 (0)1443 336000

Inspectorate Scheduling Team, Cadw
Environmental Record,
Sustainability Group,
Shropshire County Council, Shire Hall,
Abbey Foregate, Shrewsbury, SY2 6ND.

The Landscape of Special Historic Interest in the Vale of Llangollen covers much of the Buffer Zone.

The Buildings at Risk Registers for the three local authorities include three listed structures in the Nominated Site (one in Wrexham, which has now received attention and is stable, and two in Denbighshire) and fourteen in the Buffer Zone (four in Wrexham and nine in Denbighshire). However since the compilation of these registers in 2003-5, refurbishment of four structures has been completed and two others are in process.

The Registers of Buildings at Risk and reports on listed building repair work are available from:
Denbighshire County Council,
Wrexham County Borough Council and
Oswestry Borough Council.

The extensive photographic, drawn and documentary records from the 2004 conservation and repair of Pontcysyllte Aqueduct, as well as the records of the two recent archaeological surveys of the Nominated Sites and Buffer Zone, are publicly accessible. They are housed within the National Monuments Record of Wales, Royal Commission on the Ancient and Historical Monuments of Wales, Plas Crug, Aberystwyth, SY23 1NJ, UK and online at the RCAHMW website database Coflein.

Records of earlier conservation episodes in the nineteenth and twentieth centuries affecting the canal and aqueducts are held by British Waterways.

The Pontcysyllte Conservation Management Plan and the reports from the technical engineering inspections of the entire stretch of canal and associated bridges, roads and other features, are available from British Waterways.

Equalling, or in the estimation of the practical utilitarian mind surpassing, castle, abbey, or memorial stone, are the gigantic works of art, the viaduct and the aqueduct, the latter modelled after the celebrated Roman aqueduct at Nismes, and of which its architect, Telford, felt so justly proud that he adopted a representation of it on his crest – and a magnificent structure it is, combining scientific strength with fairy-like airiness and grace – the queen of arches.

The Cambrian Journal
(1858)

23

In the days before railways, such a canal as this was an engineering work of the very first importance. It was to connect the Mersey, the Dee, and the Severn, and it passed over ground which rendered necessary some immense aqueducts on a scale never before attempted by British engineers. Even in our own time, every traveller by the Great Western line between Chester and Shrewsbury must have observed on his right two magnificent ranges as high arches, which are as noticeable now as ever for their boldness, their magnitude, and their exquisite construction. The first of these mighty archways is the Pont Cysylltau aqueduct which carries the Ellesmere Canal across the wide valley of the Dee, known as the Vale of Llangollen; the second is the Chirk aqueduct, which takes it over the lesser glen of a minor tributary, the Ceriog. Both these beautiful works were designed and carried out entirely by Telford. They differ from many other great modern engineering achievements in the fact that, instead of spoiling the lovely mountain scenery into whose midst they have been thrown, they actually harmonize with it and heighten its natural beauty. Both works, however, are splendid feats, regarded merely as efforts of practical skill; and the larger one is particularly memorable for the peculiarity that the trough for the water and the elegant parapet at the side are both entirely composed of iron. Nowadays, of course, there would be nothing remarkable in the use of such a material for such a purpose; but Telford was the first engineer to see the value of iron in this respect, and the Pont Cysylltau aqueduct was one of the earliest works in which he applied the new material to these unwonted uses. Such a step is all the more remarkable, because Telford's own education had lain entirely in what may fairly be called the 'stone age' of English engineering; while his natural predilections as a stonemason might certainly have made him rather overlook the value of the novel material. But Telford was a man who could rise superior to such little accidents of habit or training; and as a matter of fact there is no other engineer to whom the rise of the present 'iron age' in engineering work is more directly and immediately to be attributed than to himself.

Grant Allen
Biographies of Working Men
(1884)

DOCUMENTATION

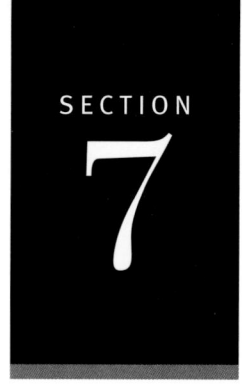

7.a Photographs, slides image inventory and authorisation table and other audiovisual material

Thirty slides of the Pontcysyllte Aqueduct and Canal are included with this document, together with a DVD of a computerised visualisation of Pontcysyllte Aqueduct prepared by the Royal Commission on the Ancient and Historical Monuments of Wales and See3D. The principal archives of imagery are held by the Welsh Assembly Government, British Waterways and the Royal Commission on the Ancient and Historical Monuments of Wales. Image collections are also held by the relevant local authorities, the Institution of Civil Engineers and the National Library of Wales.

Id. No	Format	Caption	Date	Photographer	Copyright owner	Contact
1	slide	Pontcysyllte Aqueduct	2006	WCBC	WCBC	See p.223
2	slide	Pontcysyllte Aqueduct Bicentenary Celebrations	2005	M. Dean	BW	See p.223
3	slide	Pontcysyllte Aqueduct	2001	WCBC	WCBC	See p.223
4	slide	Pontcysyllte Aqueduct Aerial View	2006/7	RCAHMW	Crown Copyright	See p.223
5	slide	Canal at Chirk Bank	2006/7	RCAHMW	Crown Copyright	See p.223
6	slide	Chirk Aqueduct and Ceiriog Valley	2006/7	RCAHMW	Crown Copyright	See p.223
7	slide	Chirk Aqueduct and Viaduct	2006/7	RCAHMW	Crown Copyright	See p.223
8	slide	Chirk Aqueduct and Viaduct	2006/7	RCAHMW	Crown Copyright	See p.223
9	slide	Model of Chirk Aqueduct	2006/7	RCAHMW	Crown Copyright	See p.223
10	slide	Main line canal formation	2006/7	RCAHMW	Crown Copyright	See p.223
11	slide	Chirk Tunnel	2007	M. Dean	WCBC	See p.223
12	slide	Whitehouses Tunnel	2006/7	RCAHMW	Crown Copyright	See p.223
13	slide	Irish Bridge	2006/7	RCAHMW	Crown Copyright	See p.223
14	slide	Pontcysyllte Aqueduct	2006/7	RCAHMW	Crown Copyright	See p.223
15	slide	Pontcysyllte Aqueduct Aerial View	2006/7	RCAHMW	Crown Copyright	See p.223
16	slide	Pontcysyllte Aqueduct	2007	M. Dean	Crown Copyright	See p.223
17	slide	Model of Pontcysyllte Aqueduct	2006/7	RCAHMW	Crown Copyright	See p.223
18	slide	Trevor Basin Aerial View	2006/7	RCAHMW	Crown Copyright	See p.223
19	slide	Public artwork, Trevor Basin	2007	M. Dean	WCBC	See p.223
20	slide	Community Event, Trevor Basin	2006	G. Lloyd	WCBC	See p.223
21	slide	Scotch Hall, Trevor Basin	2006/7	RCAHMW	Crown Copyright	See p.223
22	slide	Plâs-Ifan Bridge	2006/7	RCAHMW	Crown Copyright	See p.223
23	slide	Llanddyn Lift Bridge	2006/7	RCAHMW	Crown Copyright	See p.223
24	slide	Wern-isaf Rock Walls Cutting	2006/7	RCAHMW	Crown Copyright	See p.223
25	slide	Llangollen Wharf and Warehouse	2006/7	RCAHMW	Crown Copyright	See p.223
26	slide	Horse-drawn Boat	2006	J. Marjoram	WCBC	See p.223
27	slide	Pen-y-ddol Bridge	2006	J. Marjoram	WCBC	See p.223
28	slide	Horseshoe Falls	2006/7	RCAHMW	Crown Copyright	See p.223
29	slide	Chirk Aqueduct	2001	WCBC	WCBC	See p.223
30	slide	Pontcysyllte Aqueduct	2006/7	RCAHMW	Crown Copyright	See p.223
31	DVD	Pontcysyllte Aqueduct Visualisation	2006/7	RCAHMW	Crown Copyright	See p.223

It is not possible to assign copyright or reproduction fees of photographs that are Crown Copyright to a third party. However, UNESCO is granted the right to reproduce, and allow to be reproduced, items 1-30 free of charge for the purpose of this nomination. Any such reproduction should be accompanied by the following acknowledgement: 'Crown Copyright: RCAHMW'.

7.b Texts relating to protective designation, copies of property management plans or documented management systems and extracts of other plans relevant to the Property

The legislation relating to the protection of the proposed World Heritage Site, the relevant National Planning Policy Guidelines, and the Local Authority Unitary Development Plans and Local Plans are provided on a CD [and in the Supporting Information] and listed below:

UK Government Legislation
- Ancient Monuments and Archaeological Areas Act 1979
- The Ancient Monuments (Class Consents) Order 1994
- British Waterways Act 1995 (part relevant to conservation duty)
- Conservation (natural habitats) Regulations 1994
- Countryside and Rights of Way Act 2000
- Disability Discrimination Act 2005
- Environment Act 1995
- Freedom of Information Act 2000
- The National Heritage Acts 1983 and 2002
- National Parks and Access to the Countryside Act of 1949
- Planning and Compulsory Purchase Act 2004
- Planning (Listed Buildings and Conservation Areas) Act 1990
- Town and Country Planning Act 1990
- The Town and Country Planning (General Permitted Development) Order 1995 (GPDO).
- Transport Acts 1962 and 1968 (parts relevant to British Waterways)
- White Paper Heritage Protection for the 21st Century
- Wildlife and Countryside Act 1981

Subordinate Legislation
- Hedgerows Regulations 1997
- Town and Country Planning (Environmental Impact Assessment) (England and Wales) Regulations 1999

Planning Policy Guidance/Statements

England
- Planning Policy Statement 1: Delivering Sustainable Development
- Planning Policy Guidance 2: Green Belts
- Planning Policy Statement 7: Sustainable Development in Rural Areas
- Planning Policy Statement 9: Biodiversity and Geological Conservation
- Planning Policy Guidance 13: Transport
- Planning Policy Guidance 15: Planning and the Historic Environment
- Planning Policy Guidance 16: Archaeology and Planning
- Planning Policy Guidance 17: Planning for Open Space, Sport and Recreation
- West Midlands Regional Spatial Strategy (West Midlands Regional Assembly 2004)

Wales
- Circular 60/96: Planning and the Historic Environment: Archaeology
- Circular 61/96: Planning and the Historic Environment: Historic Buildings and Conservation Areas
- Planning Policy Wales (March 2002)
- Planning Policy Wales Companion Guide (June 2006)
- Regional Planning Guidance for North Wales
- Register of Landscapes of Special Historic Interest in Wales (Cadw, CCW & ICOMOS UK 2001)
- Register of Parks and Gardens of Special Historic Interest in Wales (Cadw/ ICOMOS UK)

UK Government Policy and Guidance
- The Historic Environment: A Force for the Future (DCMS 2001)
- Securing the Future – UK Government's Sustainable Development Strategy (2005)

Welsh Assembly Government Policy and Guidance

- Creative Future: Cymru Greadigol – A Culture Strategy for Wales (WAG 2002)
- Environment Strategy for Wales (WAG 2006)
- Wales: A Better Country (WAG 2006)
- Wales: A Vibrant Economy. The National Economic Development Strategy of the Welsh Assembly Government (WAG 2006)
- The Wales Spatial Plan 'People, Places, Futures' (WAG 2004)

Local Authority Policy and Publications

Wrexham County Borough Council:

- Economic Development Strategy (WCBC 2007)
- Emerging Physical Regeneration Strategy 2008-2011
- Local Planning Guidance Notes
- Shaping the future of Llangollen Rural (WCBC/NMC 2007)
- Wrexham Acquisition and Disposal Policy: Archives and Local Studies Service
- Wrexham Buildings at Risk Strategy 2004 (Updated 2006)
- Wrexham Countryside Strategy (WCBC 2002)
- Wrexham Heritage Strategy 2005-2010 (WCBC 2005)
- Wrexham Landmap Summary Document – SPG March 2007
- Wrexham Unitary Development Plan 1996-2011 (WCBC 2005)

Denbighshire County Council

- Caring for Our Countryside A Countryside Strategy for Denbighshire (DCC 1998)
- Denbighshire Community Strategy (DCC 2004)
- Denbighshire Unitary Development Plan 1996-2011 (DCC 2002)
- Local Planning Guidance Notes

- Raising the Standard: The Visitor Economy Strategy for the Dee Valley

Oswestry Borough Council

- Oswestry Borough Local Plan 1996-2006 (1999): Relevant policies saved beyond September 27th 2007 under the Direction of the Secretary of State (Direction dated 7 September 2007)

Shropshire County Council

- Shropshire Joint Structure Plan 1996-2011 (2002)
- Shropshire and Telford and Wrekin Joint Structure Plan - saved policies September 2007
- Shropshire and Telford and Wrekin Minerals Local Plan - saved policies September 2007
- Draft Shropshire Countryside Access Strategy - SCC July 2007
- Shropshire Biodiversity Action Plan - SCC 2006
- Shropshire Tourism Strategy - SCC 2004
- Shropshire Futures (Economic Development Strategy) - SCC 2003
- Shropshire Partnership Community Strategy - Shropshire Partnership 2006
- Supporting People Strategy - SCC 2005
- West Midlands Regional Spatial Strategy - SCC 2005

Studies

- Equal Shares for All, waterways accessibility audits (BW, WAG, 2007 – extracts relating to the Site)
- Industrial Archaeology Audit of the Area Around the Pontcysyllte Aqueduct Proposed World Heritage Site (2007)
- International Significance of Pontcysyllte Aqueduct (2005)
- Landscape Assessment (WCBC, DCC, BW, OBC, 2007)
- Pontcysyllte and its Canal: State of Conservation (2007)
- Pontcysyllte Aqueduct Refurbishment Report (British Waterways 2005)
- Wild over Waterways (WOW) schools packs for Pontcysyllte

Conservation Area Appraisals

- Cefn Mawr Conservation Area Character Assessment (2005)
- Chirk Conservation Area Character Assessment (2001)
- Llangollen Conservation Area Appraisal (1997-1998)
- Llantysilio (1997)
- Trevor Basin Conservation Area Assessment (2000) (Currently under review)
- Trevor Mill / Plas yn Pentre (1997-1998)

Management Plans (Summaries and Full Text)

- British Waterways, Wales & Border Counties Business Plan 2007-2008 to 2010-2011
- Cefn Mawr Conservation Area Management Plan
- Pontcysyllte and its Canal: World Heritage Site Management Plan (2007)
- Pontcysyllte Aqueduct and Canal World Heritage Site Nomination, Public Consultation on the Nomination and Management Proposals (2007)
- Pontcysyllte Aqueduct Conservation Management Plan, (British Waterways 2004)
- The Site of Special Scientific Interest : Management Statement for the River Dee (CCW / Natural England)

Other documents referenced in the Nomination Document

- British Waterways' Byelaws
- British Waterways' 'Code of Practice for Works Affecting British Waterways'
- British Waterways Emergency Procedures Manual
- British Waterways' Environmental Code of Practice
- British Waterways' Heritage Policy and Principle

7.c Form and date of most recent records or inventory of the Property

The Royal Commission on the Ancient and Historical Monuments of Wales undertook a comprehensive aerial and ground photographic survey of the Site between 2005 and 2007, and completed survey drawings of principal monuments in 2007.

British Waterways completed a 'State of Conservation' survey and report for the whole of the canal in 2007, consisting of text descriptions and photographs of all key features.

British Waterways maintains a rolling programme of Asset Inspections, for certain key structures on the Canal consisting of text descriptions, structural / functional assessments and photographs.

The Waterways Trust manages the National Waterways Collection which includes a range of former British Waterways and other records regarding the Site.

Welsh Assembly Government, through Cadw, are compiling an expanded inventory of all historic assets within the Nominated Site in Wales suitable for statutory designation up to and including 2007. English Heritage Inspectors have carried out the same task in England.

Wrexham County Borough Council assess the condition of all listed buildings to maintain and update the 'Buildings at Risk' register. A full re-survey is carried out every five years, the next survey being due this year.

7.d Address where inventory, records and archives are held

Royal Commission on the Ancient and
Historical Monuments of Wales
Plas Crug
Aberystwyth
Ceredigion
Wales
SY23 1NJ
www.rcahmw.gov.uk

British Waterways
Wales and Border Counties
Navigation Road
Northwich
CW8 1BH
www.britishwaterways.co.uk

Waterway Archives
The Waterways Trust
Llanthony Warehouse
Gloucester Docks
GLOUCESTER
GL1 2EJ
www.thewaterwaystrust.org.uk

Cadw
Plas Carew
Unit 5/7 Cefn Coed
Parc Nantgarw
Cardiff
Wales
CF15 7QQ
www.cadw.wales.gov.uk

The Environmental Record
Sustainability Group
Shropshire County Council
Shirehall
Abbey Foregate
Shrewsbury
Shropshire
SY2 6ND

Tel: 01743 252562,
Email: sustainability@shropshire-cc.gov.uk

7.e Bibliography

7.e.1 Literature concerned with the Nominated Site and its builders

Althea, *Thomas Telford: Man of Iron* (Cambridge, 1982)

Beckett, Derek, *Telford's Britain* (London, 1987)

Bergeron, Louis, ed., Papers from the Pontcysyllte International Canal Conference: special edition of *Patrimoine de l'industrie/Industrial Patrimony*, volume 17 (2007)

Bracegirdle, Brian and Miles, Patricia H., Great Engineers and their Works: Thomas Telford (Newton Abbot, 1973)

Britnell, W., *Vale of Llangollen and Eglwyseg Historic Landscape Characterisation* (Welshpool, 2005)

Brown, Peter, 'Thomas Telford and the Ellesmere Canal, 1793-1813' *Journal of the Railway and Canal Historical Society*, (2007)

Brown, Peter, 'How the Llangollen Canal was Saved' *Waterways Journal* (2007)

Buckley, Stanley Elvet, *Thomas Telford: canals, roads, bridges* (London, 1948)

Burton, Anthony, *The Canal Builders* (London, 1972)

Burton, Anthony, *Canal Mania: over 200 years of Britain's waterways* (London, 1993)

Burton, Anthony, *Thomas Telford* (London, 1999)

Cadw/CCW/ICOMOS UK, *Register of Landscapes, Parks and Gardens of Special Historic Interest in Wales Part 1: Parks and Gardens Clwyd* (Cardiff,1995)

Cameron, A.D., *Thomas Telford and the Transport Revolution* (London, 1979)

Cameron, A.D., *The Caledonian Canal* (Edinburgh, 2005)

Cefn Mawr, Rhosymedre and Newbridge Community Association, *Cefn Mawr Heritage Trail* (Cefn Mawr, n.d., c.2003)

Cohen, P., 'The Origins of the Pont Cysyllte Aqueduct', *Transactions of the Newcomen Society*, vol. 51 (1979-80)

Connolly, A., 'Life in the Victorian brickyards of Flintshire and Denbighshire' (Llanrwst, 2003)

Cossons, N. (ed), *Transactions of the First International Congress on the Conservation of Industrial Monuments* (Ironbridge,1975)

Davies, D., *Tafarnau Cefn Mawr* (Privately published, Cefn-mawr)

Dean, R., 'The metamorphosis of the Ellesmere Canal', *Railway and Canal Historical Society Journal* XXVIII, 6 (1985)

Dodd, A.H., *The Industrial Revolution in North Wales* (1951, 3rd edn. Cardiff,1971)

Edwards, I., 'The History of the Montsanto Chemical Works Sites, Cefn Mawr, Wrexham: A Study in Industrial Archaeology', *Transactions of the Denbighshire Historical Society*, vol.16 (1967)

Edwards, I., *Cefn-Mawr in old picture postcards* (Zaltbommel: European Library, 1989)

Edwards, I., 'The British Iron Company', *Transactions of the Denbighshire Historical Society* (1982)

Edwards, I., 'Slate Quarries in the Llangollen District', *Transactions of Denbighshire Historical Society* 34 (1985)

Ferguson, Eugene S., 'Cast Iron Aqueducts in Rees's "Cyclopaedia"', *Technology and Culture*, vol 9 (1968), pp. 597-600

Fitzgerald, Ron, 'The Pontcysyllte Aqueduct: its place in the evolution of iron technology', expert paper in preparation for the Pontcysyllte World Heritage nomination (2006)

Fox, Sir C., *Offa's Dyke* (Oxford,1955)

Gibb, Sir Alexander, *The Story of Telford: the Rise of Civil Engineering* (London, 1935)

Gruffydd, W.J., *About Britain No.7: North Wales and the Marches* (London,1951)

Gwyn, David, '*Wrexham County Borough Council LANDMAP Study: Cultural Landscapes*', (2004)

Gwyn, David, 'Pontcysyllte Aqueduct and its associated industries', expert paper in preparation for the Pontcysyllte World Heritage nomination (2006)

Gwyn, David, 'Pontcysyllte Aqueduct and its associated railway system', expert paper in preparation for the Pontcysyllte World Heritage nomination (2006)

Gwyn, David, 'Pontcysyllte Aqueduct within its historic and archaeological landscape setting', expert paper in preparation for the Pontcysyllte World Heritage nomination (2006)

Gwyn, David, 'Pontcysycllte Aqueduct: cultural context', expert paper in preparation for the Pontcysyllte World Heritage nomination (2006)

Gwyn, David, 'Industrial Archaeology Audit of the Area around the Pontcysyllte Aqueduct Proposed World Heritage Site' (2007)

Gwyn, David and Trinder, Barrie, 'Pontcysyllte Aqueduct and its associated settlements', expert paper in preparation for the Pontcysyllte World Heritage nomination (2006)

Gwyn, David and Trinder, Barrie, 'Pontcysyllte Aqueduct: conservation and interpretation', expert paper in preparation for the Pontcysyllte World Heritage nomination (2006)

Hadfield, Charles, *The Canals of the West Midlands* (Newton Abbot, 1966)

Hadfield, Charles, *Thomas Telford's Temptation* (Cleobury Mortimer, 1993)

Hadfield, Charles, 'Telford, Jessop and Pont Cysyllte', *Journal of the Railway and Canal Historical Society*, vol. 15 (1969)

Hadfield, Charles and Skempton, A.W., *William Jessop: Engineer* (Newton Abbot,1979)

Harper, C.G., *The Holyhead Road: the mail coach road to Dublin* (2nd edition, London,1902)

Hughes, M., 'Telford, Parnell and the Great Irish Road', *Journal of Transport History*, vol. 6 (1964)

James, J.G., 'Some steps in the Evolution of Early Iron Arched Bridge Designs', *Transactions of the Newcomen Society*, vol. 59 (1987-8)

Jenkinson, Andrew M., *On the Trail of Thomas Telford in Shropshire* (Little Stretton, c.1993)

Jones, J.B., *Offa's Dyke Path* (London,1976)

C. Delyth R. Jones, *Llangollen-Chirk Canal: a canal-side walk* (Mold, 1980)

Lerry, G.G., *Collieries of Denbighshire* (Wrexham,1946)

Lewis, C., 'Josiah Clowes (1735-1794), *Transactions of the Newcomen Society*, vol. 50 (1978-9)

Lewis, M.J.T., 'Cast-iron Aqueducts', *Journal of the Railway and Canal Historical Society*, vol.22 (1976)

McKnight, Hugh and Plowright, Julian, *The Ladyline Cruising Guides: 1, Llangollen Canal* (Market Drayton, nd, c.1974)

Martin, Rosemary, 'Changes in the Vale of Llangollen 1790-1865' *Old Denbighshire* 48 (1999), pp.52-73

Mavor, Elizabeth, *The Ladies of Llangollen* (London, 1971)

Maynell, Laurence, *Thomas Telford: the life story of a great engineer* (London, 1957)

Milner, W.J., *The Glyn Valley Tramway* (Poole,1984)

Morris, Chris, *On Tour with Thomas Telford* (Longhope, 2004)

Nicholson, *Guide to the Waterways: Four Counties and the Welsh Canals* (London,1997)

Noble, F., *The Shell Book of Offa's Dyke Path* (London, 1969)

Palmer, A.N., *The History of the Parish of Ruabon and The Town, Fields, and Folk of Wrexham in the Time of James the First etc* (Wrexham,1992)

Paxton, R., 'The Chairman's Column Book Review: "Thomas Telford's Temptation" by Charles Hadfield', *Institution of Civil Engineers, Historic Engineering Works Newsletter*, December 1993

Pearce, Rhoda M., *Thomas Telford: an illustrated life of Thomas Telford, 1757-1834* (Princes Risborough, 2007)

Pellow, Thomas and Bowen, Paul, *Canal to Llangollen: a portrait of the Llangollen Branch of the Shropshire Union Canal* (Crewe, 1988)

Penfold, A., *Thomas Telford, 'Colossus of Roads'* (Irobridge, 1981)

Penfold, A., ed., *Thomas Telford: Engineer* (London,1980)

Pound, Christopher, 'Pontcysycllte and the picturesque', expert paper in preparation for the Pontcysyllte World Heritage nomination (2006)

Quartermaine, J., Trinder, B. and Turner, R., *Telford's Holyhead Road: the A5 in North Wales* (York, 2003)

Quenby, Ron, *Thomas Telford's Aqueducts on the Shropshire Union Canal* (Shrewsbury, 1992)

Richards, A.J., *A Gazetteer of the Welsh Slate Industry* (Capel Garmon,1991)

Rolt, L.T.C., *Thomas Telford* (London, 1958)

Royal Society of Edinburgh, *The 250th anniversary of the birth of Thomas Telford: collected papers from a commemorative conference held on 2 July 2007* (Edinburgh, 2007)

Sakwa, Norah, *Trevor-Chirk Canal Visit* (Mold, 1985)

Sellman, R.R., *Brindley and Telford* (London, 1971)

Skempton, A.W., 'Telford and the Design for a new London Bridge', Penfold, A., ed., *Thomas Telford Engineer* (London,1980).

Smiles, Samuel, *The Life of Thomas Telford, Civil Engineer: with an introductory history of roads and travelling in Great Britain* (London, 1867)

Smiles, Samuel, *Lives of the Engineers: History of Roads: Metcalfe and Telford* (London,1874)

Smiles, Samuel, *Lives of the engineers: with an account of their principal works; comprising also a history of inland communication in Britain* (London, 1862)

Stromback, Lars, Baltzar von Platen, Thomas Telford och Göta kanal: entreprenorskap och tekniko verforing i brytningstid (Stockholm, 1993)

Telford, T., *The Life of Thomas Telford*, ed. J.Rickman (London,1838)

Trinder, Barrie, 'Ellesmere Canal and Pontcysyllte Aqueduct: their place in the history of canals', expert paper in preparation for the Pontcysyllte World Heritage nomination (2006)

Trinder, Barrie, 'The builders of the Pontcysyllte Aqueduct', expert paper in preparation for the Pontcysyllte World Heritage nomination (2006)

Trinder, Barrie, 'Contemporary perceptions of the Pontcysyllte Aqueduct', expert paper in preparation for the Pontcysyllte World Heritage nomination (2006)

Trinder, Barrie, 'The place of the Pontcysyllte Aqueduct in the history of conservation', expert paper in preparation for the Pontcysyllte World Heritage nomination (2006)

Turner-Thomas, R.J., *Pontcysyllte Aqueduct: Restoration Winter 2003 – Spring 2004* (Sofia, 2005)

United Kingdom, Department for Culture, Media and Sport, *World Heritage Sites: the tentative list of the United Kingdom of Great Britain and Northern Ireland* (London, 1999)

Williams, C.J., *Industry in Clwyd: An Illustrated History* (Hawarden, 1986)

Williams, Gareth Vaughan, 'The Ellesmere Canal Navigation – a Great Public Utility' *Old Denbighshire* 48 (1999), pp.23-36

Wilson, E.A., *The Ellesmere and Llangollen Canal: an Historical Background* (Chichester, 1975)

Wrexham County Borough Council, *International Significance of Pontcysyllte Aqueduct* (Wrexham, 2005)

Wright, C.J., *A guide to Offa's Dyke Path* (London,1976)

7.e.2 Contemporary published sources

Act, *An act to enable the company of proprietors of the Ellesmere Canal to make a railway from Ruabon Brook to the Ellesmere Canal, at or near the aqueduct at Pont Cysylltee, in the parish of Llangollen, in the county of Denbigh: and also to make several cuts or feeders for better supplying the said canal with water* (Local and Personal Acts, George III, 1804)

Atlas de la Navigation Intérieure de l'Angleterre et de la France (Paris, 1819)

Bingley, Rev W., 'A Tour Round North Wales' (London, 1798)

Bingley, William, *Excursions in North Wales* (London, 1839)

Borrow, G., *Wild Wales* (London, Everyman edition 1958)

Brewster, David, ed., *The Edinburgh Encyclopaedia*, (18 vols, Edinburgh, 1830)

de Pommeuse, Huerne, *Des canaux navigables considérés d'une manière générale, avec des recherches comparatives sur la navigation intérieure de la France et celle de l'Angleterre* (Paris, 1822)

De Salis, H.R., *Bradshaw's Canals and Navigable Rivers of England and Wales* (London, 1904)

Dickens, C. (ed), *The Life of Charles James Mathews: chiefly autobiographical* (2 vols. London, 1879)

Dickinson, H.W., 'An Eighteenth Century Engineer's Sketchbook', *Transactions of the Newcomen Society*, vol. 2 (1921-2)

Dupin, C., *Voyages dans la Grande-Bretagne depuis 1816* [Journeys in Great Britain since 1816] (Paris, 1824)

Dupin, C., *The Commercial Power of Great Britain* (translated from the French, 2 vols, London, 1825)

Dutens, J., *Mémoires sur les travaux publiques de l'Angleterre* [Reports on public works in England] (Paris, 1819)

Fairbairn, W., *On the Application of Cast and Wrought Iron to building purposes* (London, 1854)

Fairbairn, W., *Iron: its history, properties and processes of manufacture (London, 1854)*

Flachat, Christopher Stéphane, *Histoire des travaux et de l'amenagement des eaux du Canal Caledonien. Redigee d'apres les rapports de MM. Jessop et Telford... et d'apre s les rapports des Commissaires de la Chambre des Communes, etc* (Paris, 1828)

Fulton, R., *A Treatise on the Improvement of Canal Navigation &c.* (London, 1796)

Gilpin, Rev. W., 1809, *Tours on Several Parts of North Wales*

Gilpin, Rev. W., 1762, *Essay on Prints*

Griffiths, S., *Griffiths' Guide to the Iron trade of Great Britain* (1873, ed. W.K.V. Gale, Newton Abbot, 1967)

Helps, A., *Life and Labours of Mr Brassey, 1805-70* (3rd ed. London, 1872)

Hoare, Sir R.C., *The Journeys of Sir Richard Colt Hoare through Wales and England 1793-1810*, ed. M.W.Thompson (Gloucester, 1983)

Hunt, R., *Oration delivered at Pont Cysyllte Aqueduct on its first opening, November 26th 1805, to which is affixed a Letter addressed to the Rt. Hon. The Earl of Bridgewater* (Shrewsbury, 1806)

Irving, Washington, *Journals of Washington Irving* (1970)

Jones, A.R. and Tydeman, W. (eds), 1979 of:- Joseph Hucks, 1795, *A Pedestrian Tour through North Wales in a series of letters* (Cardiff)

Lewis, S., *Topographical Dictionary of Wales* (London, 1838)

Lewis, Samuel, *A Topographical Dictionary of Wales* (4th edition, 1849)

Matthew, Adam, *Industrial Revolution: a documentary history. Series 2, Papers of John Rennie (1761-1821), Thomas Telford (1757-1834) and related figures from the National Library of Scotland. Part 11, John Rennie, Thomas Telford, Joseph Black and James Watt* (Marlborough, 2003)

Mavor, W., *A Tour in Wales and through Several Counties of England performed in the summer of 1805* (London, 1806)

Mechanics Magazine, *The Mechanics Magazine* (London, 1840)

Oldschool, Oliver, *The Port Folio* (Philadelphia, 1809)

Parnell, Sir Henry, *A Treatise on Roads; wherein the principles on which roads should be made are explained and illustrated by the plans, specifications and contracts made use of by T. Telford* (London, 1838)

Phillips, J., *A General History of Inland Navigation, Foreign and Domestic* (1803)

Pigot, and Co., *National Commercial Directory: North Wales, South Wales* (London, 1835)

Provis, William Alexander, An historical and descriptive account of the suspension bridge constructed over the Menai Straits, in North Wales with a brief notice of Conway bridge from designs by, and under the direction of Thomas Telford (1828)

Priestley, J., *An Historical Account of the Navigable Rivers, Canals and Railways of Britain* (London,1831 rep. as *Priestley's Navigable Rivers and Canals.* Newton Abbot,1969)

Pükler-Muskau, Prince Hermann von, *Tour in England, Ireland and France in the years 1828 and 1829... by a German Prince* (London, 1832)

Rees, A., *The Cyclopaedia or Universal Dictionary of Arts, Sciences and Literature* (39 vols., London,1802-20)

Renwick, James, *Outlines of Natural Philosophy, being the heads of a course of lectures delivered in Columbia University, New York* (New York, 1822)

Renwick, James, *Applications of the Science of Mechanics to Practical Purposes* (New York, 1844)

Schinkel, K.F., *Reise nach England, Schottland und Paris im Jahre 1826* (ed. G. Riemann, Munich, 1986)

Anon, General *Karta ofver Göta Canal, foreslagen till sammanbindande af Wenern och Wettern med Ostersjon. Pa Konungens Allernadigste Befallning utstakad under Ofversten och Riddaren Frihre von Platens inseende af Th. Telford 1808* (Stockholm, 1810)

Simms, Frederick Walter, *A Treatise of the Principles and Practice of Levelling: particularly in the construction of roads, with Mr Telford's rules for the same* (London, 1837)

Simpson, W.T., *Some Account of Llangollen and its Vicinity* (London, 1827)

Southey, R., *Letters from England 1807* (Gloucester, 1984)

Southey, R., *Journal of a Tour in Scotland in 1819* (London, 1929)

Spiker, S.H., *Travels through England, Wales and Scotland in the year 1816 by Dr. H.S. Spiker, Librarian to His Majesty the King of Prussia* (London, 1820)

Stillman, Benjamin, *A Visit to Europe in 1851 by Prof. Benjamin Stillman of Yale College* (New York, 1854)

Telford, Thomas, *Eskdale: a descriptive poem* (Shrewsbury, 1795)

Telford, Thomas, Copy of a Letter to the Secretary of the British Society from Mr T. Telford: containing a course of experiments made by him on Mr J. Parker's Cement (London, 1796)

Thompson, M.W., ed., *The Journeys of Sir Richard Colt Hoare through Wales and England 1793–1810* (Gloucester, 1983)

Telford, Thomas, *Atlas to the Life of Thomas Telford, Civil Engineer, containing eighty-three copper plates, illustrative of his professional labours* (London, 1838)

Telford, Thomas, Life of Thomas Telford (edited by J. Rickman) (London 1838)

Tomos, D., *Michael Faraday in Wales* (Denbigh,1973)

Tredgold, T., *A Practical Essay on the Strength of Cast Iron* (2nd edition, London, 1824)

Vega, Juan de, *Journal of a Tour* (London, 1830)

Westall, G., *Inland Cruising on the Rivers and Canals of England and Wales* (London, 1908)

7.e.3 Contextual literature

Aickman, R., *The River Runs Uphill* (Burton-on-Trent, 1986)

Albert, W., *The Turnpike Road System in England 1663-1840* (Cambridge, 1972)

Andrews, Malcolm, *The Search for the Picturesque: landscape aesthetics and tourism in Britain, 1760-1800* (Stanford, California, 1989)

Andrieux, Jean-Yves, *Le Patrimoine Industriel* (Paris, 1992)

Barnes, M., 'Civil Engineering Management in the Industrial Revolution', *Civil Engineering*, vol 138 (2000) pp. 135-144

Biddle, G., *Britain's Historic Railway Buildings* (Oxford, 2003)

Blackwall, A.H., *Historic Bridges of Shropshire* (Shrewsbury,1985)

Blake, B. (ed), *Industrial Archaeology: a guide to the technological revolution of Britain* (London,1965)

Bolton, D., *Race against Time: how Britain's canal heritage was saved* (London,1990)

Bonthron, P., *My Holidays on Inland Waterways: 2000 miles cruising by skiff and motor boat on the canals and rivers of Great Britain* (London,1916)

Boyd, J.I.C., *Narrow Gauge Railways in Mid-Wales* (Lingfield,1970)

Bracegirdle, Brian (ed.), *The Archaeology of the Industrial Revolution* (London, 1973)

Bracegirdle, Brian, *The Archaeology of Canals* (Tadworth, 1979)

Braudel, Fernand, *Civilization and Capitalism, 15th-18th Century: The Perspective of the World* (translated Siân Reynolds) (London, 1984)

Breese, Gwyndaf, *The Bridges of Wales* (Llanrwst, 2001)

Bronowski, Jacob, *The Ascent of Man* (London, 1973)

Buchanan, R.A., *Industrial Archaeology in Britain* (Harmondsworth, 1972)

Burton, Anthony, *Remains of a Revolution* (London, 1975)

Burton, Anthony, *Industrial Archaeological Sites of Britain* (London, 1977)

Burton, Anthony, *The Waterways of Britain* (London, 1983)

Burton, Anthony, *The Great Days of the Canals* (London, 1989)

Chadderton, D., Outram's Iron Aqueduct at Stalybridge', *Saddleworth Historical Society Bulletin*, vol. 7 (1977)

Cipolla, Carlo M., *The Fontana Economic History of Europe, volume 4-1: the emergence of industrial societies* (Glasgow, 1973)

Clapham, Sir J., *An Economic History of Modern Britain* (3 vols. Cambridge,1930-8).

Colley, L., *Britons; Forging the nation 1707-1837* (New Haven and London,1992)

Coones, Paul and Patten, John, *The Penguin Guide to the Landscape of England and Wales* (Harmondsworth, 1986)

Cossons, N., *The BP Book of Industrial Archaeology* (1975, 3rd edn. Newton Abbot, 1993)

Cossons, N. (ed), *Perspectives on Industrial Archaeology* (London, 2000)

Cossons, N. and Trinder, B., *The Iron Bridge: Symbol of the Industrial Revolution* (Chichester, 2002)

Coulls, A., *Railways as World Heritage Sites* (York,1998)

Countryside Council for Wales-Cadw-ICOMOS, *Landscapes of Special Historic Significance in Wales* (Cardiff, 2001)

Crowe, Nigel, *The English Heritage Book of Canals* (London, 1994)

Davies, John, *The Making of Wales* (Cardiff, 1996)

De Maré, Eric, *Bridges of Britain* (revised edn. London,1975)

De Maré, Eric, *The Canals of England* (London, 1950)

Deane, Phyllis, *The First Industrial Revolution* (1965, 2nd edn., Cambridge, 1979)

Derry, T.K. and Williams, Trevor I., *A Short History of Technology from the Earliest Times to 1900* (Oxford, 1960)

Doerflinger, Frederic, *Slow Boat through England* (London, 1970)

Dyos, H.J., and Aldcroft, D.H, *British Transport: an economic survey from the seventeenth century to the twentieth* (1969, 2nd edn. Harmondsworth, 1974)

Edwards, Ifor, *Decorative Cast-Ironwork in Wales* (Llandysul, 1989)

Faulkner, A.H., 'The Wolverton Aqueduct', *Transport History*, vol. 2 (1969)

Francastel, Pierre, 'The Classicist Reaction in the 18th and 19th Centuries', in Rene Huyghe (ed.) *Art and Mankind: Larousse Encyclopedia of Modern Art from 1800 to the Present Day* (Paris, 1961; English language edition New York 1981)

Geiger, Reed G., *Planning the French Canals: bureaucracy, politics, and enterprise under the Restoration* (Newark, Delaware, 1994)

Gloag, J. and Bridgwater, D., *A History of Cast Iron in Architecture* (London, 1948)

Hadfield, C and Eyre, F., *English Rivers and Canals* (London,1947)

Hadfield, C., *British Canals: an Illustrated History* (London,1950)

Hadfield, C., *Introducing Canals: A Guide to British Waterways Today* (London,1955)

Hadfield, C., *The Canal Age* (Newton Abbot,1968)

Hadfield, C., *World Canals* (Newton Abbot,1986)

Hadfield, C. and Norris, J., *Waterways to Stratford* (Newton Abbot,1968)

Hague, D., and Hughes, S., Pont-y-Cafnau: the first iron railway bridge and aqueduct', *AIA Bulletin*, vol. 9 (1982)

Harris, Robert, *Canals and their Architecture* (London, 1969)

Hayes, L., *Ruins in British Romantic Art from Wilson to Turner*, Nottingham Castle Museum (Nottingham, 1988)

Hill, Christopher, *Reformation to Industrial Revolution* (London, 1967)

Hoskins, W.G., *The Making of the English Landscape* (London, 1955)

Hubbard, E., *The Buildings of Wales: Clwyd,* 2nd edition (London, 1994)

Hudson, K., *Industrial Archaeology: an Introduction* (London, 1963)

Hughes, S and Malaws, B., *Collieries of Wales: Engineering and Architecture* (Royal Commission on the Ancient and Historical Monuments of Wales, n.d)

Hughes, S., *The Archaeology of an Early Railway System: The Brecon Forest Tramroads* (Aberystwyth,1990)

Hussey, C., 1927, (1967 edn.), *The Picturesque: Studies in a point of view,* Frank Cass and Co. Ltd., (London)

Huyghe, Rene (ed.), *Art and Mankind: Larousse Encyclopedia of Modern Art from 1800 to the Present Day* (Paris, 1961; English language edition New York 1981)

ICOMOS/TICCIH, *Context for World Heritage Bridges* (Paris, 1997)

ICOMOS/TICCIH, *The International Canal Monuments List* (Paris, 1996)

Jones, P. Thoresby, *Welsh Border Country* (London, 1938)

Klingender, F.J., *Art and the Industrial Revolution,* ed. Sir Arthur Elton (London,1968)

Lane, Peter, *The Industrial Revolution: the birth of the modern age* (London, 1978)

Langton, J. and Morris, R.J. (eds), *Atlas of Industrialising Britain 1780-1915* (London, 1986)

Larsen, K.E. (ed.), *Nara Conference on Authenticity in relation to the World Heritage Convention: Proceedings* (Paris, 1995)

Lerry, G.G., *Henry Robertson: Pioneer of Railways into Wales* (Oswestry, 1949)

Lewis, M.J.T., *Early Wooden Railways* (London, 1970)

Lewis, M.J.T. (ed.), *Early Railways 2: Papers from the Second International Early Railways Conference* (London, 2003)

Lord, Peter, *Industrial Society* (Cardiff,1998)

Lord, Peter, *Imaging the Nation* (Cardiff, 2000)

Mackersey, I., *Tom Rolt and the Cressy Years* (London,1984)

Malet, H., *Bridgewater; the Canal Duke, 1736-1803* (2nd edn. Nelson,1990)

Millward, R. and Robinson, A., *Landscapes of North Wales* (London,1978)

Moore-Colyer, R., *Roads and Trackways of Wales* (Ashbourne, 2001)

Morgan, Bryan, *Civil Engineering: Railways* (London, 1971)

Morgan, K., *Rebirth of a Nation: Wales 1880-1980* (Oxford, 1983)

Morris, Jan, *The Matter of Wales* (Oxford, 1984)

Musson, A.E. and Robinson, Eric, *Science and Technology in the Industrial Revolution* (Manchester, 1969)

Paget-Tomlinson, Edward W., *The Complete Book of Canal and River Navigations* (Albrighton, 1978)

Pannell, J.P.M., *An Illustrated History of Civil Engineering* (London, 1964)

Pawson, Eric, *The Early Industrial Revolution: Britain in the eighteenth century* (New York, 1979)

Pawson, Eric, *Transport and Economy: the Turnpike Roads of Eighteenth Century Britain* (London,1977)

Pevsner, Nikolaus, *Pioneers of Modern Design* (London, 1960)

Pollard, Sidney, *The Genesis of Modern Management* (London, 1965)

Porteous, J.D., *Canal Ports: the Urban Achievement of the Canal Age* (London,1977)

Rajnai, Miklos, ed., *John Sell Cotman 1782-1842* (London, 1982)

Rees, D. Morgan, *Industrial Archaeology of Wales* (Newton Abbot, 1975)

Rees, W., *An Historical Atlas of Wales* (London,1951)

Reigart, J.F., *The Life of Robert Fulton* (Philadelphia,1856)

Richards, J.M., *The Functional Tradition in Early Industrial Buildings* (London, 1958)

Rix, M., 'Industrial Archaeology', *The Amateur Historian,* vol. 2 (1955)

Role, L.T.C., *Navigable Waterways* (London, 1969)

Rolt, L.T.C., 'Inland Waterways', in Brian Bracegirdle (ed.), *The Archaeology of the Industrial Revolution* (London, 1973)

Rolt, L.T.C., *Narrow Boat* (London,1944)

Rolt, L.T.C., *Railway Adventure* (London,1953)

Rolt, L.T.C., *Landscape with Canals: an autobiography* (London,1977)

Rolt, L.T.C., *The Inland Waterways of England* (London,1950)

Ruddock, T., *Arch Bridges and their Builders 1735-1835* (Cambridge,1979)

Schofield, R.B., *Benjamin Outram 1764-1805: an Engineering Biography* (Cardiff, 2000)

Sealey, A., *Bridges and Aqueducts* (London,1976)

Skempton, A.W., *Civil Engineers and Engineering in Britain, 1600-1830* (Aldershot, 1996)

Squires, R.W., *Canals Revived: the story of the waterway restoration movement* (Bradford-on-Avon,1979)

Stanford, S.C., *The Archaeology of the Welsh Marches* (London, 1980)

Stephens, John H., *The Guiness Book of Structures: bridges, towers, tunnels, dams* (Enfield, 1976)

Sutherland, R.J.M., ed., *Structural Iron 1750-1850* (Aldershot,1997)

Sweetman, J., *The Artist and the Bridge* (Aldershot, 2000)

Trinder, B., *The Making of the Industrial Landscape* (London, 1982)

Trinder, B., 'Authenticity in the Industrial Heritage', Larsen, K.E.,ed., *Nara Conference on Authenticity in relation to the World Heritage Convention: Proceedings* (Paris,1995)

Trinder, B., *The Industrial Archaeology of Shropshire* (Chichester,1996)

Trinder, B., 'Industry and the World Heritage', *World Heritage Review,* No. 2 (1996)

Trinder, B., *A History of Shropshire* (2nd. edn., Chichester, 1998).

Trinder, B., *The Industrial Revolution in Shropshire* (3rd edition, Chichester, 2000)

Trinder, B., *The Most Extraordinary District in the World: Ironbridge and Coalbrookdale* (3rd edn., Chichester, 2005)

Trinder, B., ed., *The Blackwell Encyclopaedia of Industrial Archaeology* (Oxford,1992)

Ward, J.R., *The Finance of Canal Building in Eighteenth-Century England* (Oxford, 1974)

Watkin, David, *The Buildings of Britain: Regency* (London, 1982)

Watson, Garth, *The Civils: the story of the Institution of Civil Engineers* (London, 1988)

Principal sources of archival material

National Library of Wales
Railway plans, estate plans, tithe maps, Longueville Papers

British Library
Ordnance Survey Drawings

National Coal Board, Mansfield
Colliery maps

The National Archives, Kew, London
RAIL papers for Ellesmere Canal Company and successors

Ironbridge Gorge Museum
Elton Collection

Shropshire Record Office, Shrewsbury
Deposited plans of the Ellesmere Canal, 1792

Flintshire Record Office, Hawarden
Maps

Institution of Civil Engineers, London
Manuscript book of Matthew Davidson

SECTION 8

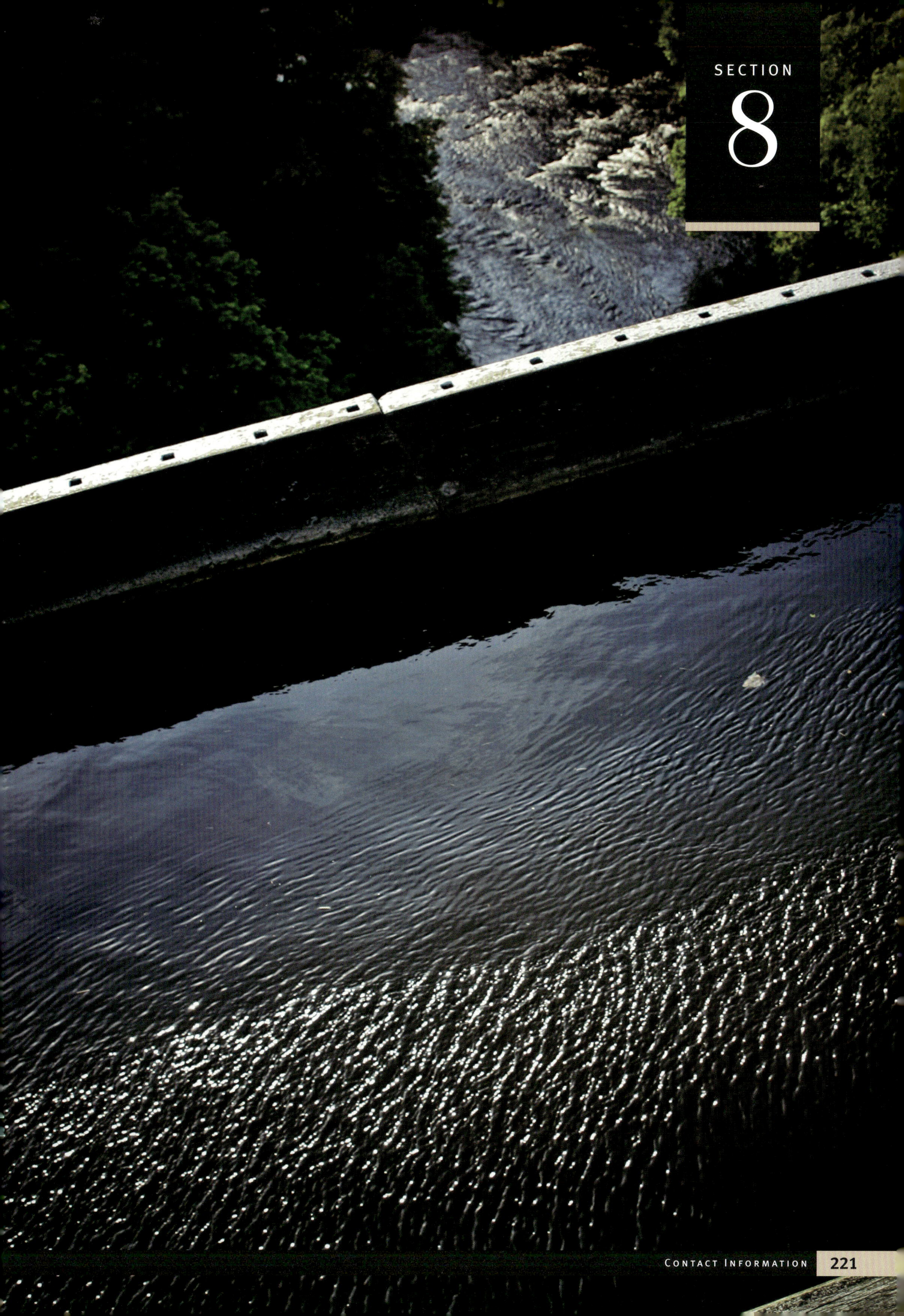

If river navigation gave birth to the profession of engineer the canals provided most of its schooling, and when the Institution of Civil Engineers was chartered in 1818 it was fitting that Thomas Telford (1757-1834), whose canal work even outshone his roads and bridges, should have been elected its president. His canal masterpiece was a pair of exhilarating aqueducts exactly suited to their function at Pontcysyllte and Chirk on the Ellesmere Canal, but his work is to be traced quite tangibly not only along the many miles of canals that he personally engineered but in the work of his contemporaries whom he undoubtedly influenced.

H.J. Dyos and D.H. Aldcroft
British Transport: an economic survey from the seventeenth century to the twentieth
(1969)

CONTACT INFORMATION

8.a Preparer

Pontcysyllte Aqueduct and Canal World Heritage Nomination
Bid Leader:
Dr Dawn Roberts
Economic Development Department,
Wrexham County Borough Council,
Lambpit Street Offices,
Lambpit St,
Wrexham, Wales, LL11 1WN
Tel: +44 (0) 1978 292460
Fax: +44 (0) 1978 292445
Email: dawn.roberts@wrexham.gov.uk

Editorial Team:
Dr Peter Wakelin - Editor
Peter Birch
Stephen Hughes
Patricia Moore
Dr Sian Rees
Dr Dawn Roberts

8.b Official local institution/ agency

Wrexham County Borough Council,
Lambpit Street Offices,
Lambpit St,
Wrexham, Wales, LL11 1WN
Tel: +44 (0) 1978 292460
Fax: +44 (0) 1978 292445
Email: dawn.roberts@wrexham.gov.uk

8.c Other local institutions

Denbighshire County Council
County Hall,
Wynnstay Road,
Ruthin, Wales, LL15 1YN
Enquiries@denbighshire.gov.uk
Telephone 44 (0) 1824 706000

Oswestry Borough Council
Castle View, Oswestry,
Shropshire, England, SY11 1JR
Generalenquiries@Oswestrybc.gov.uk
Telephone 44 (0) 1691 671111

Shropshire County Council
Shire Hall, Abbey Foregate,
Shrewsbury, England, SY2 6ND.

8.d Official web address

www.wrexham.gov.uk/aqueduct

This magnificent aqueduct was opened with great ceremony, on the 26th day of November, 1805, in the presence of about 8000 spectators. The three great Italian aqueducts have celebrated the names of as many Roman Pontiffs, and that near Maintenon has displayed the magnificence of the Grand Monarch; but neither of them had the principle of commerce for its foundation; in which light this aqueduct over the Dee is the first in Europe.

Walter Davies
A General View of the Agriculture and Domestic Economy of North Wales
(1810)

SECTION 9

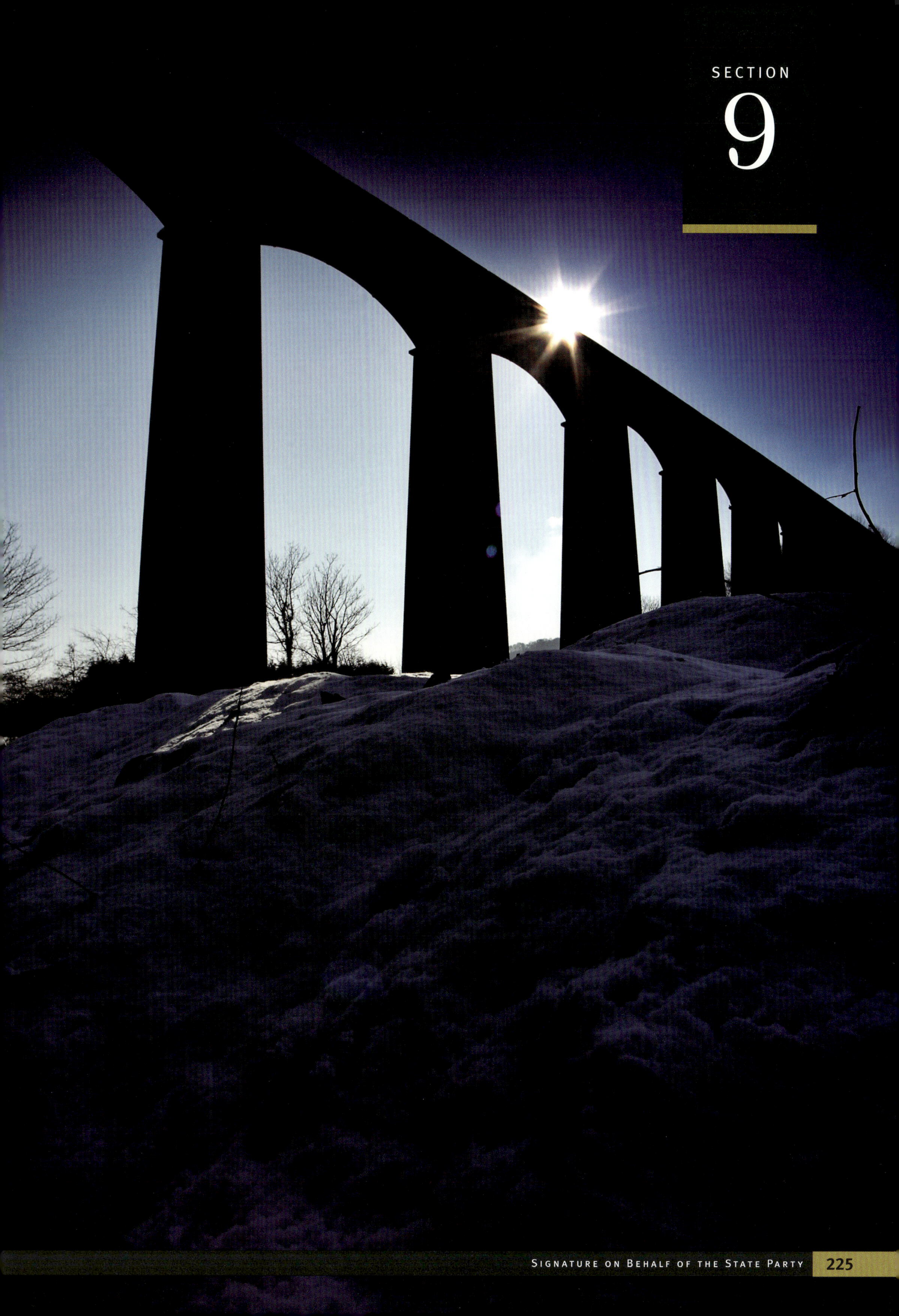

…the aqueduct of Pontcysylte, over the river Dee, one of the most stupendous works of art that was ever accomplished by man. The Ellesmere canal, which had run parallel with the farther bank of the river, is here carried over the vale by an aqueduct, supported on eighteen massy stone pillars…. On the top of the pillars is a trough or water-way, wholly composed of plates of cast iron, about twelve feet in width and five and a half in depth. The inside, over which we walked, as the water was not yet admitted, is carefully pitched; and the manner in which the immense plates are connected and closed by ledges, bolts and screws on the outside, fills the mind with wonder as it contemplates the ingenuity of man. Mr. Telford was the engineer; and if this were the only work he had produced, it would deservedly give immortality to his name. An embankment of earth extends about 1500 feet on the south side beyond the iron work, and from its height and solidity it would be a remarkable object in any other situation; but here it is little, compared with the grand part of the undertaking. As I looked over the ballustrades of the iron water-way into the bed of the Dee, I felt how little the individual man is, but how great in aggregate.

William Mavor
A Tour in Wales and through Several Counties of England performed in the summer of 1805
(1806)

SIGNATURE ON BEHALF OF
THE STATE PARTY

SECTION

9

From Llangollen, most tourists visit this stupendous work of art. It is a wonderful effort of ingenious contrivance, and offers a convincing proof of the incalculable capability of human energies, when wielded by science, and supported by power. This aqueduct was constructed for the purpose of conveying the Ellesmere canal over the river and vale of the Dee. It was commenced in 1793, from designs by Mr. Telford, and completed in ten years. Its direction is from north to south, crossing the Dee at right angles; and it forms, in connexion with the exquisite scenery surrounding it, a noble and magnificent picture. To view it to the best advantage, the stranger must descend on one side of it, into the valley beneath; he will then be impressed with its stupendous character. Though the aqueducts of the Romans were superior to it in length, in other respects they were inferior to it.

Joseph Hemingway
Panorama of the Beauties, Curiosities and Antiquities of North Wales
(London, 1844)

The Pont-y-Cysylte is not only grand as a specimen of engineering, but as a noble piece of architecture, and, situated as it is, immediately on the line of the great road to Ireland through North Wales, and in so picturesque a site, it attracts the attention and the admiration of every passenger. So well do its twenty gigantic arches assimilate with the magnificent scenery with which they are surrounded, that the vast edifice seems as if made purposely to connect the sides of the valley in the most fitting manner, and to add an essential feature to the whole, without which the observer hardly believes the former splendid view can have seemed complete. It is equally in harmony with all around, whether viewed from near its base, where an antique bridge over the Dee, a few feet only above the surface of the river, adds new grandeur by the contrast to the giant structure which rises in the air above it…. We are now familiar with somewhat similar stupendous works, in the 'viaducts' of our principal railways, but none of these can compete for an instant in appropriateness, simplicity, and magnificence, with this grand conception of Telford, albeit the constructors of the former have had all the lights of foregone experience to aid them, and the Pont-y-Cysylte was the first work of its kind on record.

The Mechanics Magazine
1839-40

ACKNOWLEDGEMENTS

We would like to thank the three lead organisations for their tremendous work, resource allocation and commitment to this nomination:

> Wrexham County Borough Council
> British Waterways
> The Royal Commission on the Ancient and Historical Monuments of Wales

We would also like to thank all the contributors for their assistance in producing this bid including:

The Members of the World Heritage Site Steering Group

- Dr Dawn Roberts (Chair) (Wrexham County Borough Council)
- Peter Birch (British Waterways)
- Dr Peter Wakelin (Royal Commission on the Ancient and Historical Monuments of Wales)
- Stephen Hughes (Royal Commission on the Ancient and Historical Monuments of Wales)
- Dr Sian Rees (Cadw)
- Dr Christopher Young (English Heritage)
- Susan Denyer (ICOMOS UK)
- Paul Blackburn (Wrexham County Borough Council)
- Peter Booth (Oswestry Borough Council)
- Peter Brown (Inland Waterways Association)
- Fiona Gale (Denbighshire County Council)
- David Gittins (Wrexham County Borough Council)
- Steve Grenter (Wrexham County Borough Council)
- Anna Irwin (Wrexham County Borough Council)
- Paul Mitchell (Countryside Council for Wales)
- Prof Richard Neale (UNESCO Cymru Wales)
- Del Roberts-Jones (Wrexham County Borough Council)
- Mike Watson (Shropshire County Council)

And to our key advisors:
- Dr Christopher Young (English Heritage)
- ICOMOS UK
- Peter Marsden (DCMS)
- Dr Peter Wakelin (RCAHMW)

Members of the Planning Sub Group
> Del Roberts-Jones - Chair
> Peter Birch, Peter Booth, Anna Irwin,
> Kate Lynch, Tim Morris, Pru Probert,
> Chris Smith, Peter Smith,
> Richard Sumner, Catrin Williams

Expert Papers and Research contributions from consultants:
> Dr Ron Fitzgerald, Dr David Gwyn
> Jane McDermott, Christopher Pound,
> Dr Barrie Trinder

'Critical friends':
> Prof John Hume, Prof Marilyn Palmer
> Dr Barrie Trinder, Keith Falconer

We would like to thank those who have taken or provided photographs and illustrations and/or given permission for their use.

Those who have helped produce the record drawings, photographs, mapping, geographical information, data inputting and collation of material:

- Paul Nelson, Dave Gittins and Rachel Cupit (Wrexham County Borough Council)
- Ian Gough (Denbighshire County Council)
- Louise Barker, Toby Driver, Gareth Edwards, Sue Evans, Susan Fielding, Stephen Hughes, Daniel Jones, Fleur James, David Percival, Geoff Ward, Iain Wright and Patricia Moore (Royal Commission on the Ancient and Historical Monuments of Wales)

All the volunteers and members of the community who have given help and advice.

Community Councils:
Chirk Town Council
Llangollen Rural Community Council
Llangollen Town Council
Llantysilio Community Council
Weston Rhyn Parish Council

Other Organisations:
Northern Marches Cymru
Inland Waterways Association.
Institution of Civil Engineers
Tourism Partnership North Wales
Visit Wales
The National Library of Wales

We apologise if we have missed naming you as a contributor.

Mapping is produced from Ordnance Survey material with permission of Ordnance Survey on behalf of the Controller of Her Majesty's Stationery Office © Crown Copyright. Unauthorised reproduction infringes Crown Copyright and may lead to prosecution or civil proceedings, Wrexham County Borough Council, Licence Number 100023429. 2007.

Copyright for the illustrations and images remains with the owners. All rights reserved.

All images are Crown Copyright © Royal Commission on the Ancient and Historical Monuments of Wales, except the following. We are grateful to all the partners and supporters who have allowed images to be reproduced on the following pages by courtesy:

Wrexham County Borough Council: 4, 11, 26 (upper), 30 (middle), 96, 108 (upper), 110, 111 (x2), 118, 134, 137 (right), 151 (right), 152 (x3), 153 (upper), 157, 159, 167 (upper x2), 172, 177, 178, 185 (x2), 192, 194 (lower), 195 (upper), 196 (lower right), 197, 200, 221, 225, 229

Llyfrgell Genedlaethol Cymru / The National Library of Wales: 17, 28, 76, 83, 86, 90 (lower), 91, 105, 107, 136

Institution of Civil Engineers: 23, 81 (upper left), 85 (upper), 94 (right), 109 (upper), 125 (lower), 127 (top)

Science Museum / Science & Society Picture Library: 25 (upper), 75, 81 (upper right), 84 (middle), 87 (lower), 119 (upper)

Ann Eastham photographs, National Monuments Record for Wales: 34, 101, 102 (x2)

Susan Denyer, ICOMOS-UK: 122 (top)

The Waterways Archive Gloucester: 25 (lower), 99 (lower), 115, 133 (upper right), 138

Tate, London 2007: 32 (upper)

Shropshire Archives: 36 (upper), 38 (lower)

Denbighshire Record Office: 81 (lower), 112 (upper)

English Heritage. National Monuments Record for England: 87 (upper)

The National Waterways Museum, Stoke Bruerne: 88 (upper)

V&A Images/Victoria and Albert Museum: 89, The Ironbridge Gorge Museum Trust: 99 (upper)

Amgueddfa Cymru - National Museum Wales: 97 (upper)

British Waterways Board: 6, 35, 104 (x4), 132 (right), 133 (upper left, middle right), 142, 145, 147, 148 (x2), 149, 153 (lower), 196 (x2 left)

Natural England: 167 (x2 lower)

Universal Music Company: 195

Crown copyright: Royal Commission on the Ancient and Historical Monuments of Scotland: 94 (left), 127 (bottom) (Scottish Colorfoto Collection)

We have made best efforts to contact the owners of all images used, but we have failed to trace the copyright holder for 26 (lower), 33 (upper), 90 (upper). We would be glad to receive information to assist us.